CW01219665

Creative Characters

▲ Poster for Jos Buivenga's Museo by Brazilian student Eduardo Uzae, under the direction of Crystian Cruz.

Creative Characters

A collection of interviews with type designers originally published as e-mail newsletters from MyFonts

EDITED BY *Jan Middendorp*

BIS PUBLISHERS

▼ Cartoon by Cyrus Highsmith

Editing, image research and production by Jan Middendorp
Cover and design concept by Nick Sherman
Layout and production assistance by Anthony Noel

BIS Publishers
Building Het Sieraad
Postjesweg 1
1057 DT Amsterdam
The Netherlands

T +31 (0)20 515 02 30
F +31 (0)20 515 02 39
bis@bispublishers.nl
www.bispublishers.nl

ISBN 978-90-6369-224-7

Copyright © 2010 BIS Publishers, MyFonts, Jan Middendorp and the respective designers

Text and type samples reproduced in this book were originally produced for MyFonts, USA
www.myfonts.com

All rights reserved. No part of this publication may be reproduced or transmitted in any form or by any means, electronic or mechanical, including photocopy, recording or any information storage and retrieval system, without permission in writing from the copyright owners.
Every reasonable attempt has been made to identify owners of copyright. Any errors or omissions brought to the publisher's attention will be corrected in subsequent editions.

Printed in China

Contents

- 6 — Foreword
- 8 — Jim Parkinson
- 16 — David Berlow
- 24 — Jean François Porchez
- 32 — Type Together: Veronika Burian & José Scaglione
- 38 — Jos Buivenga
- 46 — Gert Wiescher
- 52 — Ray Larabie
- 60 — Silas Dilworth
- 68 — Rian Hughes
- 74 — Nick Curtis
- 80 — Patrick Griffin
- 88 — P22: Carima El-Behairy & Richard Kegler
- 96 — Nick Shinn
- 104 — Hans Samuelson
- 110 — Ellinor Maria Rapp
- 114 — Alejandro Paul
- 122 — Mark Simonson
- 130 — Eric Olson
- 138 — Mário Feliciano
- 144 — Dino dos Santos
- 152 — Christian Schwartz
- 158 — František Štorm
- 164 — Tomáš Brousil
- 170 — Ronna Penner
- 174 — Cyrus Highsmith
- 182 — Underware: Akiem Helmling, Bas Jacobs & Sami Kortemäki
- 190 — Acknowledgements & copyrights

Foreword

Anyone who earns a living designing, producing or selling digital typefaces must have met the Baffled Person at the Party who won't stop asking questions, in an increasingly exasperated tone, about what it is we do. "Making *fonts*? Is that… a *job*?" Or: "*What!?* You wrote *an entire book* about fonts?" After some explanation, the Baffled Person may get cheeky, and start on the critical examination: "Why more fonts? Aren't there already too many of them as it is?" Whereupon we may have to resort to the answer put forward, as legend has it, by Adrian Frutiger: "Are there ever too many wines?"

But the Baffled Person is becoming rarer. More and more people are, to some extent, knowledgeable about fonts. Anyone owning a computer today has a selection of fonts at their fingertips that equals or surpasses the typeface collection of a small professional typesetting office in, say, the 1950s. It is only natural that some of these users develop a curiosity about their tools, and want to know more about them – maybe even buy some fonts for their own use. In the graphic design world there has been a change as well. As little as fifteen years ago, only a minority of design students were interested in typeface design. Today type and lettering are immensely popular, which has led many design colleges to introduce type design as a subject.

For typography newbies, the World Wide Web has become an important ally. During its early days in the 1990s, typography on the web was a confusing mixture of rather forbidding professional sites and hastily-made free-font pages (and some stuff in between) with little help offered to sort the wheat from the chaff. Today, in the era of Web 2.0, users help each other, sharing their insights and preferences through blogs and networking sites, and content providers have to follow suit. With the emancipation of the web user, sincerity and directness have become essential elements for successful, credible communication. The meteoric success of a blog like ilovetypography.com is a case in point. At the time of writing it has over 57,000 RSS subscribers – attracted, no doubt, by its personable and enthusiastic tone of voice, as well as the natural way it mixes informality and knowledgeability.

In the history of typography, the 1990s represented a phase of unprecedented democratization of the type design and production process. What used to be a cumbersome affair, involving costly machines and lots of overhead, became a one-man operation using hardware and software that any budding professional could afford. It seems that the 2000s have accomplished a similar step for the user. Enjoying letterforms, choosing fonts and putting together your own library of favorites used to be a thing that was strictly reserved for design professionals. Today, many managers, secretaries, bloggers or scrapbookers have preferences regarding the fonts they use.

In 1999 Bitstream, the Massachusetts company founded in the 1980s by Matthew Carter and Mike Parker as the first independent manufacturer of digital fonts, created MyFonts.com. Its concept was born when Charles Ying, Bitstream's Chairman of the

Board, wanted to find a font for a particular project. To his annoyance, the only way to find typefaces on the web was to know their names – or browse alphabetical lists. Ying's idea was to make finding fonts "as easy as shopping for shoes. I should be able to point at a font in a magazine and say, 'Show me more fonts like this.'" This was what MyFonts set out to make possible. Powerful tools such as WhatTheFont (an online typeface recognition program) and a straightforward user interface helped make fonts more accessible to non-specialists. On the supplier side, MyFonts wanted to provide an open marketplace where fonts from many vendors compete side by side, instead of the more typical single-company walled gardens of the 1980s and '90s.

MyFonts went on to play a pivotal role in empowering both users and vendors. Its principle of a "level playing field," offering hassle-free procedures to participating foundries, has been instrumental in changing the distribution model. Ten years ago only the most enterprising designers started a foundry of their own. During the past decade, many more type designers took that step, relying on MyFonts as their main outlet. It enabled them to become independent from the larger foundries or boutique distributors; to go from producing a font to marketing and selling it within days instead of having to wait up to a year for a decision; and, if they are so inclined, immediately react to trends in the market.

While being respected by foundries and customers for its user-friendliness and technical sophistication, the MyFonts website suffered from an embarrassing image problem design-wise. The site looked "as if it was designed by your mother" (Nick Sherman) and the clumsy vignette adopted as a temporary placeholder for the logo remained in place for years. All this was amended when, in 2009, a wholly new website was launched, including a new logo by the Underware studio. The site began attracting more users from the world of professional design; several foundries that had hesitated because of the site's amateurish look, now signed up.

The site's leap in quality had been preceded by the evolution of MyFonts' newsletters. What had basically been an illustrated sales pitch had become a more sophisticated publication. The type designers took center stage when, in mid-2007, the Creative Characters newsletter was installed as a platform for the ideas and insights of "the faces behind the fonts." As the largest-audience publication in its field – the newsletter goes out to more than 750,000 individual users – the series has met with wide acclaim and, at times, genuine gratitude for allowing font lovers a peek behind the scenes. Hopefully the series has also been instrumental in spreading the insight that fonts are made by interesting people, not anonymous companies – and so are worth paying for. And maybe it has served the occasional Baffled Person.

This book is the printed version of the first two-plus years of these interviews, expanded with partly unpublished visual material. Conducting and editing the interviews has been a fascinating and instructive experience. We want to extend our thanks to all the type designers involved for sharing their thoughts and work. Many thanks, also, to the graphic designers and publishers who made available images of fonts in use. From the author, a big thank-you to the colleagues at MyFonts, to Nick Sherman who designed MyFonts' new look as well as an early version of this book, and to Anthony Noel, who stepped in to help us get it over and done with.

Enjoy!

Jan Middendorp

▼ Illustration by Rian Hughes

Jim Parkinson

PARKINSON CONDENSED LIGHT

AVEBURY BLACK & OPEN

Jim Parkinson has probably designed more magazine and newspaper nameplates than any other designer alive. Some of his designs have become true icons, like the logos he made for *Rolling Stone*, the quintessential American rock magazine, and for Ringling Bros and Barnum & Bailey Circus. Drawing on artisanal techniques such as hand-lettering and signpainting, Parkinson's typefaces often evoke past styles and shapes, subtly updated to fit present contexts. Meet Jim Parkinson, an expert forger who likes fooling with time. *April 2008*

PARKINSON ROMAN

Jim, I envy you. You were born in 1941, the same year as Bob Dylan, Paul Simon and Don Van Vliet (aka Captain Beefheart). You graduated in 1963, the year in which it all started happening. You lived in the Bay area when it became the epicenter of hipness. You worked for *Rolling Stone* when that magazine was just about the coolest in the world… What was it like to grow up alongside rock'n'roll? Did you feel part of the "scene" at some point?

The closest I ever got to the epicenter of anything was a moment at *Rolling Stone* in the early 1970s, in San Francisco. Jann Wenner had called a staff meeting in his office. I have no idea what I was doing there. It may have been by accident. But never mind. There I was, sitting on the floor in Jann's office along with all of the great artists and writers and staff who were working there at the time. Everyone was packed into the room sitting on chairs, on tabletops, on the floor, and standing or leaning against the walls. Hunter Thompson, Annie Leibovitz, and of course Roger Black, Vincent Winter and Greg Scott from the art department. I was just looking around, taking it all in. I don't even remember what the meeting was about. I just remember this moment with

Parkinson's sketches for the *Rolling Stone* logo

so many of my heroes in one room. I didn't really feel like one of them. I felt more like a groupie, just really lucky to be there. Thinking, "Wow".

Many people who worked for *Rolling Stone* in the early years still think it was the coolest job they ever had. I've never been around such a talented group of people. Many, like myself, were living life completely without boundaries, yet we were able to get it together enough to produce this amazing magazine. Whatever you thought it might have been like, however cool you think it was… it was probably like that, just a little bit wilder. The Endless Boogie. The Capri Lounge. The Cosmic Giggle. You had to be there. I still work for *Rolling Stone* fairly regularly after 37 or so years. In fact, I'm doing a job for them right now and while I work I can drift back into that special head space. Not by wearing bell-bottoms and granny glasses, but spiritually. It's nice.

You graduated from the California College of Arts & Crafts in Oakland with a degree in advertising design. Was lettering design part and parcel of the curriculum back then – or were you an exception?

We're talking Stone Age here. Type design was not an option in 1959. Not as a course of study and certainly not as an occupation for a kid like me. Lettering was at the absolute bottom of the food chain. My first exposure to lettering came much earlier. When I was around four years old and living in Richmond, California, there was a showcard lettering artist who lived across the alley from me. Abraham Lincoln Paulsen. I used to sit in his studio for hours, watching him work. I was fascinated. Mr. Paulsen kindled an interest that would fester for years, eventually taking me over. When I finally started at CCAC there were no more than a half-dozen classes devoted to Advertising Design, as it was called. There was only one lettering class offered at the school. It was three hours, two days a week for one semester. That is all the formal lettering education I have. The rest I just picked up along the way. I'm still learning every day, in fact. That's part of what makes this so damned much fun.

Since college I bumped into the most amazing series of mentors an aspiring lettering freak like myself could imagine. Myron McVay, Rob Roy Kelly, Hermann Zapf and Roger Black all taught me volumes and helped drive my passion. And these individuals all happened into my life quite by accident.

Cover of *Rolling Stone* magazine's tenth anniversary issue, designed by Roger Black with lettering by Jim Parkinson. The first of two logos Parkinson designed for the magazine debuts here.

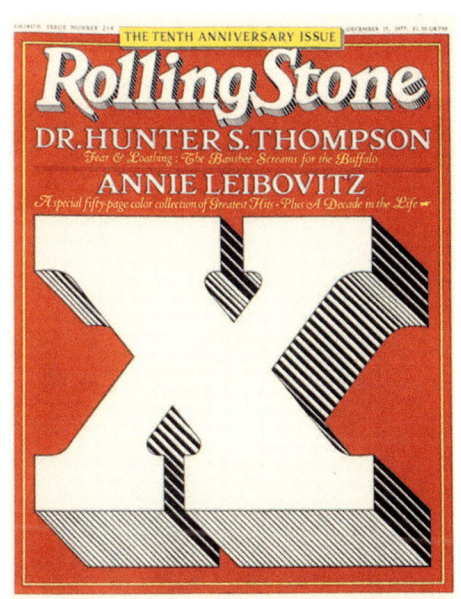

"Journalism"
HEARST
Not Quite Libel
PULITZER
News!
SENSATIONAL

Balboa

▲ "Boldface" was one of the typographic inventions of the early nineteenth century, a style of advertising type created for maximum impact on billboards and magazine pages – the earliest mass media. Parkinson's Balboa was inspired by those primitive sans-serif letterforms, which in their time were dubbed "grotesques" or "gothic" because of their striking looks. Parkinson gave the designs contemporary touches to make a distinctive modern design. With its five weights in three widths, Balboa is a flexible display family which lends a special look to books, magazines or brochures.

Today I paint, draw, take photos, write and build things, in addition to designing logos and fonts. Unless a typographic project is client driven, I approach it the same way I approach a painting. I have a mental image, a vision that I want to capture. Something I am trying to understand. Often it's a letter detail so personal and obscure that I'm the only one who sees it. But it's gotta be there. A new font is mostly the answer to some creative question I've asked myself. Or at least an attempt at an answer.

Your first job after graduation was in the greeting card business, at Hallmark. Many people in the type business seem to have done a kind of apprenticeship at that company. What influence did it have on your later activities?

When I graduated from CCAC, most of the commercial art jobs available to beginners were cutting amberliths, doing mechanicals, paste-up. Pouring cup after cup of instant coffee for some pompous cigar smoking twit. Arghh! A nightmare. On the other hand, Hallmark was a job where you could do art right away. When I took the job, I didn't have a clue about what I was getting into. Once I had an apartment in Kansas City and started work, I discovered that they wanted me to paint happy, fuzzy greeting card rabbits. Well, it turned out that I was not a fuzzy greeting card rabbit type of guy. I was packing my bags to leave for Oakland when they offered me a job in the lettering department, like it was purgatory or something. Because of my experience watching old Mr. Paulsen and my brief encounter with lettering in art school, I felt that it was something I could enjoy. "Don't give up too soon," I thought. So that's how I became a professional lettering artist... by failing the Fuzzy Rabbit Test.

At that time, the primo lettering artist in the art department at Hallmark, Myron McVay, was working on a new project designing greeting card type styles for Filmotype machines. Mechanizing hand lettering. Hallmark thought of all lettering as either Formal or Informal referring to the type of greeting card the lettering appeared on. Myron thought I had a knack for inventing Informal greeting card lettering styles and he plucked me out of the production line and taught me how to go from making lettering to making type. Of all the people I have been lucky enough to bump into, Myron patiently taught me more about lettering and type design than everyone else put together, save Roger Black. I still do most things the way Myron taught me.

After Hallmark, you returned to the Bay area, where you eventually became a very successful independent lettering artist, designing logotypes and nameplates for clients such as Fast Company, Esquire, Newsweek and the San Francisco Examiner. How did that evolve?

When I first got back to Oakland, the only thing I was sure of was that I didn't want a real job. I had this idea that I would do lettering for people and they would pay me for it. It took about ten years of struggling to make that happen. In the meantime I was

"Whatever you thought it might have been like, however cool you think it was... it was probably like that, just a little bit wilder."

PARKINSON CONDENSED BOLD

LA

Los Angeles Times

Atlanta

The Metropolitan

Los Angeles

The Gazette

El Gráfico

Esquire

BOHEMIAN

▶ A selection of nameplates designed by Parkinson

▲ Jim Parkinson's photorealistic oil paintings

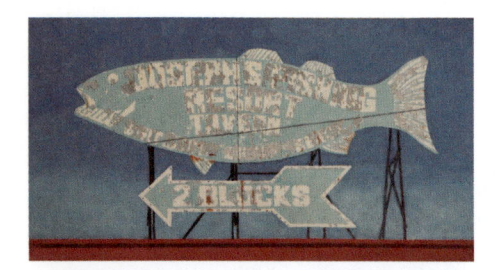

Sculling Gondolier
Traghetti
Venezia, Italia
Skiffing under bridges
Floating taxi

Benicia

▲ Benicia reflects Jim's ongoing fascination with the Golden Type/Jenson genre of the late nineteenth and early twentieth centuries – sturdy adaptations of Nicolas Jenson's book face from 1470s Venice. Jim felt that "the ATF Jenson thing needed more flogging" and managed to whip the Venetian model into a versatile typeface that works well in both display and text sizes. Its simplified shapes and sober italic makes it more twentieth century American than fifteenth century Italian. Benicia is named after a historic town in northern California.

doing design, illustration, whatever. Just as long as it involved doing some kind of art. I worked for money and for trade. I lettered for beer. I lettered for furniture. I did a logo in exchange for a 1946 Chevy. For a while I painted big canvas "grand opening" banners for a chain of Pizza Palaces. I did about two banners a month and I was paid with free pizza coupons. So for several years I lived on pizza and beer.

Eventually I started to get jobs where I was paid with money. But not much. I was doing lettering for album covers, book covers, advertising, packaging – you name it. Once I started working for *Rolling Stone* a lot in the early '70s, I started to get an idea of what my Lettering Heaven might be like, but the publication logo jobs didn't really start showing up until the '80s. And it wasn't until the early '90s when I was on a Mac that I was able to focus completely on logos for publications and on designing fonts.

Before desktop computers came along, how did you work? How were your pieces reproduced – and how were your alphabets turned into fonts?

Every alphabet or typeface I did from Hallmark on until the End of Analog was done in essentially the same way. First, the initial designing, maybe just vowels. The vowels appear the most and therefore contribute the most to the quality and personality of a font. I like to start with the capital 'I'. It's not too challenging and offers the designer instant reward and the encouragement to go on.

After the vowels, I add an 'm' and an 'n'. Then I can start tracing long strings of letters to establish spacing, relative weight and proportional characteristics, and so on. I always start with "minimum." Myron's word. The parade of verticals helps establish spacing and color. After that, it is page after page of tracing lettering strings, adding new characters and adjusting old ones the whole time. Then I would go to the light table and ink the best tracings on pieces of single-ply, plate finish, Strathmore paper. Inking was a craft that I slavishly worked at perfecting. By the time I was back in Oakland,

I was getting pretty good at it. For example, I inked both the *Rolling Stone* logo and the Ringling Bros and Barnum & Bailey Circus logo without needing even a spot of retouch. They both required a lot of beer, but not a speck of white retouch.

Alphabets were turned into fonts in a number of ways. Actually a lot of my early fonts were just alphabets masquerading as fonts. There were no bearings. The spacing was all visual, left to the whim of the designer/typesetter. For an alphabet to become a font, the space needs to be designed and included as part of the letter. At least, as far as I'm concerned.

Anyway… First step was stats. Sometimes multiple prints were made and the words pasted up, one letter at a time. Sometimes the letters were pasted up in long horizontal strings with plenty of space between each letter. A film negative was made, reduced so it could be trimmed out into a two inch filmstrip to make a Typositor font. Sometimes the stats were pasted up with multiples of each character so transfer type sheets could be made. There was no end to the ingenuity applied to the making of these "fonts".

When desktop publishing and digital font production came along, how did you respond to that? Were you in awe of the new technology?
In awe? I don't think so. I thought computers were toys. Like Speak & Spell. I resisted until I was exposed to Fontographer in about 1989 or '90. Then it was like, "Man overboard!" I took the plunge. Not only was it a gazillion times easier than drawing and inking by hand, but you could charge more money. Go figure. So after twenty-plus years of drawing and inking by hand I was finally free. The new technology not only made my work easier, but it also allowed me time to do more of what I went to art school for in the first place, and that is painting. What do I paint? Mostly pictures of letters.

When I finally started making digital fonts, I realized quickly that it didn't make sense to try and do something that's already popular. By the time you manage to bring your entry to market, that style will be out of fashion. I also realized that it was very likely that I might be the only person to ever see the fonts I designed, so it might as well be a font that I would enjoy designing. So, maybe something easy, for starters. Over the years I had experimented with dozens of styles that I thought someday I might want to turn into fonts. Many were big display styles and the first four or five I made digitally were in the style of classic showcards. I like their irreverence and I like their spirit. My first three digital fonts were Showcard Gothic, Poster Black and El Grande, three showcards for the Font Bureau. Then the Moderne Gothics for FSI and Jimbo for Adobe. I still have a little bit of showcard left in me, but I think I have a couple of more interesting threads I would like to follow until they play out.

Among your many fonts – what is your favorite?
My favorite fonts are still in my head. I can hear them knocking. They want out. "I'll get to you as soon as I can," I shout back.

Your logos and typefaces cover an amazing range of styles. What is the one you are you most proud of? Do you feel like an actor sometimes – taking on a completely different persona for each job?
First, a couple of things about the typographic logos. They are not just my logos. Every job is a collaboration between a designer or art director or publisher and a type guy. Just as there are many people to blame for a bad logo, so are there many people to

Avebury

▲ Avebury is wicked: a cheeky, ultra-black blackletter that will work on a rock t-shirt as well as a beer label or art catalog cover design. Avebury Black and Avebury Open were inspired by an early blackletter from the Caslon Foundry, as well as early blackletters from the Bruce Type Foundry. The gothic letterforms were subtly modernized but although Avebury is more readable than many other blackletter revivals, Parkinson advises against setting a bible in it: "Caution. For display only."

Modesto

▲ Modesto is based on a hand-lettering style that Parkinson often used in the 1960s and '70s for ads, book covers and posters. "It was my fall-back position, hand-lettering-wise. It was easy and readily accepted," says Parkinson. Eventually, it became the Ringling Bros logo, which, in turn, became the Modesto type family. Its classic forms and small serifs recall Goudy's Copperplate Gothic, although it is more fancy in its details. Modesto Text has an idiosyncratic lowercase alphabet, the Initials font has a gorgeous outline and the Open Caps have distinctive inlines.

DROP OUT OF LIFE

Mojo

▲ Like almost all Bay area lettering artists, Parkinson mastered this lettering style that was popularized by 1960s artists Wes Wilson, Victor Moscoso and Rick Griffin. The style is rooted in the Art Nouveau period, particularly the work of the turn-of-the-century Czech/Viennese poster designer Alfred Roller. Later, the lettering became a font – Mojo.

▼ Two examples of Parkinson's Roller-style lettering: a hand-drawn wave-shaped version and a past-up of single letterforms. They are both pre-Mojo: the digital font in the same style was produced years later.

credit for a good logo. That collaboration, the logo history of the publication, the personality the publication wants to project, plus any number of other factors help make each logo different.

It is not my signature I am lettering. It is somebody else's signature.

Maybe I feel less an actor and more a forger. Nobody comes to me and says, "I want my logo to look exactly like everybody else's." If they did, I probably wouldn't be interested. I can't keep learning if I'm always doing exactly the same thing. Also, publications want their logos to look fresh and new and old and established all at once. Interesting problem. I love wrestling with that one. When I work on logos, I always try to find subtle little things I can do to make them timeless. Old, but new. It spills over into my font design. When I design a font, I can't see its future. I don't have a clue how its life will develop after I let it go. Will anybody like it? Will anybody buy it? Who knows? So, I might as well design something I feel like designing. After all, the fun of the design process and the learning that comes with it may be the only reward a particular font has to offer. My old lettering jobs offer a rich variety of letter styles that I want to make into fonts. It may give my work a nostalgic look, but my view of the past is much more precise than my view of the future.

One example. I designed a font called Poster Black, early on. A sharp-edged gothic with concave strokes. I wondered what it would look like if it was softened up a little, like it was inflated with air. Poster Black with gas. The result was El Grande, a soft gothic showcard style. It looks so mid twentieth century, that even the Font Bureau's own catalog makes the mistake of attributing it as a revival of a style popular in mid-century comic books and grocery store ads. So what looks old may not be exactly what you think. Fooling with time. It's the journey. I love the way things develop unexpectedly. Enjoy the trip.

> "I worked for money and for trade. I lettered for beer. I lettered for furniture. I did a logo in exchange for a 1946 Chevy."
>
> RICHMOND MEDIUM

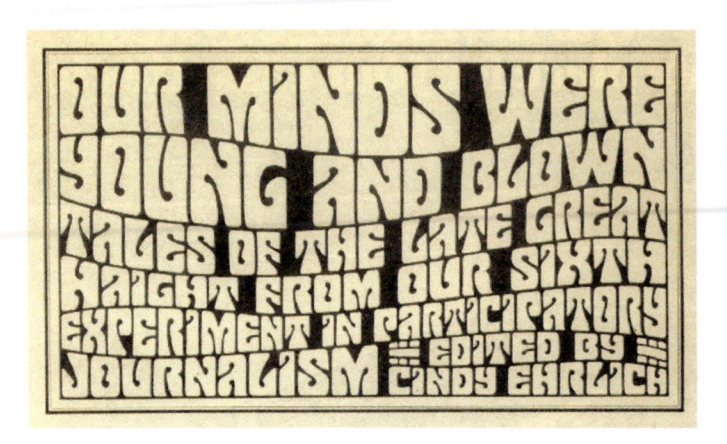

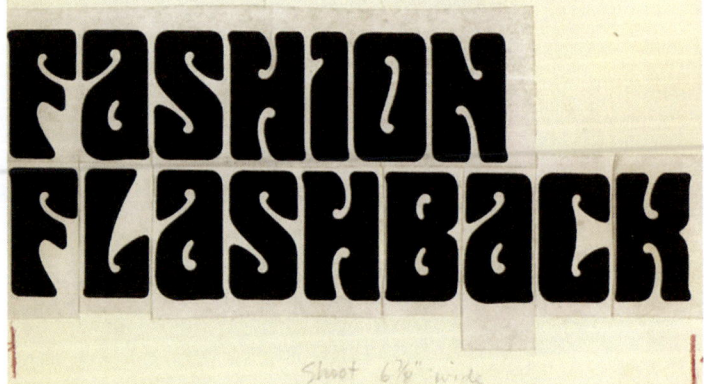

▶▼ FROM TOP RIGHT: the Xerox reference Jim originally worked from; Sutro used in a magazine; the *Manacled Mormon* cover; the *Newsweek* logo; a Sutro specimen.

The story of Sutro

as told by Jim Parkinson

SUTRO BOLD

SUTRO LIGHT ITALIC

Roger Black was the Art Director at *New West* magazine in Los Angeles in the late 1970s. The magazine was planning to run a lurid cover story one month called *The Case of the Manacled Mormon*. Roger had an idea for a typographic cover treatment. He sent me a Xerox of a page from an old Nebiolo specimen book. Nebiolo was a type foundry in Italy and the name – Egiziano – is Italian for Egyptian, or slab serif. The specimen was incomplete, as specimens usually are, and the fax was funky. Roger wanted a fairly complete character set inked, and, not surprisingly, he was in a hurry. I had almost a whole week to do it, including designing all the missing characters and inking them all. I wondered, *Why Egiziano?* But even in the limited time I had for reflection, I could see that this was a much different design than the mechanical and cold slab serifs I was so used to seeing. There were a lot of nice details going on that made it special. Once the job was done, I continued to play with those letter forms on various other jobs.

About a decade later, Roger asked me to work with him on a redesign of *Newsweek*. Of course Roger did the designing, but I did a display typeface and a logo. The logo was a slight variation on that original Egiziano. Finally, after nearly 25 years of puzzling over the details of that typeface, I took a stab at making an Egyptian that had similar warmth and eccentricity. I called it Sutro.

SUTRO LIGHT

David BERLOW

ELDORADO

GIZA

Although David Berlow is obviously too young to be counted among the grand old men of American typography, he is certainly one of its most influential figures. As a designer with Linotype and Bitstream, he witnessed and influenced the early developments of digital typography. As co-founder and principal of Boston's Font Bureau he has conceived and directed an impressive number of quality type designs. His status as one of today's type gurus was underlined when, during TypeCon 2007, he received the SoTA Award of the Society of Typographic Aficionados. We spoke with David from his hideaway on Martha's Vineyard. *September 2007*

VILLAGE

When and why did you decide to become a type designer?
Well, I didn't grow up or go through my education knowing it was possible to be a type designer, because I never really thought it was until I toured Linotype's New York Letter Design Office in 1977. There was however, this moment of unmistakable joy I still remember quite vividly carving block prints at the age of 7 – that if I positioned the palm trees just so, and the monkey swung just so, I could repeat the same block as many times as I wanted for a longer picture! I found this again when I opened a drawer of type in the first year of university but still didn't think to pick up punch cutting. I found it again at Linotype with a lot of fine art, commercial art and art historical education in between.

Who taught you how to do it? What were the most important things you learned from them?
It's not over 'til it's over. Going backwards, I'm still learning a lot from the people I'm supposed to be teaching. Each person has a lot to give and the first time one learns

something is not always right, or complete. I think this is especially true in a field as wide as ours historically, stylistically and culturally. So in a big way, all the designers whose work is published through Font Bureau are my latest teachers. From them I learn how to look at things related to type today from a variety of stylistic and entrepreneurial perspectives.

Before that, there was a core of designers who lived through Linotype and Bitstream during the formative years of the digital era, some of my "graduate experience" including Matthew Carter, Mike Parker, Cherie Cone, Larry Oppenberg, Alex Kaczun, Richard Stetler, Walter Petty and George Ryan. I was together with these designers, and many others, roughly from 1978 until 1989. At the beginning of that, I learned a lot about the qualities of any design and the lines themselves from John Quaranta, the master designer at Linotype when I arrived, who, past 65 at the time, did not make the leap to Bitstream, but who was patient and tolerant enough to make the leap to Ikarus.

During the eleven-year period mentioned above, I was also fortunate enough to be exposed to the design and technology ideas of Karow, Knuth, Bigelow, Holmes, Stone, Zapf, Frutiger, Jim von Ehr and many more.

That's the living. Type designers who lived hundreds and occasionally thousands of years ago are still teaching me, because type design is pretty much infinite, and all it takes is a letter you've never seen before to incite learning, I think.

Eagle

▲ In 1933 Morris Fuller Benton drew his famous titling alphabet, Eagle Bold, for the National Recovery Administration. In 1989, David Berlow took Benton's ideas as a starting point for a full typeface. He designed a lowercase, completed the character set, and added a Book weight for setting text. In 1994, Jonathan Corum followed up with the Light and Black weights.

▲ LEFT: Since founding The Font Bureau with Roger Black in 1982, Berlow designed dozens of type families, many of which found their way into Font Bureau's retail catalog. This printed specimen shows about 35 type families by Berlow and his co-designers.

"Type design is pretty much infinite, and all it takes is a letter you've never seen before to incite learning."

ELDORADO TEXT

Big fiasco
Prohibition, 1920
RUM
75% alcohol
Is that really you, McCoy?
FAST BOAT

Giza

▲ In the early nineteenth century, archeological discoveries triggered a genuine Egyptomania. Type founders capitalized on that craze by using the name "Egyptian" for several fashionable new display fonts. Over time, the word "Egyptian" has become synonymous with slab serif. Named after the Cairo suburb where the great pyramids stand, Font Bureau's Giza is a slab serif of monumental proportions. Its sixteen styles bring back the colorful power and variety of the original "Egyptian" typefaces. Berlow based the family on showings in Vincent Figgins' specimen of 1845. The truly thunderous bolder weights were designed for maximum effect in the largest of sizes.

▼ For the Giza family of heavyweights, common weight designations such as "Bold" or "Black" would obviously be of little use. Hence the number system, indicating first weight, then width.

When you and Roger Black founded the Font Bureau in 1989 – what were your objectives? What was it like, back then, starting an independent font foundry?

We're talking about all this happening midway between the introductions of PostScript and the web, so there was no web, just email. I'd been told that magazines were being composed and output using PostScript, but had never seen it. The type used in the graphics of newspapers was also being composed in PostScript, but I'd also not seen this. I had personally never sold any fonts or written or read a contract or licensing agreement, I'd only made two or three fonts in Fontographer. Adobe controlled the PostScript Type1 format, Apple had no competition and the basic hardware for a letter designer cost $7,000. So it was a little scary.

But Roger and I had the simple objective of making fonts that were useful to customers, and there was just enough cooperation going around to get things done repeatedly enough to bolster the confidence of lots of composers (a.k.a. customers), to move to PostScript.

Initially, customers were newspapers and magazines, Roger's clients, and I had brought a few clients with me too, including Apple and Hewlett-Packard. So, our simple objective became tied early on to the changes in technology, which is perhaps a good thing for founders already somewhat knowledgeable about type.

Many typefaces in the Font Bureau catalog, and your own fonts in particular, are revivals or interpretations of typefaces from previous centuries. What is so fascinating about the past?

What is fascinating to me about the types of the past is that they take me to a particular place and time where a type was required to solve some problem. The solution, quite often, then became visually associated with the person, publication or place where the solution was needed. Then, if the design was still cool several decades or centuries later, the design was revived for new technologies. Having the first one happen over 400 or so years ago, and then the second one 150 years ago to 50 years ago, we now have several layers of technologically and culturally motivated inventions and revivals to peer through for inspiration. And of course, with the physically vacant nature of type's modern form, all of the pieces of the past that were used to make and use type, even the rottenest old job case, are fascinating to me as well.

OneOne	OneThree	OneFive	ThreeOne	ThreeThree	ThreeFive	FiveThree	FiveFive
a	a	a	a	a	a	a	a

FiveSeven	SevenThree	SevenFive	SevenSeven	SevenNine	NineOne	NineThree	NineFive
a	a	a	a	a	a	a	a

> *"What is fascinating to me about the types of the past is that they take me to a particular place and time where a typeface was required to solve some problem."* — ELDORADO TEXT

More specifically, several of your own designs are inspired by nineteenth-century typefaces – I'm thinking of designs like Bureau Grotesque, Rhode, Giza. So… what's so fascinating about the nineteenth century?
To continue what I was saying, I think viewers in many cultures have reactions to types from different times and places that infuse some of the cultural soul from those places, to the new places in which the type is used. In your example, the slightly decorative uses of type in the world that preceded Helvetica, had roots in the nineteenth century, and I, being inclined towards Anglo-American tastes quite a bit, made Grotesques, Egyptians and Industrial sans in response, because lots of people between me and the viewer wanted to take the viewer to a slightly more soulful place, perhaps.

Font Bureau specializes in the design of custom type for newspapers, magazines and corporate clients. Is designing fonts for clients very different from working without an assignment – from being your own client, so to speak?
I've not worked without an assignment since Font Bureau was formed, really. When I've gone off on some big new font family, it's always been for a group of clients who wanted enough parts of it at once to make it worth risking.

When you begin working on a new typeface, do you have a specific method, a fixed sequence of characters that you draw first? A ritual, maybe?
Absolutely. Unless there is a logo involved, and assuming a whole typeface family is required with all the characters, I have a specific method. Logos and projects with limited styles to draw can require a different method. But usually, I start with H-O-D and then n-o-p, and then all the lowercase of the lightest and blackest styles of roman and italic from a to z.

At this stage I'm thinking of the possible typologies of each glyph, the detail of each of the unique features of each character, the weight spectrum and of course the roman-italic relationship, as much as possible in the context of its main use, whatever that has been determined to be. This is when I usually spend a lot of time looking at other solutions and historical references, and once a full set of lowercases are done, I do interpolations if I need to look at a middle weight right off, and a lot of proofing, and tinkering. I sometimes finish only the unique forms in each style, and sometimes I draw, space and build tables for everything, this decision depends on the design itself, how much detailed attention is required by the form of the type, and what kind of client relationship there is.

The knight returns
NOTHINGNESS
GRAY
32 flights
Some day, I swear, I will get the better of you
Intentionally stalling
Rack

Eldorao

▲ W. A. Dwiggins, the most idiosyncratic type designer of mid twentieth century America, cooperated with Mergenthaler Linotype on a long series of experimental typefaces. Many of his experiments never went into production, but Eldorado – which he worked on during World War II – was released in 1953. Based on a classic Spanish face, its atmosphere is distinctly different from Dwiggins' more radical families such as Metro and Electra. With Tobias Frere-Jones and Tom Rickner, Berlow revived Eldorado in 1993–94 for Premiere magazine, developing versions not only for text and display, but also a sturdy "Micro" weight for type sizes of six point and smaller.

CUMULATIVE MILES TRAVELED IN 2008

THIRTY-EIGHT THOUSAND FIVE HUNDRED AND TWENTY-FOUR*

*INCLUDES 1,030 MILES TRAVELED WITHIN THE VIDEO GAME GRAND THEFT AUTO IV.

An exhaustive compendium of travel and activity in 2008, including: 366 days of walking, 545 subway trips, 107 taxis, 12 flights, 19 buses, three car service journeys, two ferries, 38 chairlifts, four days of skiing, 20 days of driving, 46 trips with other drivers, 64 visits to the gym, three pools, an ocean, one hayride and 62 hours of Grand Theft Auto IV.

AVERAGE SPEED
4.39
MILES PER HOUR

PEDOMETERS PURCHASED
THREE

MOST MILES WALKED IN ONE DAY
11.7
BARCELONA, SPAIN: JUNE 21

TRAVEL: AVERAGE MILES PER DAY
835

NYC: AVERAGE MILES PER DAY
11
EXCLUDING VIDEO GAME MILEAGE: 7 MILES PER DAY

MILES WITH MOUSTACHE
179

SUBWAY MISHAPS
3
MISSED STOPS: 2
WRONG DIRECTION: 1

AVERAGE MILES WALKED PER DAY
3.13

AIRLINE PRICE PER MILE
$0.05

DRIVING PRICE PER MILE
$0.15

SUBWAY PRICE PER MILE
$0.93

GYM PRICE PER MILE
$5.26

HOURS AT WORK: 46%
JAN — DEC

HOURS FREE: 44%
JAN — DEC

HOURS ON VACATION: 10%
JAN — DEC

AVERAGE TEMPERATURE (°F)
54.7

LOWEST TEMPERATURE (°F)
7°
PARK CITY, UT: FEBRUARY 5

SPORTING ACTIVITIES
23
4 DAYS SKIING
1 SUPERBOWL PARTY
1 NIGHT OF POKER
1 BOWLING GAMES
1 HOCKEY GAME
6 DAYS SWIMMING
9 MATCHES WII TENNIS

SICK DAYS
FOUR

BEST MOVIE
MICHAEL CLAYTON

MICHAEL J. FOX SIGHTINGS
ONE

HIGHEST TEMPERATURE (°F)
96°
NEW YORK: JUNE 9, JUNE 10 & JULY 19

MUSEUM VISITS
SEVEN

PROPER HOUSE CLEANINGS
SEVEN

TRIPS TO THE CINEMA
14

PURCHASED CLOTHING ORIGINS
11
CANADA (1 ITEM), CHINA (5 ITEMS), ENGLAND (1 ITEM), ITALY (1 ITEM), KOREA (1 ITEM), LAOS (1 ITEM), MAURITIUS (4 ITEMS), MEXICO (1 ITEM), TURKIYE (1 ITEM), USA (5 ITEMS), VIETNAM (1 ITEM)

BIRTHDAY PARTIES ATTENDED
20

AVERAGE BIRTHDAY PARTY AGE
31
YOUNGEST: LUCIA, 2
OLDEST: PHIL, 40

TWO THOUSAND AND EIGHT

MUSIC

ITUNES TRACKS PLAYED
33,817
UP 14% FROM 2007

The verdict on 12 months of listening habits as recorded at last.fm/user/feltron.

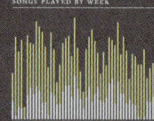

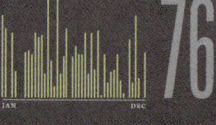

ARTISTS PLAYED
511

SONGS PLAYED BY WEEK
TOP 10 ARTISTS | OTHER ARTISTS

CDS PURCHASED
2
DIPLO & SANTOGOLD
DEERHUNTER

ALBUMS DOWNLOADED
46
EMUSIC (15)
OTHER MUSIC (12)
AMAZON (5)
ITUNES (3)

GENRE DISTRIBUTION OF TOP 100 ARTISTS
ELECTRONIC 22%
POST-ROCK 8%
HIP-HOP 15%
ALL OTHER 26%
INDIE 14%
IDM 9%
EXPERIMENTAL 6%

TRACKS PLAYED BY TOP 10 ARTISTS
BRADFORD COX (ATLAS SOUND & DEERHUNTER) 26%
RADIOHEAD
DAEDELUS
FLYING LOTUS
ELLIOTT SMITH
CARIBOU
THOM YORKE
VAMPIRE WEEKEND
THE NOTWIST

BEST ALBUM
ATLAS SOUND
"LET THE BLIND LEAD THOSE WHO CAN SEE BUT CANNOT FEEL"

BEST MIXTAPE
DIPLO & SANTOGOLD
"TOP RANKING MIXTAPE"

CONCERTS ATTENDED
8
DEERHUNTER
LE LOUP/RUBY SUNS
GLEN EDEN QUAY
THE NOTWIST
SIGUR RÓS
VAMPIRE WEEKEND
WEST DAKOTA (W/DJ)

NIGHTS DJ'D
EIGHT
5X LAPTOP & 3X VINYL

TWO THOUSAND AND EIGHT

READING

A set of determinations drawn from the reading of 2,440 book and 1,079 magazine pages.

BOOKS READ (WHOLLY OR PARTIALLY)
FOURTEEN
ABU GHRAIB (234 PAGES), THE BLACK SWAN (20 PAGES), COLLECTIONS OF NOTHING (74 PAGES), DRY STOREROOM NO. 1 (118 PAGES), DOWN AND OUT IN PARIS AND LONDON (218 PAGES), THE END OF OIL (270 PAGES), FROM HEAVEN LAKE (192 PAGES), IN DEFENSE OF FOOD (205 PAGES), IN PATAGONIA (193 PAGES), I MUST'VE BEEN SOMETHING LIKE (54 PAGES), KING LEAR (179 PAGES), THE MARTIAN CHRONICLES (182 PAGES), THE MEZZANINE (144 PAGES), THE VILLAGE UNDER THE SEA (60 PAGES)

NEW YORKER READING BY ISSUE
JAN — DEC

MAGAZINES READ
76
FAST COMPANY (76 PAGES), GOOD (85 PAGES), NEW YORK (64 PAGES), NEW YORKER (855 PAGES), NY TIMES MAGAZINE (9 PAGES), WIRED (46 PAGES)

BEST FICTION
THE MEZZANINE
BY NICHOLSON BAKER

BEST NON-FICTION
FROM HEAVEN LAKE
BY VIKRAM SETH

TWO THOUSAND AND EIGHT

PHOTOS

A summary of photographic activity with four cameras and online at flickr.com/photos/feltron.

PHOTOGRAPHS TAKEN
1,468
CANON SD870 IS (665 PHOTOS), CANON EOS 5D (605 PHOTOS), LEICA M8 (178 PHOTOS), BLACKBERRY (20 PHOTOS)

LAST PHOTO OF THE YEAR
THE GOLDEN GATE BRIDGE
DECEMBER 29, 2008

FLICKR FAVORITES
TYPE & DESIGN 33%
ARCHITECTURE 9%
OBJECTS 8%
CARS, TRAINS & OTHER VEHICLES 7%
PEOPLE 17%
CATS, DINOSAURS & ANIMALS 4%
OUTDOORS 15%
FOOD, ASTRONOMY & ALL ELSE 9%

DIGITAL PHOTOS BY WEEK
JAN — DEC

PHOTOS POSTED TO FLICKR
9%
124 PHOTOS & 6 VIDEOS

20

◀ At the end of 2005, designer Nicholas Felton published his first *Annual Report*, visualizing details of his professional and private life in appealing infographics. In 2006 the *Feltron Annual Report* became a printed publication, to huge international success. Shown here is the 2008 edition, designed with Berlow's Titling Gothic. The serifed typeface used for smaller text is Brioni Light from Typotheque.

49er luck
GOLD FEVER
BANG!
Sometimes crime pays
Sheriff
You look mighty cute in them jeans
CHAIN GANG

Rhode

▲ Not only did the trend-setting nineteenth century Londoner Vincent Figgins introduce the first recorded slab serifs, he also pioneered a style of elephantine grotesques, which found their parallel across the Atlantic in the American Railroad Gothic. Both styles stand out by their striking combination of straight verticals and generous curves above and below. Working from these forms, Berlow shrunk center strokes (as in 'A', 'E' and 'e') and minimized counterspace to emphasize the massive forms. The result is Rhode, a complete family of sans serifs which Font Bureau proudly describes as "a manly series of great dignity and presence."

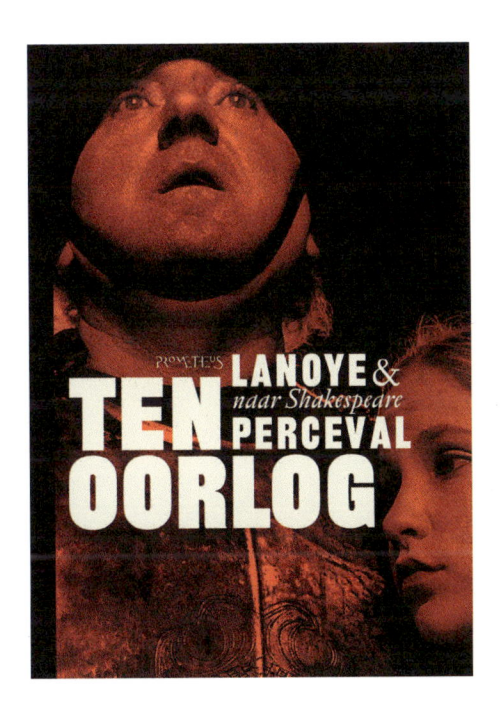

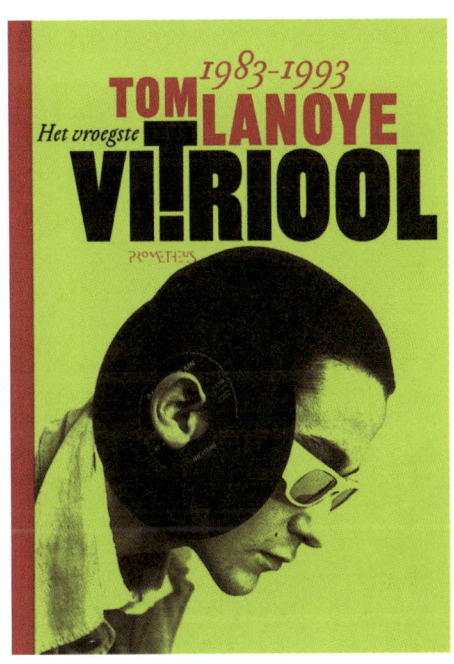

◀◀ Graphic designer Gert Dooreman from Ghent, Belgium, used Rhode to great effect in a number of book and poster projects for Prometheus publishers and the Toneelhuis theater company.

What?! Who is that wearing #23?
JORDAN
Dunkin' on you, left & right
TONGUE OUT
Endorsement checks are nice.

Bureau Grot

▲ Bureau Grotesque was first developed by David Berlow in 1989. In his quest to capture "the essence of tooth and character in an English nineteenth century sans," Berlow worked from original specimens of the grotesques released by Stephenson Blake in Sheffield during the 1800s. Bureau Grotesque met with immediate success at the Tribune Companies and Newsweek. Between 1994 and 2006, the family was further expanded under Berlow's supervision by Jill Pichotta, Christian Schwartz and Richard Lipton, at which point the family's name was shortened to Bureau Grot.

But the first several hundred characters are the most fun – getting the "monkey to swing right" repeatedly, so to speak, through the first styles and then through all the rest of the common glyphs in a family, and watching a style or family of styles behave on the screen or from the printer is the most fun, and I think, the very most fun when done methodically. By that, I mean not n-o-p then a to z, which is just an order of convenience for me. But methodically as in knowing what to compare to what and what to use as a starting point to draw a new character and how to differentiate between making changes and not chasing your tail.

As the Font Bureau's principal, one of your tasks is to criticize other people's design. What are the things you pay most attention to? What are the common mistakes made by beginners? And… do people think you're harsh?
Just to be clear, we receive one submission every day, there are a dozen or so projects going on at once, and hundreds of fonts are involved. These go through a screening process that gets a lot of things done that I never see. In reviewing submissions, for example, all the types that "don't fit" in our library, that are too close to what is already in our library, and other kinds, never get my criticism. What gets criticized is what I'm asked to look at, and my own work.

When I do look critically at type, I pay attention to suitability for the purpose it was intended, both technically and stylistically, and to see if the monkey swings, i.e. does the type work to form letters, words, lines or whatever, of the kind required? "Do people think I'm harsh?" is a question only "people" can answer. I am certainly direct when it comes to critiquing a font, but I try not mix harshness for a font with harshness for a person.

▶ Packaging for Warp Records artists Savath&Savalas designed with Bureau Grot. Art direction and design project by the Brooklyn agency GHAVA. Album cover photograph by Maya Hayuk.

Beside the computer – what's your main tool in designing type?
The rest of the world, I guess. I spend time doing things that allow me to think better about letter, typeface and font design. I generally do not, for example, sit down at the computer and think, "draw some letters", I go there when I can "draw these letters!" With this and the world's steady stream of typographic stimulation from old and new media and the revival of old media in new, I can't even think of another tool.

Among your older colleagues – who do you admire the most? And which type designers of the younger generation do you think are particularly talented?
Aldus to Zapf? Does older include passed? I can't choose there, it'd be like one of 'dem old Greek stadia filled with 'em, and I'd have to point at the whole thing or they'd stone me. Younger is also difficult because there are creators, there are craftspeople, there are technology people and I know five or ten of each that would be hard to separate. Other people, I think, are far more objective than I'd be.

You've witnessed something of a revolution in the type world since you started at Mergenthaler Linotype in the late '70s. What are the most dramatic changes? Do you like what's happening?
Well, perhaps not surprisingly, the web is the most dramatic change. The only thing I don't like about the web is that is makes it much easier for bad information and bad practices to spread very quickly and it is very difficult to correct. This is not unlike information and practices in many other fields, but in type, it is so easy for amateurs.

Among your typefaces, which are your favorites?
My fonts that are done.

Finally: you live on Martha's Vineyard, an island off the coast of Massachusetts. It is a beautiful spot, I'm told. Apart from that – does the place and its relative isolation help you in your work?
I'd grown up in small towns and rural environments until age 24 and then I moved to Manhattan. I lived in cities for 16 years and kept an apartment in Boston until four years ago. Urban living always supplies some amount of inspiration, but as the work itself (for me), requires a lot of concentration and an isolated if not isolationist environment, I find the quiet default more conductive to a 24/7/365 requirement to work, than anything else I've tried.
P.S. I utterly hate working in headphones.

▲ Cover of Geek Mafia, a self-published novel by Rick Dakan. Designed by Austin McKinnley with Berlow's Agency.

Agency

▲ This family was designed on the basis of a single titling font designed by Morris Fuller Benton in 1932. Berlow liked the squared, monotone forms of the narrow capitals and made Benton's concept his own, creating five different weights – all with lowercase – to produce Agency, an immediately popular hit.

Jean François
PORCHEZ

AMBROISE STANDARD

PARISINE PLUS STANDARD BOLD

Ever since he vaulted onto the type scene some fifteen years ago with a series of award-winning typefaces, Jean François Porchez has been among the most prominent type designers in France. He designed custom type for clients ranging from the *Baltimore Sun* to Louis Vuitton and the Paris Métro, and drew some of the best-known logos in his country. His one-man foundry, Porchez Typofonderie, offers an ever-growing library of type families that are both original and spectacular. Meet Jean François Porchez, our man in Paris. *July 2009*

APOLLINE STANDARD REGULAR

Photo © Jan Middendorp

François, shall we start at your beginnings?
Sure. My first serious encounter with type took place in the late 1980s when I was studying graphic design at a school called EMSAT. We had a guest teacher there named Ronan Le Henaff, who had been a trainee at the ANCT in Paris, a school specializing in type design – I'll get to that later. He introduced me to calligraphy and type design and made me realize that there were other career paths beyond graphic design or advertising. All the kids in my school wanted to become illustrators or art directors; nobody was seriously interested in type. So I thought: hey, here's my chance to do something special. When you start studying you want to be different. To choose type design was, at that time, pretty extraordinary.

There was another important reason. My mother ran her own bookshop; my father, who was in politics, had this huge library which, for example, included the complete collection of the famous literary review *Les Temps Modernes*. A very French, very intellectual background. Type design was a way to reconnect to that culture of the book, and do it on my own terms. I liked that.

Zero bits, really
5 SQUEAK
"Face your feet"
42¢ Tax
Going for Easter
Knight
REQUEST?
Peanut & Jelly

What did the French type world look like when you came out of art school?
At the time, the dominant tendency was a calligraphic one. The most influential school was in the city of Toulouse in the South of France: the Scriptorium de Toulouse founded by Bernard Arin. In Paris, a group of type specialists named CERT had persuaded the Ministry of Culture in 1985 to found ANCT, the Atelier National de Création Typographique, in an attempt to revive type design and technology in France. The sector had been in dire straits ever since the demise of the Deberny & Peignot foundry in 1974. During the first years of the ANCT (which later became ANRT and moved to Nancy), José Mendoza and Ladislas Mandel were important teachers, as was Albert Boton. Early trainees included Franck Jalleau, Jean-Renaud Cuaz and Thierry Puyfoulhoux – an entire wave of young type designers whose view of type was based on handwriting.

I studied at the ANCT for a year. But as I already knew how to design type (I had made my first typeface, Angie, while at the graphic design school), I didn't learn much. At one point I took a week off without telling anyone, to visit the Scriptorium de Toulouse. That's where I started my second typeface, Apolline.

Meanwhile, your international career had already taken off…
I soon felt that there was not a lot of room for me in the French type scene. The main positions were taken, and in Paris there was a kind of clan that you were or were not part of – and they had a tendency to reject you if you weren't. So it was natural for me to look abroad.

Ambroise

▲ The Didot family of typefounders and printers were pioneers in what came to be known as "Modern Face" – the neoclassical style of vertically contrasted typefaces. Designed in 2001, Ambroise is a contemporary interpretation of various types belonging to the late Didot style. It borrows some of its peculiar details from typefaces conceived circa 1830 by the Didots' punchcutter Vibert. The family's conception was based on the Black weight. Fat Didot faces in several widths could be found in the catalogs of French type foundries from the mid-nineteenth century until the demise of the great French foundries in the 1960s and 1970s. Each variation of the typeface carries a name in homage to a member of the illustrious Didot family. The condensed variant is called Ambroise Firmin; the extra condensed is Ambroise François.
ABOVE LEFT: Front page of an A3 format Ambroise specimen designed by Porchez in 2001.

▶ Hand-lettered logo sketches for Passionata, which Porchez created at Dragon Rouge design agency in 1994.

Eastern breakfast
ROCK
The final crag
Quench stone

Angie Sans

▲ Angie Sans is the sans-serif version of FF Angie, Porchez' first typeface. Angie Sans is a "glyphic" face in the tradition of Optima and Pascal, and has the elegantly tapered stems of that rare genre. It was given optimum legibility at text sizes by keeping letter shapes open and distinct from one another. Thanks to its subtle detailing, it is also a striking headline face for advertising and magazines. The italics are lighter, narrower and more flowing than the romans.

Contrary to many French designers, I always had a strong interest in what was happening elsewhere – in the English-speaking world or in the Netherlands. One book that introduced me to international type culture was Sebastian Carter's *Twentieth Century Type Designers*, a great didactic collection of short biographies that taught me a lot about the history of type design, about the various cultures and influences. I was also fascinated by the writings of John Dreyfus and Lawson's *Anatomy of a Typeface*.

So right after finishing the first version of the Angie typeface, even before I enrolled at ANCT, I submitted it to various international type foundries. It wasn't accepted, but it won a special prize at the 1990 Morisawa Awards in Tokyo, the Brattinga Prize.

I began frequenting the Rencontres Internationales de Lure, a yearly type conference in the south of France. I got on very well with its organizer Gérard Blanchard, who was a man of great culture – and a kind of mentor to many young designers at the time. At Lure, I met people like Matthew Carter, FontShop's Jürgen Siebert and people from Agfa. These contacts would eventually lead to the publication of my earliest typefaces at various international foundries.

In the mean time, what did you do to make a living?
At a certain point I was ready to cross the Channel to work at British Monotype. It didn't happen, for a number of reasons. Instead, I found a job at Dragon Rouge, a Paris design agency specializing in packaging and corporate identity. Remember that in the early 1990s computers and software were not as accessible as they are today, and there were hardly any independent type foundries. In France, working at a packaging agency was the best option if you wanted to make a living designing type. At Dragon Rouge I did a lot of hand-lettering – it enabled me to draw letters all day. Most importantly, it helped me to break away from calligraphy.

When you work at a packaging design company, you have to propose a wide variety of forms all the time, which opens up you mind and pushes you to make new discoveries. I stayed for three years. By then I had realized that letterforms do not necessarily have to evolve from the chancery script or the renaissance roman.

Working at Dragon Rouge also introduced me to the computer. There were just three Macs at the studio; I got to use one of them. With my own money I bought the type designing system Ikarus-M, which I installed on their computer. I actually preferred Ikarus to Fontographer – which I discovered later – because it was better for digitizing drawings on paper.

"We have to interpret traditional forms in our own way, which will necessarily be different."

PARISINE PLUS STANDARD BOLD ITALIC

How did you make the transition from working at an agency to being an independent type designer?
I was always looking for opportunities to design type. In April 1994 I read an article in *Le Monde*, a major French daily, by the new editor-in-chief Jean-Marie Colombani. He announced that later that year there was going to be a major overhaul of the paper's design. So I decided to make them a new typeface: a drastic reworking of Times New Roman, which was their current typeface, optimized for a French newspaper and for current technologies. In July I wrote to the editor saying I wanted to propose a new typeface to suit the paper's new formula. A typeface made for the French language, respectful of French culture. I mentioned that it might be high time to replace Times New Roman, which had originally been designed for a conservative, royalist English newspaper. Of course I knew that *Le Monde*, with their independent, politically committed stance, would be sensitive to that.

Le Monde agreed to receive me, I did a big presentation and at the end of it they said "Banco!", which in French means, "OK, go for it!" They were in a hurry. They asked me to design three weights during my August holidays. So after a month of hard work at Corsica, carrying my very first notebook computer, I submitted three fonts for testing in September. They gave me the definitive go-ahead a couple of weeks later, and within a week I'd quit Dragon Rouge. After that, I made them one weight each week, eight series including serif and sans-serif versions.

You never yielded the Le Monde typeface's copyrights to the paper and you negotiated the right to publish it yourself after some years. It takes considerable business acumen for a budding designer to insist upon that kind of clause.
I'd talked to some very experienced designers, like Sumner Stone and Matthew Carter, and also Ladislas Mandel in France, who had designed phonebook typefaces for major telephone companies. They made me understand that the best option was to give them a discounted price in exchange for a limited exclusivity period. In France, type design is part of copyright laws; copyrights are unalienable, and protected until 70 years after the death of the author. If you have that kind of protection, why not benefit from it?

From 1995 onwards you were an independent type designer, publishing your typefaces at different companies: FF Angie through the FontFont library; Apolline at Creative Alliance (Agfa-Monotype); Anisette at Font Bureau. You obviously didn't want to put all your eggs in one basket.
I wanted to be independent right from the start. It is a bad idea to have all your fonts with just one publisher. A colleague of mine had published several fonts at a German

Sea finding
LINER
Steam Journey
Bon voyage!
TRAVEL BY SHIP

Anisette
▲ Inspired by a mid twentieth century Art Deco font named Banjo, Porchez designed the multi-weight display font Anisette in 1996. Anisette is a double alphabet of capitals: wide and narrow. As requests kept pouring in to add lowercase characters, Porchez drew Anisette Petite, based on a new intermediate width of the capitals. The Anisette Petite lowercase possesses the sobriety of many geometric typefaces, adding unmistakable dynamic tension in the curves. Subtle imperfections seen in the 'r', 'l' and 'g' help create an original typeface.

Marshmallow
2 Graham crackers
Chocolate
Open flame

Le Monde Journal

▲ Le Monde Journal is the typeface on which the entire Le Monde family is based. By definition, it is intended for newspaper use and at small sizes. As it was designed to replace Times New Roman, it has the same typographic "color". Yet it is distinctly different in its detailing, being optimized for greater fluency and reading flow. The counters in the glyphs are large and open, as if they illuminate the letters from the inside. To meet the challenges of newspaper printing, the Bold sharply contrasts with the Regular, while the Demi weight is better suited for titling. Le Monde Journal was designed in 1994 as the text face of the daily *Le Monde* and was used by that newspaper for over ten years.

foundry which then folded and was taken over, and in the process he lost all his royalties. I soon realized that even with the most respected foundries, you never know what may happen to them. That's why I've always advised younger designers to diversify in order to better protect their rights, and have a broader range of options from a marketing point of view.

You soon decided to start up your own foundry, Porchez Typofonderie. When did that happen?
Let's see… I discovered the internet in 1996, took my domain name in early 1997… I had my first website up in the summer of 1997. It was a hassle to have a website hosted in France at the time, so I went to a Canadian provider that was also used by my colleague John Hudson.

In the beginning I worked without any distributor at all, just selling to customers directly. Kind of crazy when you think about it. It was my way to safeguard quality and be independent. I even withdrew a couple of typefaces from one of the foundries I worked with because they didn't operate in a correct way. I saw the royalties diminish each month. It turned out they were calculating the percentage not based on turnover but "after marketing" which is, of course, impossible to check. It was disrespectful of the rights of the designer, so I left. I did embark on the MyFonts adventure from the very start, though with only two font families.

For almost ten years, I was radically against working with distributors, in order to have total control over my work. I changed my attitude a couple of years ago. After many discussions with people in the business, I've become more open. I'm distributing through FontShop and I'm making more and more stuff available through MyFonts.

Pirating has always been a concern, but I realized that you'll always have a certain percentage of leakage through pirated fonts. Whatever your sales volume, the ratio is more or less the same. So it's better to open up instead of trying to seal yourself off.

Let's touch on the creative aspects of your work. How would you summarize your philosophy of type design?
The main task of a type designer is to enable people to read a text. So the letters have to be readable. This may mean – and for a long time I exclusively took that approach – that you use open letterforms of a humanistic character, related to writing. You pay a lot of attention to the rhythm, the frequency of particular signs in particular languages, the varying widths. You shouldn't borrow too many details from calligraphy, the way I learned it in the beginning, but mainly the force, flow and structure of writing.

When I do a piece of lettering using new letterforms, for example, I try not to concentrate on the effect but on what's behind it, on the inner workings of the alphabet.

"Type design was a way to reconnect to the culture of the book and do it on my own terms. I liked that."

PARISINE PLUS STANDARD BOLD ITALIC

Open up the counterforms – the "white" of the letters – which has always been a focus of pragmatic type designers such as Gerard Unger or Ladislas Mandel. It relates to a philosophy of making things accessible.

I think this practical aspect of usability is crucial to type design, even when working from a historical model. When I'm working on a Baskerville revival like Henderson Serif, for instance, I'll open up the counters to improve legibility, I may accentuate the diagonal stress. I don't just scan a typeface and digitize it respectfully. That's more or less the approach you find a lot in North America; I think that from a design perspective it lacks the added value which you may find in revivals that have been made the European way. I think it's not so interesting to just take old letterforms and adapt them to a new technology. You can leave those typefaces alone, they're fine where they are. You have to come up with new elements instead.

Your revivals, such as Sabon Next – based on Jan Tschichold's Sabon, itself a Garamond revival – and Ambroise have been criticized for taking too many liberties.
I'm aware of that, and I'm comfortable with it. I've consciously taken on the task of adding something meaningful that befits our times. We have our own experiences and our own culture, with its reading habits and printing technology. We have to interpret forms in our own way, which will necessarily be different. You can criticize it and comment on it – fine. But it's added value. Is it better or not? That's for the critics to decide.

It's a bit like *haute cuisine*. In a good restaurant, they don't cook a Boeuf Bourguignon just like that. They interpret the dish in a creative way, maybe adding some oriental flavors… that's what constitutes the work of a great chef. He doesn't simply take the recipe from a cookbook. It's what he adds that makes it into something contemporary and special.

Could you describe your steps when you begin a new typeface?
The first thing I do is to formulate a challenge that is different from others – if it's possible. When I make a custom typeface for a client, they are not going to tell me exactly what to do, because they're not type designers. So I often need to write my own brief

Big up yourself
It's been a while coming
Didactic
Skills paying billz
Nice technique
Breaker up
Park Square
Aiming for first
Top Pick
325 km/h
24 hours of Le Mans
Qualifiers
Ending of the track
GO FASTER

Parisine and Parisine Plus
Porchez designed Parisine in 1996 for the Paris transport authority RATP with the specific purpose of improving the legibility and ease of use of the public transport signage system. In 1999, the family was revised and extended for use in maps and external communication. Bold versions are available as Parisine Sombre, lighter versions as Parisine Clair. Parisine Plus is a playful variation on the Parisine typeface, designed independently from the series of custom fonts developed for RATP. It was meant to be a reaction – a kind of self-criticism – to the functionalist objectivity of Parisine. While Parisine tries to embody neutrality (a very relative term, in fact) Parisine Plus has fun with contrasts and ornamental details that are not so obvious for a sans-serif family.

It's in the basement
Marge
Tyrannosaurus talk
The heart of Texas
Dance shoes
GIVE CHASE
Paging Mr. Herman

Le Monde Sans

▲ Le Monde Sans was designed in 1994 and was derived from the serifed family – a practice that has now become commonplace. The design of Le Monde Sans follows the proportions common to the entire family, which allows the user to effortlessly combine and alternate these subfamilies within the composition.

Eat 25 Nonpareils
Sugary Pureé
Crazy figs
Gorgeous Aubergine
THE UNION of FOOD
Work Quest

Le Monde Livre & Livre Classic

▲ As Le Monde Journal was developed specifically for use at small point sizes (below 10 points), Porchez decided to develop a companion sub-family for everyday work at larger sizes, from books to posters. Le Monde Livre has subtler details and brighter contrasts. Additionally, Le Monde Livre's italics are of a totally new design, closer to Renaissance models. The Classic version is a fancier variant, with special ligatures and other typographic effects.
Porchez originally designed it for his daughter's birth announcement.

stipulating as many constraints as possible in order to give the design a certain direction and a force of its own. I've found that writing a brief is especially useful when working with a graphic design agency. Graphic designers have a lot of expertise when it comes to symbols and colors and figurative connotations; but they're often at a loss when they're faced with a series of black abstract forms like an alphabet. So you have to give them a parallel road to arrive at understanding why this or that shape has a specific evocative power.

For instance, when I designed the corporate typeface for France Télécom's new identity in 2000, their brief was to develop an alphabet which evoked both technology and the human aspect. They had gone from being a company that sold stuff – machines, hardware – to selling communication between people. My way of translating that was to combine round forms and angular forms within the letters. You also found that in a lot of French car designs at the time: Twingo, Mégane, Kangoo; there was a Ford Focus across the street from my studio that had similar characteristics. So… you have to create a visual concept.

In general, working for a client is always better. You have a specific need to fulfill with specific constraints. Constraints are what allow you to design. Imagine a graphic designer making a corporate identity without a client? Design a book without an author? They can't work like that. You can't design something unless you know what has to be done, what the thing's function is going to be. It's the same with type. Making a typeface without having a clue about what it is for is impossible. It's not design! A designer is there for solving problems, for making something perform a certain function. After that, you put in your own individuality, of course, because you're a unique person. But the first step is to respond to a particular need.

Apart from having designed some spectacular typeface families for retail as well as dozens of corporate typefaces and logos, you've also been very active in other capacities. Among other things, you edited a book on French type, founded the community blog *Le Typographe* dedicated to French typography and type design, and for several years were president of the international typographers' organization ATypI. In what ways have these activities been meaningful to you?

I believe in sharing knowledge, and there are many ways to exchange and share information. I began teaching during my first year as a professional designer. Teaching allows me to compare opinions, structure my thinking, pass on knowledge. Those associations founded in the 1950s, such as the Rencontres internationales de Lure and ATypI, have allowed us to exchange experiences and build a community – however small it still is. I think it is very rewarding to take part and give your time without expecting anything back because if an association works well, our community as a whole profits from it, receives recognition, becomes more visible and more alive. I took the initiative to set up *Le Typographe* in 2003 when I was the French delegate of ATypI because I thought a French-language website would help to enhance that association's visibility in this country. Also, I am convinced that speaking about type, and about the fonts we and our peers create, pushes the media to treat type design as an important subject. To acknowledge that meaningful things happen in France as well – not just in New York, Berlin or Amsterdam. ෴

▶ Poster designed in 2004–2005 for an exhibition of Porchez' work.

Mini spécimen du Le Monde Livre Classic, 1999.

Le Monde

Empattement du Le Monde Journal.

Nouveau logotype dessiné en 1994 pour la nouvelle formule du journal *Le Monde*.

Des livres
Some books on Type
finer French type cast by Mathis Porchez
& TES CARACTÈRES
LM Livre 012 ÆThßŒŷ Classic
LM Livre 0123456789 & Classic
LM Livre 0123456789 & & Classic
LM Livre ÆThßŒŖfclesty Classic
LM Livre 0126 ÆThŒŧyŸ Classic

Empattement du Times.

Superposition des 4 dessins de base.

Toutes les séries.

Le Monde
Le Monde
Le Monde
Le Monde
Le Monde
Le Monde
Le Monde
Le Monde
Le Monde
Le Monde
Le Monde
Le Monde
Le Monde
Le Monde
Le Monde
Le Monde
Le Monde
Le Monde
Le Monde
Le Monde
Le Monde
Le Monde
Le Monde
Le Monde
Le Monde
Le Monde
Le Monde
Le Monde
Le Monde
Le Monde
Le Monde
Le Monde

Accentuation des horizontales pour une meilleure lisibilité du caractère Le Monde.

nandnenon
nandnenon

Comparaison dans la taille réelle d'utilisation du journal *Le Monde*.

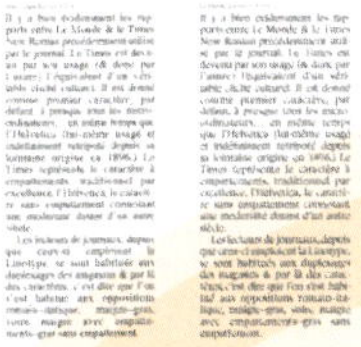

Capitales plus petites. *Smaller capitals.*
Empattements décalés. *Gap serifs.*
Contre-formes plus ouvertes. *Open-counterforms.*
Horizontales affirmées. *Strong horizontality.*

HOphagnef

Empattements plus contrastés. *Contrasted serifs.*
Pente moins forte. *Lesser slope.*

HOphagnef

Formes plus découpées. *Contrasted forms.*
Empattements simplifiés. *Simplified serifs.*

Comparaison du Times en gris avec Le Monde en noir.

Il y a bien évidemment les rapports entre Le Monde & le Times New Roman
Times.
Il y a bien évidemment les rapports entre Le Monde & le Times New Roman
Le Monde journal.

La famille Le Monde utilise l'axe oblique comme principe de construction pour dynamiser le processus de lecture.

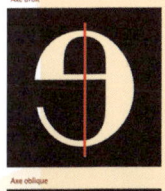

Axe droit
Axe oblique

Exemples des différentes séries de la famille Le Monde.

L'Illustration
Grande Mobilisation !
AFFAIRE TRÈS EUROPÉENNE
Journaux
Prise de la Tour de Malakoff
Guerre au Moyen-Orient
Transatlantique
dʒupmɑɡ
θmɛҫbɑɣn ŋ͡l ɔ̃guiҫҫ
La chaise
LE BULLETIN
Un traité d'art décoratif
Stabilité d'une composition graphique
Rhinocéros fou
À titre indicatif, 3500 F DONNE 530,30 €
La belle Italique
Les Classiques
ŒUVRES ADMIRABLES DU SEIZIÈME SIÈCLE
L'année dernière, j'ai lu 2467 romans
Some books on Type
finer French type cast by Mathis Porchez
Renaissance du livre
26 caractères
Les Classiques
Some books on Type
finer French type cast by Mathis Porchez
LA TYPO & TES CARACTÈRES
Ligatures
Beau Garage
not monospaced
Courriers
Chère grand-mère, nos vacances se passent bien
The incompetent Student
Letter setting
WELL FITTING CLOTHES ARE AN ACTUAL NECESSITY
typewritten imitation

Quelques uns des différents logos de sections (suppléments) utilisés jusqu'à la nouvelle formule de janvier 2002.

Le Monde Journal
ABCEGMRhàmbürgêfioñstiv1234

Le Monde Journal Ipa
ɑbҫɛɢɰrhɒmβʉɪɡeføŋʃtʊvʐҫɜɸɑ

Le Monde Sans
ABCEGMRhàmbürgêfioñstiv1234

Le Monde Livre
ABCEGMRhàmbürgêfioñstiv1234

Le Monde Courrier
ABCEGMRhàmbürgêfioñstiv1234

Le Monde Livre Classic
ABCEGMRhàmbürgêfioñstiv123
ABCTEGMhàmbürgêfioñstiv12345

La une du journal *Le Monde* jusqu'en 2002. Depuis, le caractère Le Monde n'est utilisé que pour le texte.

LISTE DES CARACTÈRES DE BASE POUR CHAQUE SÉRIE.
abcdefghijklmnopqrstuvwxyz
ABCDEFGHIJKLMNOPQRSTUVWXYZ
æœÆŒfffiflffiffl
0123456789&0123456789&0123456789
$¢£¥€ƒ%‰¹¼½¾†‡¹²³⁰⁽⁾...
-*‡§†¶§@©®™ªºµ\<÷×>¬
áâàäåçéêèëîïìñóôòöõśŭûùüÿ
ÁÂÀÄÅÇÉÊÈËÎÏÌÑÓÔÒÖÕŚŬÛÙÜŸ

TypeTogether:
Veronika Burian & José Scaglione

BREE LIGHT

BREE EXTRA BOLD

She is one of the type world's most cosmopolitan type designers, having lived in Munich, Milan, London, Boulder, and recently moved back to her native Prague. He is a designer in Rosario, Argentina. Both interrupted successful careers in graphic and multimedia design to become two of the first graduates of the MA program in Type Design at the University of Reading, UK. Having spent several years as an in-house designer at the Dalton Maag foundry in London, Veronika teamed up with José in 2006 to found TypeTogether and start a fruitful long-distance partnership. *October 2008*

CRETE THIN

Veronika, you were born in Prague, grew up in Southern Germany, worked as a designer and teacher in Milan and learned the fine points of designing type in England. To what extent has each of these cultures influenced your work?
These different experiences deeply influenced my general personality and made me, I believe, tolerant and open-minded. I think this also manifests itself in my work, because I don't feel I have a specific style in my typefaces (but please correct me if I am wrong!). One could possibly summarize it this way: From the Czechs I learned expressionism and vitality, from the Germans perseverance and methodology, from the Italians openness and warmth, and from the Brits I got contacts and marketing skills.

Your initial education was in Industrial Design. What made you switch to type? Do you think your approach is different from other type designers because of that background?
I came to designing type via some detours. I was getting disillusioned with the reality of product design and moved increasingly towards graphic design. A friend, who is a

type enthusiast, then introduced me to the world of type design and it was like falling in love. I knew I had found something I really enjoyed and felt at home with. There is actually a link to my previous education as product designer. Both fields ideally endeavor to improve the experience of an object from the user's point of view, be it a good piece of typography or a comfortable chair. Creating things that have meaning and a function is very satisfactory.

I don't think I am particularly influenced by my previous education as product designer. However, it surely sharpened my eye for detail, proportions and sense for shapes in a way that is different than a graphic designer would have. The main link I see between the two is the versatility and human expression that manifests itself in something practical.

You perfected your type designing skills at the University of Reading, one of the few institutions that offer a specialized course in type design. Would you say there is such a thing as a "Reading School": a specific methodology or stylistic approach?
Well, I guess many people would say there is. The MA course was at its beginnings when I was there, so the curriculum wasn't very fixed yet and [program director] Gerry Leonidas improves it continuously as a result of his students' feedback. Something particular to Reading, though, is the focus on non-latin typography. They have amazing resources there and people like Fiona Ross are fabulous teachers in that particular field. Also, the academic part of the course is rather strong. Personally I enjoyed that and found it important for my general development in the field. They've reduced it a bit since I was there, though. Other than that I don't really think there is a specific design style being imposed on the students. They are left free to experiment and find their own sources of inspiration. However I did notice, in some of the students' work since my time there, a clear influence from Gerard Unger, who has a special style himself.

Many type designers are self-taught. Would you say that a formal education in type can help you acquire skills or open up perspectives that are hard to arrive at when finding out things on your own?
I wouldn't say that a self-taught type designer is by default worse than somebody that was formally educated. However, I do think that it is faster and easier to learn when attending a type course such as the one offered in Reading. There is better and broader access to resources such as archives, teachers and guest-lecturers. This will deepen one's knowledge and skills and it will establish future contacts. There is also intellectual and direct exchange with people with similar interests, who will give you

Far-reaching
Quirky
fisticuffs
Walking & Talking
13th goal

Bree

▲ Based on the TypeTogether logo, Bree can be considered the foundry's signature typeface. Like many of TypeTogether's faces, Bree was a joint project by Veronika Burian and José Scaglione. Bree's design is clearly influenced by handwriting and has many characteristics of an upright italic: a single-story 'a', cursive 'e', curved outstrokes on 'v' and 'w', and more. When a more classical look is desired, alternate lettershapes are available for each of these.

▼ The poster below, made for a Type Together exhibition, shows these stylistic variants.

Quickly jumping zebra
Quickly jumping zebra

> "The main link I see between *type* and *industrial design* is the versatility and human expression that manifests itself in *something practical.*"
>
> KARMINA REGULAR & ITALIC

33

Released @ 3:15 AM
Sensation
½ Man, ½ Whale
Print to fit
THE MAGIC BULLET
Daily & Weekly
HOT STORY

Ronnia

▲ Ronnia, another joint design by Scaglione and Burian, is a versatile sans-serif in two widths (Normal and Condensed) and five weights, from Light to Heavy. Ronnia has the qualities of a typeface engineered for newspaper and magazine applications: economic in use, highly legible, and approaching the reader with friendliness and charm. Ronnia's personality performs admirably in headlines, but thanks to its humanist touch and open shapes it is also highly legible in continuous text. Ronnia features about 800 glyphs per weight, including small caps, fractions, and many styles of numerals.

important feedback. I learned almost as much from my fellow students as from the teachers themselves. Also, not to forget the fact that doing an MA or similar, guarantees one year of concentration on type design. This rarely happens in the real world and therefore it takes much more effort to learn type design on your own. However there are online forums, conferences and small courses that surely allow for some degree of exchange and learning.

Who have been your main teachers, either through their personal teachings or through their work and writings?
At Reading there were mainly Gerry Leonidas and Gerard Unger, both of whom were influential teachers for me. I still admire Gerry for keeping his confidence in me and encouraging me despite my amateurish sketches at the beginning. Also I should mention Maxim Zhukov, who was incredibly helpful when I was designing Maiola Cyrillic. He made me understand the subtleties and typographic rules of Cyrillic. And last but not least, there has been the example of two designers who are long gone – Oldřich Menhart and Vojtěch Preissig, who influenced me through their passion and vigor in their work.

What is the most satisfying aspect of designing typefaces?
The most satisfying aspect of designing typefaces is to see them used well; to see that it works in a particular environment.

You mentioned Menhart and Preissig as influences; you even wrote a lengthy essay on the former. What is it that attracts you in their work? Is part of the attraction in their specifically Czech or Central European spirit? What are the most important things you've learned from them?
When I started at Reading, I didn't know anything about Czech type design. So I was delighted when I found some books in the library that showed some beautiful Czech specimens. I looked into it further and discovered Menhart's and Preissig's legacies. Their work attracted me not only because they were Czech, but also because they showed such vitality and vigor. At the same time as being expressive, their typefaces – in particular Menhart's – are also very legible and functional on the page. This combination fascinated me. In addition to their approach to designing diacritics properly, Menhart's typefaces also taught me that calligraphy, in a broader sense, is important; it is where the origins of our alphabet lie. Studying the flow of a broad-nibbed pen is crucial for understanding the correct letter structure and contrast. However, I do not fully embrace his credo of calligraphy being the cradle of type design.

> "The most satisfying aspect of designing typefaces is *to see them used well*; to see that it works in a particular environment."

KARMINA REGULAR & ITALIC

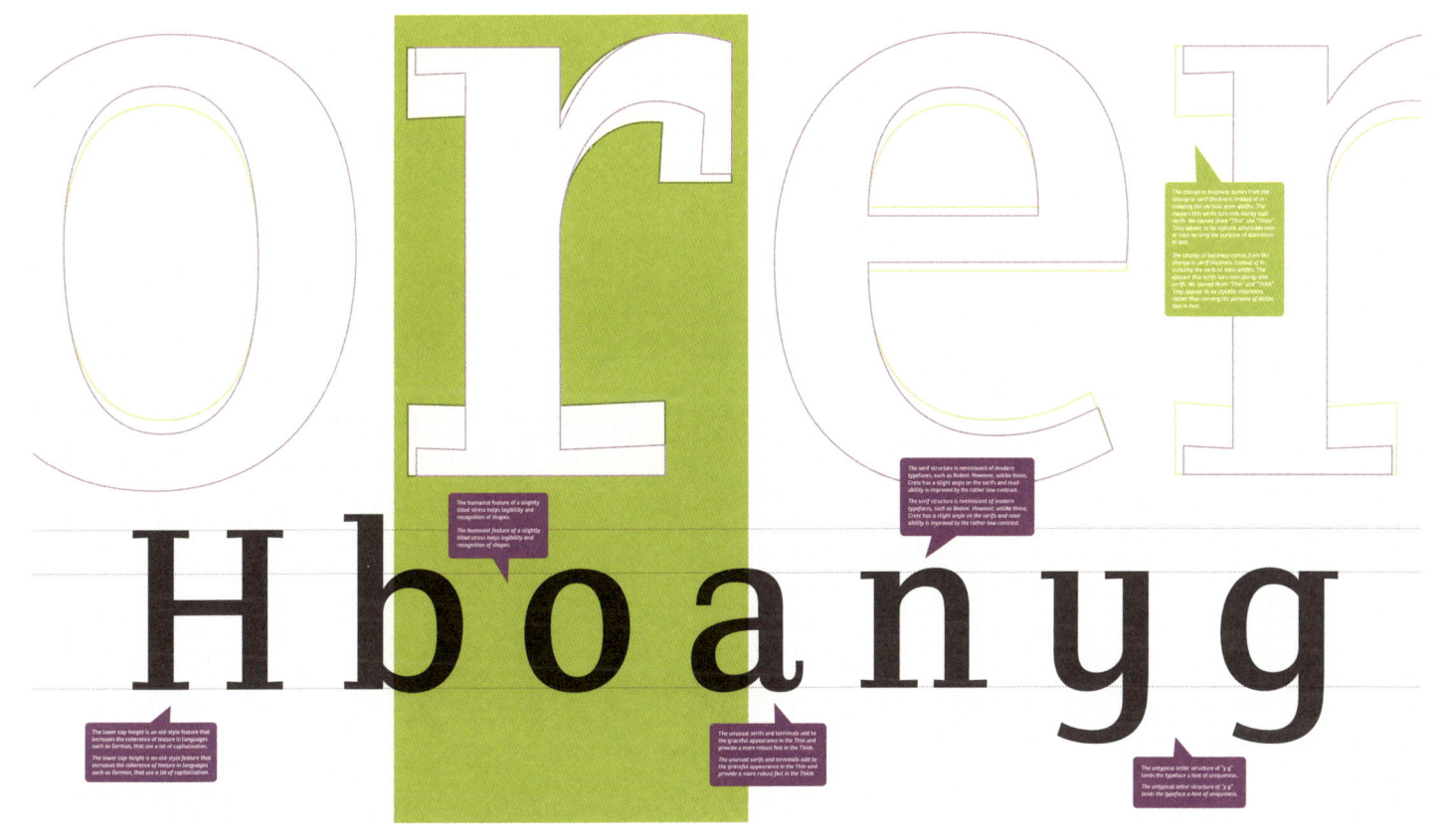

For several years, you worked for Dalton Maag in London, developing mainly custom typefaces such as Tondo. Does designing a custom typeface require a different attitude or approach than making a self-initiated font for retail?
Well, one big difference is time, I'd say. With client work there is always a deadline, often a very tight one. It is common to design a four-weight family within a few weeks. Also you have to be flexible, and sometimes design something you don't particularly like or agree with. Ideally the client trusts your judgment and authority on this subject, but it also happens that you have to explain typographic terms and conventions to them; all of which can be very difficult.

Having published one typeface, the wonderful Maiola, as part of the FontFont library, you founded TypeTogether with José Scaglione, whom you met while you were both studying in Reading. What made you decide to create your own foundry, and do it together?
I always enjoyed working independently more than being employed. I decide what I want to do and when; and quite honestly, financially it's more lucrative too. José told me about his wish to create a foundry some day, and at some point I thought it would be a great idea to share our skills and experiences. So we started to work on the project that later became Karmina. It worked out really well and things developed from there.

You recently moved to Prague after having lived in the US for some time; José is based in Rosario, Argentina – do you actually meet sometimes to work together?
This past May, I went to visit José in Rosario on the occasion of our exhibition and that was the first time we saw each other since we started TypeTogether, over 2 years ago. It was great to actually sit in the same office and discuss projects directly, but I don't think it's necessary in order to have a fruitful collaboration. It is more important to

EARTH
Branches
Island
King's Fruit
Salty

Crete

▲ Burian designed Crete after spotting an interesting piece of wall lettering in a chapel on the Greek isle of that name. The result is an unusual display font in two variations: Thin, with flat, Bodoni-like serifs, and Thick, sporting sturdy slab serifs. Both varieties have exactly the same width, so they are fully interchangeable without causing the text to reflow – opening up great possibilities for experimental mixes. However, Crete also works nicely in a more conventional text environment.

Affective sauce
Visceral
Food & Drink
3 drops should do the trick
Concoction

Athelas

▲▼ Athelas originated as a project by Scaglione and was completed as a joint venture with Burian; it is probably the most traditional-looking of Type-Together's faces. Inspired by the great literary classics, Athelas is an homage to fine book printing. According to its designers, "Athelas takes full advantage of the typographic silence, the white space… between the columns, the lines, the words, the lettershapes and within the characters themselves." Athelas will look best in carefully designed book editions, printed on a quality offset press.

ABCDE
FGHIJK
LMNOP
QRSTU
VWXYZ
abcdefg
hijklmn
opqrstu
vwxyz
01234
56789

have mutual trust and respect, and obviously a fast internet connection with Skype! As a design process, usually one of us has an idea for a new typeface or thinks it necessary to expand an existing one. José or I then prepare some characters, we discuss the design direction, start to expand the character-set and give each other feedback. Basically we send the files back and forth and mark the glyphs we worked on. We also talk almost every day and discuss the workload.

Your typefaces are all quite serious and well wrought. Would you see yourself designing a display or script typeface?
One should keep the options open and I have done some display style typefaces for Dalton Maag. However, there are already some very good script and display faces around, so I don't feel I can contribute as much as I can with text typefaces.

When you co-design a typeface, who does what?
We don't really look at it in terms of splitting tasks. We like working on several typefaces at the same time and doing different stuff so we don't get bored. Both of us can take care of any part of the process. The basic and most important rule is that the one who designs a shape should not correct it. In other words, if I design a few glyphs it is up to Veronika to check them and fine-tune them, and vice versa. The font goes back and forth many times until we are happy with it. I think we trust each other's judgment a lot, and that makes it a very easy and interesting collaboration methodology. Plus, it can accelerate the type design process significantly.

José, you're now permanently based in Argentina again after a prolonged stay in Reading. What do you think about the recent developments in Latin American type design?
We are seeing very exciting times on the Latin American font scene. This year's type exhibition Tipos Latinos showed that more and better fonts are being produced than ever, with more than 400 fonts submitted. There are now three schools in Latin America where it is possible to study type design, and I understand attendance was very good for 2009. I also see that the rest of the world is observing the growing Latin American type scene with a lot of interest. For instance [the worldwide typographic association] ATypI hosted last year's conference in Mexico, the first time ever in a Latin American country. All this being said, I have no doubt that type design in this region is still in its adolescence, and I expect an improvement in quality over the next couple of years, partly driven by these new design courses and the growing interest in the field.

(Updated early 2010)

Karmina: Serif to Sans

aendz

When creating a sans from a serif counterpart a designer makes several obvious changes – chopping off serifs, changing terminals, maintaining the same x-height and similar stroke-width, and decreasing the stroke contrast, whilst keeping the same axis angle.

Additionally, special care is taken to preserve the subtleties of the original serif typeface, such as small curves on in- and outstrokes, ink traps and the blunted bowl on 'e'.

Apart from all of these, particular decisions were made to ensure a well-balanced design. For example, the kink in the bowl on 'a' is smoothed out, the bottom connection on 'd' is less deep, the eye on 'e' is bigger and the horizontal strokes on 'z' are more subdued.

Economic
Penguin, **Victor Hugo**, "Les Misérables"
(Popular Classics)
£63.98?!
The cover shows a detail from "FIGHTING AT THE HOTEL DU VILLE"
DENNY & POPPER
Písmař

¿PARA TEXTO?
Národní DIVADLO začalo s vydáváním
10^{5}/$_{6}$ miles Æreo of the
découvert
laisser la date EN SUSPENS
¶905•613
Tipografías, desde la

Jos Buivenga

FERTIGO PRO SCRIPT

MUSEO 900

The way Dutchman Jos Buivenga rose to prominence on the type scene is quite remarkable. For years, his online friends and fans could follow the development of his typefaces via his website, and download the results at no cost. When his one-man foundry exljbris began selling his first commercial typeface Museo through MyFonts in 2008, several weights were offered for free. The generosity paid off: Museo became a meteoric bestseller. Eighteen months, five typefaces and one bankrupt employer later, he found himself a full time type designer – and doing very well, thank you. Meet Jos Buivenga, going with the flow on the river of life. *September 2009*

CALLUNA REGULAR

Jos, you joined MyFonts in early 2008. By then, you had already created quite a following on your website and blog, where people could comment on your type design process and download beta versions of your fonts. When did it all start? Was there any kind of master plan behind it?

It all started back in 1994 with the wish to make a typeface of my own. I just wanted to see what it would feel like to use a font of my own on my first Mac. Of course this isn't the best brief to start a font. So I considered making my first typeface, Delicious, to be just a learning process. I was completely new to type design, which is the main reason why it took me two years to create a font family that I was happy with. It sounds like a long time but it was a great experience, being in a creative process, doing highly concentrated work, exploring caveats and finding solutions. It never really crossed my mind to sell it because I didn't know if it was good enough.

My second typeface, Fontin, which I began a decade later, still felt like a typographic exploration that I preferred to share rather than sell. Another reason for preferring to give it away was probably that I still didn't consider myself a real type designer. After I had finished Fontin, my fonts got listed on several blogs. That's when things really took off. I realized that people really liked my work, fortunately not only because I offered it for free. Site traffic started to build up and grew steadily year after year. At that stage I still worked full-time but the thought of selling some fonts to be able to work a day less each week began to occur more and more often.

So as a type designer you're completely self-taught. Have you missed education, once you became serious about type, or do you think that designers who are talented and interested will always be able to figure things out on their own?
You won't hear me say that ignorance is bliss. But as a non-intellectual person, when creating things I need to find a sound balance between knowing and not knowing. I found out long ago that this is the best way for me to explore my creative capabilities, and make the design process worthwhile. With wonderful online resources like Typophile, I never really felt I missed education. My experience is that if you're interested, the effort it takes to figure things out is reduced drastically. And that's really a blessing for someone like me who is otherwise lazy by nature.

Also – and this is not out of laziness, but to have more time for type design – I am always exploring the possibilities of outsourcing technical stuff and repetitive tasks. For my latest fonts I've been using iKern, the kerning and spacing service of Igino Marini. That proved to be a big time saver, which is great because time really is probably my most valuable asset. I have so many ideas that I want to fulfill, that if I were able to split myself into three entities I would still have enough type design work for years to come.

You're in your mid-forties, and as a type designer you were a late starter. Do you think things would have been much different if you had begun getting serious about type earlier on?
I've always regarded life as a river on which I don't try to canoe upstream too much. Things have always happened to me at their own pace. The one thing I always try to do is to keep an open mind towards everything. I started my first font at 29 – which might already be regarded as late. Then for a decade I did not feel the urge to make a new one because I wasn't inspired. It all changed with a little sketch which finally resulted in Fontin. From then on I was hooked.

Before diving head-first into type, you worked in advertising for fifteen years. Looking back – what were the things you liked most about the advertising world, and what did you like less about it?
Ever since I was a teenager I wanted to be an artist. After I graduated from high school, the right place to go seemed to be art school, but my father wanted me to learn a "proper" job. So we compromised and I got to go where I wanted, but to study

Efficient garden
RISQUÉ
Industry Norm
Get ready
Pages 32–85

Anivers
▲ Buivenga describes his Anivers as "robust and rigid, forgiving, flexible and elegant…". We especially like "forgiving." As a graphic designer, you can't ask much more from a typeface. Anivers' whimsical shapes evolved out of an earlier free font, Diavlo, although it took major tweaking and redrawing for one font to become the other.

"If I were able to split myself into three entities I would still have enough type design work for years to come." CALLUNA SEMI BOLD ITALIC

39

M

Museo Slab – a robust slab with Museo's friendliness

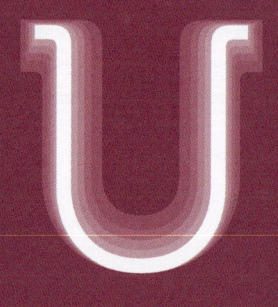

U

MUSEO... it all started with my love for U

S

Museo Sans – the sans with a familiar look

40

graphic design, not painting. After four years – I didn't graduate – I decided that it was time for me to become an artist. I did that for about six years until it became more than clear that I wasn't able to make a living out of it. So I bought a Mac, taught myself the basics of desktop publishing and arranged an internship at an advertising agency. After a few years I got a job as an art director.

Working in the advertising business never really was my cup of tea, mainly because of the commercial attitude and the fact that all the work was based on very specific assignments. The best thing about it was the puzzle-solving aspect of commercial projects. But creating something and being in a creative process is what makes me feel alive, so I always made sure that I had something to do "on the side" that interested me. That could be painting, writing or type design.

When you joined MyFonts with Museo, you were the first designer to offer most weights of an extended family for free. On the strength of the paid fonts alone, Museo became one of the best selling fonts of 2008, and Museo Sans did even better. What made you choose this strategy? Did you expect that kind of success?
Before Museo was ready for release I often thought about what would be the best pricing strategy. I had to take into account that most people who knew me, knew me for my free fonts, so my guess was that it would be best to offer more free than paid weights. Next thing to consider was which weights should be free. I myself always hate it when free things are not complete or not as useful as they could be, so I decided to offer the three middle, most common, weights for free. And that was received better than I could have imagined. I had a bit of a hunch of Museo's potential success because of all the positive feedback I got on my blog, but I didn't expect it to be this big. The two fonts I released later that year – Anivers and Museo Sans – were also received very well. When the advertising agency I was working for went bankrupt in April 2009 it was clear that the time was right to become a full-time type designer.

In the close-knit landscape of Dutch type design, you were completely unknown until a couple of years ago. Now you're probably one of the country's best-selling designers. Do you still feel like an outsider?
Yes, sometimes it feels like everything I've done has led up to the point where I'm at now, creating type in a world where it is not so necessary any more to relate to other type designers in order to function well. Besides, I am a person who really likes to do things his own way. On the other hand, I do feel connected to everyone who loves type and type design. Also, I immensely enjoy working together with Martin Majoor on a project at the moment.

Oneironauts
SLEEPER
Lucid dreaming
The Night

Museo

▲ Museo is a spirited semi-serif typeface with lucid, open forms and idiosyncratic details – especially the pipe-like, bent half-serifs. Three out of the five styles were, and still are, free. Museo is great for cool-looking magazine and poster headlines but also very effective in medium-sized texts. It supports a wide range of languages and comes with several extra ligatures and alternates.

32 miles
SACRED GEOMETRY
Picking
Just try me

Museo Sans

▲ Museo Sans was introduced a few months after Museo. While the original Museo's most striking characteristics are in the unusual shapes and placement of the asymmetric serifs, Museo lacks those signature accessories. That makes it less immediately recognizable – but not bland. Its clarity and legibility are remarkable, its detailing is quite original and its wide range of numerals is both attractive and practical.

◀ Museo specimen covers by Jos Buivenga.
◀ CLOCKWISE FROM CENTRE TOP: *Cultivon les Objets* brochure by Studio Punkat; *Pictographic Index 1* by Hans Lijklema, published by Pepin Press; *Digital Atlas of Economic Plants*, R.T.J. Cappers, R. Neef, R.M. Bekker, published by Barkhuis Publishing and the Groningen University Library; *Five Secrets of the Waters (For Mnemosyne)* at the 10th Sonsbeek International Sculpture Exhibition, by artist Ana Maria Tavares. Photo by Jos van Roij.

65½ giant flicks
BE GONE
Handspring
✴ ✺ ✵ ✴ ✳

Fertigo Pro

▲ The calligraphic roman Fertigo Pro has been one of Buivenga's most popular fonts for years. It has the flow and humanist touch of italic handwriting, and the roundness and regularity of a roman book face. It is almost too good to be a free font and yet, that's what it is — you can show your gratitude by adding the lovely and very affordable new Italic to your collection.

Large zip
Start & finish
QUOTH

Fertigo Pro Script

▲ While working on Fertigo Pro Italic, Buivenga suddenly saw possibilities for yet another Fertigo variety — a connected script. The resulting Fertigo Pro Script is charming yet vigorous, and great for packaging or branding.

That project is Questa, a new "modern face". Could you tell us a bit more about the typeface and about the way you collaborate?

Early April this year I was asked to give a lecture at the 33pt. symposium in Dortmund, as was Martin Majoor. We knew each other from way back at art school in Arnhem, with the difference that I wasn't into type design then. It was great meeting each other again and we both felt that the time in Dortmund was too short for all the things we wanted to share. Back in Arnhem after a few meetings we decided to do a type design project together. Going through the options we stumbled on Questa, a squarish Didot-like font that I originally had planned in one display style only. Martin saw enough possibilities to use that as a basis to create a text version too, as well as a sans-serif, all with true italics. We both have busy schedules and Martin spends a lot of time in Poland, but when he's in Arnhem we try to team up twice a week to work on Questa in harmonious collaboration – although fortunately there is also some healthy discussion going on. Because I'm self-taught it's great to witness closely how another type designer handles the whole process of making a large font family.

During the past few years, you've made exemplary use of online communication and networking tools to get your fonts out there: a blog, a free fonts website, a Flickr pool, Twitter, contributions to ilovetypography.com… What's more, it doesn't feel like a calculated strategy. You seem to thoroughly enjoy this kind of communication.

In the early days people had to e-mail me to get my free fonts. Soon I started to receive more than twenty requests per day, so I decided to offer the fonts as a direct download. The emails still kept coming in, but now from people who just wanted to comment on my work. A blog is of course the better place for that, plus it also offers me the opportunity to have a direct response to type designs in progress. That's also the reason why I embrace Flickr, Twitter and the like. To be able to interact like this is a thing I value tremendously. Later – with the release of Museo – I discovered that it also works very well to help market my fonts.

A detail for type geeks: Your typeface Calluna has a sloped crossbar on the 'e' – one of the primary characteristics of early Venetian or "Humanist" typefaces, as the history books never tire of teaching us. Did you actually look at Jenson's type as a model for Calluna? Do historical models play a role in your work at all?

One day when I was playing around with Museo to see if I could make a slab serif out of it, the bent serifs with the newly attached slabs resulted in a serifed roman letterform that had a nice forward direction. I used that little accident as a base for Calluna.

Ee ∞

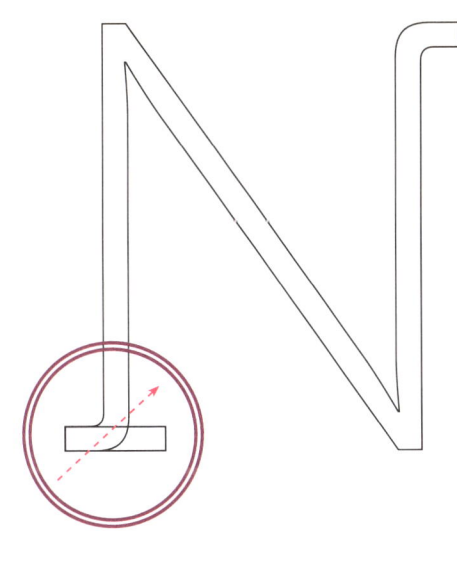

Calluna

A BEAUTIFUL ACCIDENT

Calluna was born more or less by accident. When I needed a break from Museo I was just fiddeling around a bit with Museo to see if maybe a *slab serif* would be something to have a look at.

The first thing I did –of course– was to put slab serifs on the stems of Museo. When I did, I saw something nice. A slab-serif with a nice **direction**.

I ended up with using the idea for something I always wanted to do. A –rather serious– text face. I used the direction idea to shape the characters. I thought that maybe it could help the eye a bit to move easier in the direction in which one reads. This is absolutely not scientific or so… Just an idea. A starting point for **Calluna**.

DETAILS ON DISPLAY

The goal was to make a text font, but one with enough interesting details. And that is really finding a balance between robustness to function as a text face and rafinement to look good as display font.

THE IVY GREEN
~

Oh, a dainty plant is the Ivy green,
That creepeth o'er ruins old!
Of right choice food are his meals, I ween,
In his cell so lone and cold.
The wall must be crumbled, the stone decayed,
To pleasure his dainty whim:
And the mouldering dust that years have made
Is a merry meal for him.
Creeping where no life is seen,
A rare old plant is the Ivy green.

Calluna

◀▶ Calluna, Buivenga's first fully-fledged roman for text and display, emerged from the Museo design process. Out of the experiment to create a hypothetical Museo slab serif grew a totally new typeface – a robust, clean and contemporary face with interesting details and a forward flow. Calluna makes for comfortable reading even at very small text sizes; its striking details ensure that it can also be used as a display font with personality. As for Calluna's name: it's simply the name of the street in Arnhem, the Netherlands, where Jos happens to live and work.

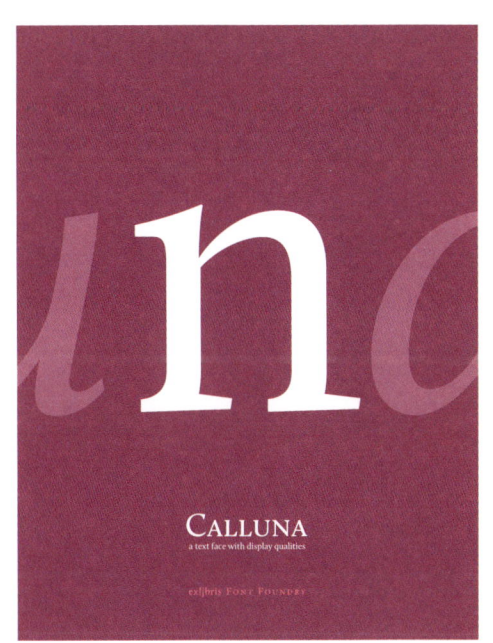

Calluna
a text face with display qualities

exljbris FONT FOUNDRY

Gravlax
From '*trench*' & lax '*salmon*' (fish)

Calluna
Is also the name of a so-called heather plant.

HAMSTRING
A (QUADRUPED'S) HOCK!

luckiést
Q&A: 32 questions should be answered

APIUNT ERGON
TE CAELUM ET
UONIAM NON T
U IMPLES EA? AN
MPLES ET RESTA
APIUNT? ET QU
E? AN NON OPUS
TERRA, QUONIA
NDIS QUIDQUI

43

Questa

Historic sparfun. qa'fligéz

stacguw

The Close Ranks Struck Forward.

handgloves
DISPLAY

handgloves
TEXT

handgloves
SANS

These are my handgloves
REGULAR

These are my handgloves
ITALIC

Questa, a unique collaboration

Questa is a new typeface that was designed in close collaboration between Jos Buivenga and Martin Majoor. Majoor is best known as the designer of FF Scala, a family of serif and sans typefaces that has come to be recognized as a modern classic. Majoor, who lives in Arnhem and Warsaw, designed several more typefaces, including a family for Dutch telephone listings called Telefont. He is also a writer and a teacher. Although Buivenga and Majoor had known each other when studying at the Academy of Fine Arts in Arnhem in the 1980s, they had lost touch when embarking on very different careers. They met again more than 20 years later when both were invited to give a lecture at the typographic symposium 33pt. in Dortmund, Germany. Their friendship was renewed and after a few meetings the two decided to do a type design project together. The result is Questa, a typeface-in-progress, still unpublished at the time of writing. Questa is based on a squarish Didot-like font that Jos had originally planned to be produced in one display style only. It turned out to be a perfect basis to apply Martin's type design philosophy about the form principle of serif and sans, as advanced in an article for Eye magazine about the origin of the sans serif and Helvetica's lack of originality.

▲ Dutch tandem: Martin Majoor (left) and Jos Buivenga working on Questa. Above: screenshots of Questa-in-progress.

Not only did this determine the shape of the regular serifs, it also shaped lots of other details like for example the bottom serif of 'p' and the crossbar of 'e'. I wanted the proportions of the capitals to be classical, therefore I had a glimpse at Garamond capitals. I don't really look at other typefaces as a model; I only look at what other type designers' solutions are for specific things I'm struggling with at that moment.

"I've always regarded life as a river on which I don't try to canoe upstream too much."

CALLUNA SEMI BOLD ITALIC

You've been working with MyFonts for a year and a half now. What are the main things this collaboration has brought you?
When I was ready to release Museo I was still working four days a week so I needed a partner that would relieve me from the hassle of setting up and maintaining a shop. MyFonts looked ideal to me because of the fact that I was able to do my own marketing and because MyFonts' commissions on sales are fair. They offer good possibilities for people to try out type before buying – which has gotten even better with the new site – and also the opportunity to set up one's own foundry page. Because of that I could keep my own site fairly simple and that saved me time… precious time to design more type.

Gert Wiescher

BODONI CLASSIC CHANCERY

ANNABELLA AND BRIGITTA

He's probably Germany's most prolific type designer. He worked at international advertising and packaging design agencies before setting up shop in Munich as a full-time type designer. Just the same, he likes to go diving in Hawaii or can be found browsing the Paris flea market for samples of handwriting and lettering. Meet Gert Wiescher, a man of the world. *December 2008*

BODONI CLASSIC ROMAN

Gert, your biography tells a fascinating story of wanderings around the world, of meeting Salvador Dali in Paris and designing dog food packaging in South Africa. But how did you get into type?
While I was a student in Berlin, I met Erik Spiekermann one evening in a café. Erik was still at school then but he was already a total "typomaniac". I must admit that at first I had no idea what he was talking about. To me in those days, uppercase and lowercase were drawers in my kitchen cabinet, and capitals and small caps were big cities and not so big ones. But Erik's enthusiasm was, and still is, compelling. He sparked something in me right there and then in that coffee shop on the Kurfürstendamm. And then – maybe two years later – I moved into the same house with Erik, wife and kid. This guy had a complete printing shop in his basement, uppercase and lowercase, a press and what have you. That place was *type*, period!

▸ One of Gert Wiescher's famous notebooks filled with type sketches

Did you get an academic education in lettering or type design?
I was at the Berlin Academy for Fine and Applied Arts, and of course we had calligraphy classes and very good typography courses. I learned a lot about tension, about inner and outer space, about proper letterspacing. But again – without Erik's constant advice and knowledge, all the well-intended typography classes would have been in vain. Erik taught me what to do with those theories in the real world. It was like having my private tutor right at home.

Your career as a type designer proper began much later, when your first commercial fonts were released in the early 1990s. What took you so long?
Sure, I started publishing fonts very late in my life. For a decade I was traveling: my friends were not surprised to get mail from me out of some obscure country. But all that time I had – and still have – this little black book in which I made notes about ideas for typefaces (and other things) in the form of little drawings or written descriptions.

After my traveling years I became a partner in an advertising agency, but I secretly kept drawing in that little black book.

Then along came the Apple Lisa and the Macintosh. I realized that the times of sketching headlines for ads, which then had to be ordered from a typesetting firm, were over. I immediately adopted the new technology. I converted the fonts I needed into pixel versions using a forerunner of Fontographer – can't remember the name [probably Fontastic – ed.]. In that way, I could simply type the headlines, which made life as an art director much easier.

One day in Paris I stumbled onto the Bodoni problem. All Bodonis that were on the market in those days had square serifs. But Giambattista Bodoni never designed a typeface with a square serif! After all those years, I wanted to give the world its first real

Ellida

▲ Bend it like Bickham! Ellida was inspired by the elaborate scripts of 18th century English calligrapher George Bickham, with additional influences from nineteenth century American calligrapher Platt Rogers Spencer. Wiescher put a lot of effort into making the letters join in a natural flow: he called it his most brain-consuming script font so far. It combines well with his Fleurons series of elaborate ornaments.

▲ Fleurons V.

"Along came the Apple Lisa and the Macintosh. I realized that the times of sketching headlines for ads, which then had to be ordered from a typesetting firm, were over." BODONI CLASSIC TEXT BOLD ITALIC

Young Virtuoso
MAESTRO *of the* CHAPEL
REVERIE
Ringing in my head
Eroica
Lend me your Ear
TESTAMENT

Bodoni Classic series
▲ When the first of Wiescher's Bodoni Classic fonts came out in the 1993, there was nothing like it. Up to then, virtually all Bodoni revivals had been given clear-cut forms and square serifs. But Bodoni's originals from the late 1800s were never as straight and simplistic as is often assumed: they had rounded serifs and slightly concave feet.
Wiescher digitized a wide range of Bodoni letterforms, including a wonderful script-like family called Chancery and a nice series of Initials. Having accomplished his mission twelve years later, he began making personal additions to the family, such as the more decorative Bodoni Classic Swashes.

Bodoni. Erik again helped by lending me Bodoni's *Manuale Tipografico*. And I adapted everything Bodoni had ever done, bringing his outstanding designs into the digital age. Some years later I added some decorative designs to my Bodoni Classic family.

When and why did you start your own foundry?
As could be expected, I published my early fonts, such as New Yorker and Bodoni Classic, at Erik Spiekermann's outfit FontShop International as part of the FontFont library. I never cared much about what happened to the fonts once I had finished with the design. I just kept making new typefaces and stored them on my hard disk where they simply collected virtual dust. So I had been designing typefaces for many years before I started publishing them myself. Besides the Bodoni Classics, there were only four or five of my fonts on the market, while I was running my advertising and design agency in Munich.

Then one day, about five years ago, I became a victim of globalization. My biggest design client concentrated all his European design business in London and I was stranded with just a few small accounts that barely kept me afloat. So I had to change the way I earned my living – fast!

I remembered all those typefaces on my hard disk and started preparing them to be sold commercially. Amazing how many typefaces I found on my hard disk! I started offering the business through my usual channels, but there was not much enthusiasm. I figured that I had to start doing my own font marketing – regain control over my work. That is what I did and never looked back once I had sold my first font through the MyFonts platform. Now I am the guy with the global business!

A few decades ago, you settled in Munich in southern Germany. What is so special about working in Munich?
I am a very restless guy, I love to be in a different place every four weeks, but I have two beloved sons in Munich who tame my roaming ambitions. My favorite places in this world are Munich, Nice, Paris, Hilo and Zürich, in that order! Munich is great in summer, Nice warms me in winter, Paris gives me lots of new input, Zürich is for that little extra bit of luxury and Hilo is where I meet good friends and do some diving.

Much of your work is based on historical materials. What steps do you take in adapting and digitizing them?
Sometimes I find an entire alphabet, but that is rather rare. Mostly I find two or three letters, maybe a word or a headline that intrigues me. Then I make little drawings with overlapping forms to get a clear (or not so clear) picture of how that font could look. Then, bingo!, I sit down in front of my computer and design the basic 52 letters mostly in a single throw (usually right on screen). And then I forget about that font! It collects dust on my hard disk, gets overgrown with mold and starts to virtually smell. But all the time I think about it, juggle curves in my imagination and change weights. Then at some point, on a rainy day or at three o'clock in the morning, I sit down and try out all these workings of my subconscious mind. And then either I am satisfied or the whole thing starts over again. I never (or almost never) just digitize a given font. It is not a very interesting thing to do. The "almost" applies to some ornaments which I found I had to save from getting lost.

Digital Bodoni

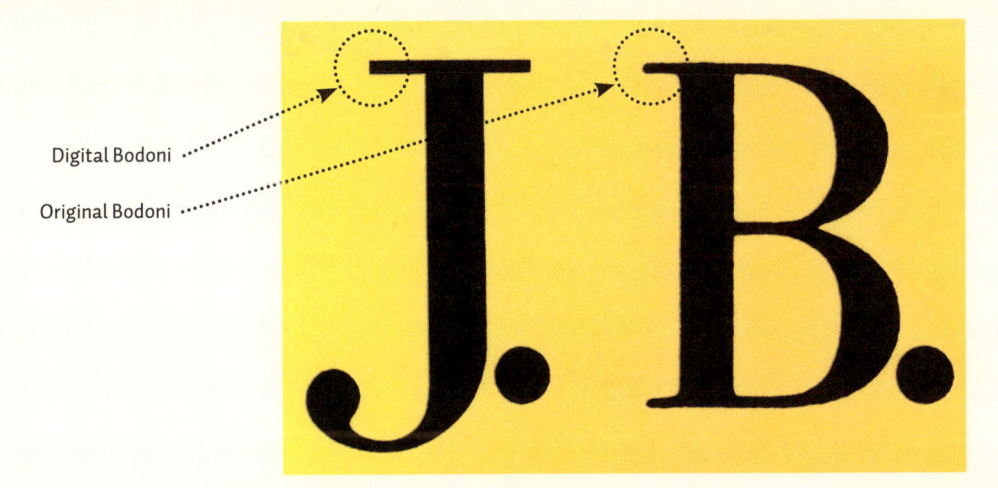

Original Bodoni

The story of Bodoni Classic

As told by Gert Wiescher

BODONI CLASSIC

In 1993 I was in Paris once again. I love Paris! Its air, its wide and high streets, its hecticness and imperturbability, its intimacy and anonymity are things I just miss in Munich. In the Centre Pompidou I discovered a small exhibition about typography and in the museum's bookshop I found a booklet about Giambattista Bodoni. Now the French call Bodoni "Jean Baptiste" and that was where I got lucky.

The publisher's graphic designer had substituted a 'J' for the 'G' that must have been in the original letterpress sample used for the cover. He had pasted a letter from a modern Bodoni font in place of the 'G' that had been there before. Rightaway I noticed that the capital 'J' had rectangular serifs, and the rest of the name did not. I became curious. Back in Munich, I did some research and found that all modern Bodoni revivals have straight serifs.

So where did those rounded serifs come from? Close examination of the facsimiles in my newly acquired booklet taught me that Mr Bodoni had never drawn a perfectly straight corner in his life.

To make sure I wasn't crazy, I consulted with my good friend Erik Spiekermann. Erik agreed to lend me his facsimile of the *Manuale Tipografico* until I had finished. It took me twelve years in all, because I still had my design studio to look after and could not work on the typeface full-time. The Bodoni Classic originally came out as part of the FontFont library founded by Erik, and later became part of my own type library. I am not quite sure how many styles are in the Bodoni Classic family now, but it must certainly be the most complete and most faithful Bodoni revival currently available. I added a few variations of my own – not all of which might be to Mr Bodoni's liking, but I find that the Bodoni design principles tolerate a lot of ornamentation and variation without losing their character. As a tribute to "Signora Paola Margherita Dall'Aglio", Bodoni's widow, who published the Manuale Tipografico, I designed a script in Bodoni's style based on his English initials and called it Donna Bodoni.

BODONI CLASSIC TEXT

▶ Photographs taken by Gert Wiescher at the Bodoni Museum in Parma, Italy.

Good Luck! Beloved Mother

Annabella & Brigitta

▲ Both Annabella and Brigitta are based on letterforms written with a Japanese brush on rough watercolor paper. The two joining classical English scripts were first scanned and then finished by hand on screen, taking care to keep the "rough" touch. Annabella and Brigitta are complementary fonts that can be mixed freely.

You don't seem to be the kind of person who spends years developing a huge, all-purpose text family. Do you envy designers who do have that kind of patience? Do you currently have any plans for text typefaces?

I want to develop "Pura" into a real big family; I already have a dozen new cuts in the works. My problem is not the actual design work, but the production. Naming and generating the actual files, spreadsheets, ads, font sample PDFs and all the rest is such a hassle that I simply prefer to make single cuts. But just yesterday I made an attempt at getting more know-how in the production field by attending a private class with someone who knows his way around FontLab. Very interesting. I learned a lot! Maybe one day I can talk my youngest son into doing that kind of stuff!

Since you began working as a designer in the early '70s, a lot has changed, typographically speaking. Do you have moments of nostalgia for certain aspects of the good old days? Or wouldn't you want to work in any other era?

I would really like to work in the future. I am very curious about what is going to happen to the world in general, and especially to type design in fifty years. Some things in type design and design in general were easier in the past, less complicated, more straightforward and not so time consuming. Today there are unlimited possibilities to change forms or make alternative weights – and they are sooooo easy to implement – it is no longer necessary to think first and design later. A designer can produce an endless number of variations and then choose what looks best. The problem seems to be that this process takes long and consumes a monstrous amount of time. Lost time, I call it. If you work that way, computers steal a lot of your time instead of saving time.

"I try to excuse that 'need for speed' I have in me, by saying that I generally am a lazy bastard who wants to get the job done as fast as possible just to be able to be lazy again."

BODONI CLASSIC TEXT BOLD ITALIC

In picking out what kind of design to work on next, are you guided by market behavior, by "fashions" that you perceive? In other words, do you sometimes choose to work in a specific genre because it is what the public wants?

Well, to put it quite bluntly: I live off type design. So of course I react to the market. If I design, for example, Fleurons and customers buy those all of a sudden like crazy, it is only natural that I give those clients more Fleurons. Other than that, I simply design the typefaces that I fancy. Or like I said earlier, I finish ones that have ripened. I pretty much do what I want, one day it is a blackletter and maybe in the evening I work a little on a text face, the next morning I finish a script or whatever. Only in cases when I really experience an explicit demand in the market do I try to fulfill that demand. MyFonts fortunately gives me enough information to immediately see which font picks up in sales, which makes it easier to react.

In general, how does MyFonts compare to other retailers on the internet?

I don't normally tend to rave about anything. But MyFonts is absolutely f#@%$ fantastic!!! If it wasn't for MyFonts I couldn't and wouldn't have been able to publish all of my fonts. Once I have finished designing a typeface I want it to be on the market as

Floralissimo

▶▶ Gert Wiescher has designed so many ornament packages that it is impossible to list them all here. One of the most successful is Floralissimo, based – like most of his other ornamental fonts – on vintage material from old books and catalogs. The flowery ornaments are an elegant addition to any design that is meant to exude romance, nostalgia… or subtle irony. Here Floralissimo combines well with circular devices from another of Wiescher's packages, Fleurons Four.

fast as possible. It takes MyFonts an average of two days to do that, whereas I have retailers that take a whole year for the same job – and I am not talking about small retailers in a remote African country. MyFonts is simply the best – friendly, reliable, fast, efficient and they give type designers a really fair deal.

When I mentioned to Erik Spiekermann that I was interviewing you, he wrote: "Gert is the fastest designer I have ever met. Whatever he touches illustrations, photos, ads, fonts – he gets them done in hours." Do you think of yourself as fast? Do you think your speed influences your style?
I try to excuse that "need for speed" I have in me, by saying that I generally am a lazy bastard who wants to get the job done as fast as possible just to be able to be lazy again. But the truth is that I am absolutely concentrated when I work. I don't see or hear anything (for example I don't listen to music while working) so I get results very fast. As to the influence on style: in some instances I make decisions a little too fast but I don't see any effect on style. Since I have started to let my fonts "ripen," speed doesn't influence the design quality.

You recently created Autographis, a special foundry for handwriting fonts. Where do you find all those styles of handwriting? And why did you decide to create a new label?
I can write in many different ways. I can combine two or three scripts into one and I find old scripts that I change into a new one. It is good fun and I find script fonts easy to design. No kerning!!! I find old scripts in old newspapers and on flea markets. The Paris *Marché aux puces* is as good as any other market. Oh, and I look at the writing of friends and change that into a font.

As for the new label: when your name starts with a 'W,' you get used to always being called last in school. So when you get older, you know it is a pretty good idea to have a second name that starts with a letter from the beginning of the alphabet. Hence: Autographis!

If you had a message to your colleagues in the type world, what would it be?
Like in every trade there are many people that take "their thing" too seriously. Type is very important to transport content, and it is a significant aspect of our culture, but it shouldn't dominate one's life. I have a friendly request to typographers who still dream of, and live in, the past of lead type, who keep repeating that the good old rules of typesetting are too often ignored: Give our young people a chance, accept them, teach and guide them, but please let them do their own "thing."

Refreshing Spring Flower buds

Ayres Royal/Royal Bavarian
▲ John Ayres was a 17th century English calligrapher who produced superb acrobatic calligraphy, samples of which were collected in instruction books such as *The Accomplish't Clerk* from 1683. Wiescher digitized Ayres' initials and combined them with a lowercase based on his elegant Ayres Royal.

Ray Larabie

A decade ago, he was the prince of free fonts. Today, his Typodermic foundry is one of MyFonts' most successful type libraries, although hundreds of his freeware fonts are still out there. His output is awe-inspiring, his tastes as diverse as can be, and his sense of style spot-on. His tool of choice is the computer. Don't look for pencil sketches or brush-drawn alphabets in this chapter; it was all done on the screen – with a trackball. Meet Ray Larabie, a Canadian in Nagoya, Japan. *May 2009*

Ray, I've been aware of you as a type designer for twelve years or so. I remember spotting your early free fonts all over the internet and downloading some of them from your Larabiefonts website. Were these your first endeavors in type design? You must have been pretty young back then.

I was in my mid-twenties when I started publishing fonts. I feel younger now. I think back then I was less in sync with the contemporary than I am today. I sort of had to kick the retro habit. My fonts had a liberal "post-'em-on-your-free-font-site" policy so they ended up on every site.

What got you into type design?

When I was about five years old, living near Ottawa, my grandmother brought me stacks of partially used dry transfer lettering sheets from the government department where she worked. Helvetica, Clarendon, Franklin Gothic, Futura, Univers. I really got to know those fonts well and I was able to recognize them in the environment. That was around the time of my earliest memories, so my brain is kind of hard-wired

◀ The Larabies in traditional Japanese ceremonial kimonos

Small Bully Conference
THE BATTLE OF GUS VS. ROLLY PART 2
"Big headaches require smaller & more flavorful pills"
TUNE RADIO EVERY MINUTE?
"Legs of gnomes & a zillion teeth make my formula complete!"
ZOMBIE RIBS

▲ One of Larabie's very many promotional pieces – this time for Enamel and Fenwick

for fonts. My folks bought me a computer in the early '80s and I made some bitmap fonts, mostly knockoffs of Letraset fonts. Letraset was the most popular brand of dry transfer lettering... these plastic sheets that you'd rub down to transfer letters onto a surface. The catalogs came out once a year, they were free at art supply stores. I was just crazy about those Letraset catalogs, still am.

In spite of your love of type, you embarked on a career in animation and video games. Was that your other big fascination at the time?

When I was sixteen I worked on Alien Fires, a game that nobody remembers. But it made me confident that I could work in games. And you know... explosions are fun to make. In high school, I asked my layout teacher (it was an art/high school) about the prospects of designing fonts for a living. This was in the late '80s, before digital design really took off as a career path. She told me I could become a typographer or submit designs to Letraset and maybe they'd accept it... but I probably wouldn't be able to live off that. Back in those days the number of fonts released in a year was about the same as what gets released at MyFonts in a week today. It just wasn't a practical career path in 1988.

I wanted to get into computer graphics and the particular college I was interested in required 3 years of animation training. I graduated at the beginning of the 1990s recession at a time when more and more animation work got outsourced to Korea. I did a lot of watercolor painting to pay the bills and I made free video games for fun. That got me a job in video games and the fonts were put aside for a few more years. I really enjoyed working on games. You had these really tight technical restrictions to deal with; I like being forced to innovate. Saving a kilobyte in those days felt like a major victory.

RUMBLE ROAR ゴジラ

Meloriac

▲ Meloriac is a straightforward Ultra Black all-caps face – until you use the E (and who doesn't?). Then it suddenly becomes something special: a streetwise, unicase display font. Says Ray: "My goal with Meloriac was a dry geometric sans. With a geometrical font, if you try to make it neutral and balanced you're always going to end up looking like Avant Garde or Futura... that's just the way it goes unless you give it a definite flavor. But I wanted it to be neutral. Heavy and neutral. So you get this kind of comfortable familiarity but just not the way you remember it." Meloriac is ideal for tight headlines and logos. Check out the trendy J-pop Katakana letters.

Bike Gang
Visions
TOKYO
QUARANTINE
Level 4

Korataki

▲▼ Korataki is a tribute to a mid-1970's retro-futuristic classic, M. Mitchell's China. It is wide, angular, almost monolinear and utterly cool. Executed in five weights, from the feathery Ultra Light to the euphemistically named Regular (an Extra Bold, if you ask us), Korataki's simple design appeals directly to the imagination. As its designer wrote, tongue firmly in cheek, "it transfers messages invisibly without a trace of manipulation. Readers are left aware of only a bright future stretching out ahead of them."

When you finally got into type design for real, you began making fonts like crazy.
Once I tried font software for the first time, I was completely hooked. I never had a long term plan, I just started working on fonts because I couldn't stop. Also, most of my early fonts really weren't very professional. Over the years I've been fixing them up or completely rebuilding them. Most freeware font sites still carry that old junk… which is why I encourage people to pick up fresh versions at MyFonts.

As a type designer, you've "grown up in public": people with an eye for type have been able to watch you learn, acquire more skills and get rid of mistakes. Did you ever feel uncomfortable about that?
I guess I didn't have as much of an eye for type design as I had thought. Everyone has some kind of artistic blind spot. The thing about blind spots is… you don't see them. I considered going back to school but I took a driving course and was reminded how much I truly hated school. What was really helpful to me was the occasional e-mail from very brave people who pointed out faults. In 2000, I remember someone letting me have it about my overshoots. That's what I needed to hear. I had been making overshoots…. but so tiny. I wasn't uncomfortable with it because I never thought real type designers would ever notice my work. The world of freeware font design, back then, was disconnected from the mainstream. There was a divide and if you trace it back I think you'll see that MyFonts and MyFonts alone broke that divide. It seems really clear to me. MyFonts took the "quality bar" and put it in the control of the customer. We'll let the historians deal with that one.

RADIO JERKS
Fine Vinyl Helmet
EARLY TRANSISTOR
Year of Universal Oil
Phase Lunar King
コジセント

You have made over 1,000 fonts. Why so many?
The first few hundred were easier because there was so much less to make back then. I'd bash out an alphabet, autokern it, come up with a funny name and upload it to my website. I didn't have to deal with accents, proper kerning, proper metrics, OpenType coding, promo graphics, ad copy, keywords, testing, multiple formats, etc. Within minutes of finishing a font it was on my site. One Saturday I created three fonts.

To judge from your output, you still work faster than most. Are you impatient? Do you ever wish you could spend six months or a year on a single type family, like some designers do?
I was pretty slapdash back then. Impatient? Yeah, a bit, but not like I used to be. I certainly don't make three font families in a day. I do like to get 'em out the door though, that's true. A year, every day in Fontlab… on one font. Hmmm. I don't make a lot of text fonts. Mine are mostly catchy display fonts. Plus, you never know what people are going to buy. Some of my most popular fonts are ones I didn't have high hopes for, and vice versa. It may sound crass but a year spent on a font that doesn't sell is a wasted year – to me anyway. If you can't be realistic about that aspect of font design then you probably can't make a living from it. It's a big gamble. I guess some people can do it but that's not for me.

A related question about pricing: For a serious type foundry, Typodermic's prices are extremely low. Most of your fonts cost less than $9, and if a customer decides to buy one of your value packs, the price may go down to as little as 33¢ per font. In a world where $30 to $70 is considered a fair price for a fully featured OpenType font, that's a pretty good deal. And probably some of your peers find it really annoying. What's the thinking behind that policy?
My prices have gone up and down over the years. Of course, changing the price has an effect on sales and I've adjusted them accordingly over the years; the market determined the price. But consider this: I make mostly display fonts. I think designers buy them because they have a particular need based on whatever project they are working on. Text fonts are different. They're an investment for a designer. Spending a couple of hundred bucks on them is worthwhile because of the years of rigorous use you're going to get out of them. Display fonts are… well, they're more like art supplies. Like those dry transfer lettering sheets back in the day. They were about $10. Fonts didn't have to be an investment – sometimes artboard was more expensive than a font. The number of jobs you can use a font for isn't limited like it used to be with dry transfer sheets, but what matters is how most people use them. And most people buy a display font for a specific use.

Captions: **closed**
And so that's when I say
Year of Fun
Maybe we should go outside
REMARK
Official Report
Don't want
Documentarian

Cinecav X

▲ The Cinecav X family is based on Cinecav™, a typeface created for closed caption television applications, used to produce optional subtitles for viewers with hearing difficulties. The idea to provide an alternative to the fonts normally used for CCTV came from Larabie's agent David Delp, who is well-connected in the American TV world. "The US government has mandated a set of technical specs," explains Larabie, "which TV manufacturers selling sets in the US are forced to abide by. I had a lot of experience in the video game industry dealing with on-screen type. From what I had seen from competitors' CCTV fonts, they were going about it wrong. I tested the Cinecav fonts on less-than-ideal equipment to make sure they could take punishment. My toughest test was a color TV I'd picked out of someone's trash, with playback on 1980s thrift shop VHS tape." Cinecav X is the affordable consumer version of that remarkable family.

"I never had a long term plan, I just started working on fonts because I couldn't stop."

CORZINAIR BOLD

Kingdom

GRIST

forest country

Yer Fuzz

Querying the foreman

Madawaska

▲ Although he is best known for his prolific output of display fonts, Larabie has actually produced several families of eminently legible text fonts. The popular Madawaska, a rather idiosyncratic slab serif family, has a bit of both. It has some of the funky qualities and techno vibrancy of his display work, combined with the extensive structure and clarity of a text family. With 34 styles, including some very subtle hairline versions, it's versatile and widely usable.

My Lover

Affront 32 times

Glittery

Amienne

▲ The successful Amienne is a remarkable departure from such techno-oriented and streetwise display fonts as Neuropol X or Bomr. Amienne was designed to resemble handwriting done with a watercolor brush. Charmingly informal, Amienne is a lively and graceful brush script font that moves with a nimble rhythm. It comes with some handy arrows and there is an additional set of old-style numerals.

It seems you are gradually moving toward a more personal, thoughtful idiom. Yet you still do quick-and-dirty reworkings of existing typefaces, like Soap – a kind of unicase Cooper Black – or Tight, a washed-out version of the 1970s font Quicksilver by Dean Morris. Is that because you like seeing quick results? Because of an anarchistic streak? Or because there's still a 1990s typographic DJ in you, remixing old favorites?

I really just try to think of what designers are going to find useful or inspiring. Often I see designers modifying type in a way that indicates a need for a certain kind for thing. With Soap, I had seen many cases where designers had messed around with Cooper Black to give it more funk. Tight, Reagan, Rinse and Teeshirt were designed to evoke a certain era. I could easily have come up with my own fonts or plundered my own catalog but the effect wouldn't be nearly as good. If you want to make a '70s or '80s worn t-shirt font, you have to use fonts that would have been used in that era. I knew using those fonts would cause some members of the typographic establishment to look down on me (even further) but I had to do it. My goal was to make '70s and '80s t-shirt fonts… of course I was cringing a bit: those fonts are my heroes. They're actually a lot of work because I have to create a fully functional, clean version of the font before I do the grunge thing. My samples are pretty blurry and the character sets, very sparse. On the other hand – though not in the cases you mentioned – I do like to mess around with very familiar forms to freak people out. Order is based on Univers Condensed proportions. So from a distance, it looks like Univers but when you get close, you realize it's all robotic. Jillican has that sort of thing going on. Yes, it looks like Gill but that's the whole point. I could have easily come up with my own fonts in those cases but the familiarity is the whole point. I think some people get what I'm try to do… I hope so.

Where do you find your inspiration? Are you a great collector and/or photographer of typographic ephemera?

There are exceptions but usually a typeface is an accumulation of influences from multiple sources and thoughts I've been keeping in mind for a while. I try not to copy directly from source material if I can help it. I've always got a few fonts that I'm mentally constructing. I don't do sketches. I like to keep those ideas flexible and somewhat nebulous. A font starts to form while I'm working on it and I can test it in words. That way I don't get pushed into a design corner I can't get out of… the ideas kind of gel on their own during creation.

I'm not a collector of typographic ephemera. Most of my old font catalogs and books have been scanned and destroyed. I'm a real computer guy but I still have my old Letraset catalog by my side. I'm not one of these font designers who has a reverence for type history or physical books on paper. I couldn't care less about that stuff. I just want to make fonts that designers find useful. That's it… plus have some fun along the way.

For inspiration, I look at how fonts are currently being used by designers. When they start dragging up old fonts, it often means there's a need for something new to do the job.

▶ Another of Larabie's specimen graphics, featuring Gnuolane and Stencil

Howard's thrilling 89 days in jail.
Must Be the Season of the Jerk
Freeze Dried Instant Weiners
Arizona Zomboid Wrestlin'
1973 TRANSISTOR BUSTING CHAMPS
Entertaining Dipsticks?
Presenting: famous nudes of 2015
Untamed Janitor Partnership '46
STOP TRUCK WAXING!
"Read my Lips: Marmalade Wallpaper"
MALADJUSTED QUALITIES UNION!
Chrome Grilles & Rusty Pipes
Yeah, I Know. Lumpy Potatoes

AUTOMATE YOUR VCR!
Machine Volts?
centipede war stories
CONSIDER THIS FIRE BUTTON MASHED
MICROCHIP AVATARS
TRS-80 Coco Dating Service
DEATH OF VIDEO: BIRTH OF RADIO
Shakin' with laser battle shell shock!
FAMICOM CARTRIDGE
just a trick of the electrozipper
GORKAMORKA 1983
"Knights of the Perisphere?"
Giving me winter instead of summer
OVER THE OTAWA WALLS
Jungle Climber Tears Were Shed

Among your many fonts, do you have any absolute favorites?
I always like my newer ones because they're more in sync with what's going on today. I really like how Movatif turned out. I don't think everyone's going to "get the joke"… you know? Mashup music had its heyday a couple of years ago but I got back into it recently. If you don't know what mashups are, think of a Jackson Five vocal spliced over a Nirvana riff. So I was in a mashup kind of mood when I came up with Movatif. I had just finished a remake of Coolvetica, an old Larabie Font based on a scratchbuilt sort of Helvetica thing… which was in turn based on a 1970s trend where logo designers and even font designers were goofing around with Helvetica shapes. So I started obsessing on doing the Avant Garde Gothic slanted 'A' with something built off Coolvetica to generate a kind of 1980s "rad" feeling. I was travelling through Osaka and came up with a few ideas from old store signs. So the whole effect you get when you use it is kind of a custom logo look that gives people an unnerving sense of deja vu. It looks like a bunch of things you've seen before in an alternate universe or in a dream. That kind of effect really excites me.

You're Canadian, but you recently moved to Nagoya. Please tell us about Japan, and your relationship with it.
This is my wife's hometown and I've only been here for a little over half a year. It's a really friendly, comfortable, interesting place to live. I've been learning so quickly… I thought there would be some kind of culture shock, but for me, not really. Every day I see something new and exciting. As for fonts, I've had a chance to get a clearer image in my mind of the evolution of industrial minimalist display fonts. I didn't set out to do that but it surrounds me so it's hard not to take notice. Back in Canada, I'd only seen glimpses of Japan, so the image was distorted. I now live in an area which is partially medium residential and partly light commercial. So I can take a walk and see these really small, quiet industrial spaces with barrels, old signs, rusty machines. I can kind of make out a timeline, not accurately, but an idea of how the industrial minimalist style came to be, and its relationship to Katakana lettering, a more simple, linear character set often used to display English words phonetically. So the first font I created in Japan was Uniwars, a culmination of the best aspects of that style. Living in Japan is helping me grow as a font designer, and as a person too.

What are your plans for the near future, type-wise?
I don't think more than one font ahead. I figure it's part of my job to try to pick up on design trends… long term plans work against me.

Sinzano
For those who use InDesign or other layout programs with full OpenType functionality, Sinzano is a treat. It has over 400 interlocks which automatically replace the letter combinations you type. The comics-inspired style is certainly not new (Larabie himself already experimented with it in his mid-1990s fonts, and others have since) but the programming on this one is something really special.

"I'm not one of these font designers who has a reverence for type history or physical books on paper. I couldn't care less about that stuff." CORZINAIR BOLD

Movatif brings the mashup meme (a meeshup?) to typography, not only combining elements of Helvetica with Avant Garde, but throwing Larabie's own Coolvetica hybrid into the mix, as well as a few disco and glam references to boot.

Silas Dilworth

HEROIC CONDENSED THIN

FACEBUSTER

Silas Dilworth has the kind of technical instinct that many of us are envious of. He can repair your car or motorcycle. He taught himself the technicalities of high-end font production and web programming. Yet he has also trained as a painter, and it shows. His letterforms are economic yet elegant: with minimal means, they provide typographic style and character. He is one half of TypeTrust, a platform for high-quality typefaces. Meet Silas Dilworth, a type designer who does not believe in retirement. *March 2009*

BREUER TEXT

Silas, it seems you have tried out several career options before becoming a type designer. You studied painting and digital imaging, experimented with photocopiers and even worked for an insurance company. How did all of this add up to get you interested in type?

Before I viewed art as a career path, I was always more interested in computers and engineering. I grew up with Lego, BMX bikes, and video games. My father is mechanically minded and he taught me a lot about cars and motorcycles. He encouraged me to be an engineer by the time I started high school. I excelled in math and really enjoyed technical drawing. I spent a lot of time building complex Lego Technic contraptions and plastic model kits, or drafting concept cars and dream houses with a ruler and compass. It seemed a likely trajectory to study mechanical engineering or even architecture, but in the end I grew tired of calculus and more interested in unbridled artistic expression.

But after my first semester at art school, I got restless and wanted to get a taste of the real world. So I went to work for an insurance company. In retrospect, that job has been rather influential. I started as a data-entry temp working on health insurance claims processing. The backbone of the operation was a Kodak microfilmer/scanner the size of a refrigerator that was hooked up to a PC with Optical Character Recognition (OCR) software. We were processing thousands of claims per day submitted by hospitals and doctors' offices all over the US. This was the mid-90s, and the majority of the claim forms were still poorly filled out by dot-matrix printers that were misregistered or sorely needed a fresh ink ribbon. The job entailed eight hours at a monochrome PC terminal, manually correcting the OCR errors in the digital version against stacks of hardcopy claims. I started to appreciate the subtleties of letterform structure and legibility when the machine would mistake an 'S' for a 5, or a 'Z' for a 2. A well-designed and clearly printed typeface saved us a lot of time making those little corrections.

I eventually landed the position as the microfilming technician on the second shift. Perfect hours for a night owl. The slower pace and typically lighter workload allowed me some time to tinker with the OCR software and the Kodak machine. The whole process was essentially the opposite of printing but very similar in a mechanical sense. I was operating this complex contraption that figuratively lifted the words from the printed page and returned them to digital form. I've never worked in a print shop, but I think that subconsciously this experience gave me a similar, somehow backwards, understanding of the printed word.

Then you went to back to art school?
Quite naturally I grew tired of the monotony of office life. I wanted to surround myself with curious, creative people. I wanted to learn how the art world functioned. I focused my studio classes on drawing and painting because it was familiar and accessible. I was always recognized for my drawing abilities since childhood, and I've always enjoyed making images and thinking and talking about them. I was even more interested in seeing what other people would create and hearing what they have to say. I was never quite as interested in the academics of art history or traditional studio techniques as much as understanding "why we make art."

In the end, art school taught me that I was most interested in the mechanics of visual communication, where written language and picture-making collide. Design school, as I understood it, was about the practice of effective visual communication. A fine arts curriculum – especially at the School of the Art Institute of Chicago – was less about guidance and tradition and more about exploration and discussion. Although this experimental setting appealed to me, my work became more attuned to graphic design in traditional media from a painter's perspective.

Witch's Hazel
Kinder & Märchens
GRIMM
Froschkönig
BREADCRUMB TRAIL

Everafter

▲ Everafter is a display typeface that poses as an old-fashioned text face. It doesn't have a single straight line. The vectors were all drawn and tweaked by hand (and mouse) for a soft, wobbly appearance. The result is a serif typeface that doesn't take itself too seriously – a picturesque font for fairy tales, herb teas and incense. Though it is kind of naive, it is not stupid: OpenType features include oldstyle figures, fractions and ornaments.

> "I had always viewed typefaces as the most basic, vital elements of graphic design, and I was innately curious as to how they worked." RESERVATION WIDE BOLD

Cooter Deuce

▲ Cooter was conceived as an homage to what Dilworth calls "suburban graffiti," the kind of quick hand lettering that you might find plastered across sale signage at the hipster boutique of your local mega-mall. Cooter Deuce is a reworked, more sophisticated version of that earlier pop hit. The original Cooter's randomly-distributed solid and counter-punched letterforms have now been extended to encompass two complementary fonts: Regular, with counters; and Plugged, where the counters are, well, plugged. In addition, Cooter Deuce has been re-drawn with more consistently square proportions, and a handful of glyphs have been entirely redesigned.

Breuer Text & Headline

▶▶ In this age of no-frills sans-serif typefaces, it is not an easy task to come up with something new; with Breuer Text and Breuer Headline, Silas Dilworth has done an impressive job. Breuer Text has a straightforward nuts-and-bolts structure but, despite the underlying squarish skeleton, is also rather elegant and reader-friendly. It will make an excellent secondary typeface in a complex editorial design project, for pull quotes, running titles and subheads (check out the small caps and small caps figures) but will also work well for moderate lengths of body copy.

So you gradually gravitated towards graphic design and typography?
Right. While I spent my studio time navel-gazing in the company of painters, I started spending more of my time working as the Communications Director with the Student Union Galleries. Quite consciously, I was balancing the professionalism and clarity that were required in this role with the playfulness and poetics that painting allowed. I was also working for Whole Foods Market as a sign-maker. I had access to brand new Mac G4s, Quark, and Adobe applications at both jobs and I started becoming more acquainted with – and fond of – computers than paint and paper. Although I had very little critical feedback regarding the merit of my design work, I was learning. More importantly I was also fiddling with a large collection of often inadequate fonts.

I've always been the type of person that needs to know how things work from the smallest part on up. I had always viewed typefaces as the most basic, vital elements of graphic design, and I was innately curious as to how they worked. When I started playing around with fonts and type design, I discovered a world of nearly limitless expressive freedom and purposeful, indisputable technicality. I saw a marriage of creative opportunity and practical constraint.

Between 2001 and 2004 you worked at T-26 as a font technician, type designer, webmaster and administrator – your introduction to the world of fonts. What were the most important things you learned there?
Most of my time was spent with font submissions and new releases. I worked intimately (and obsessively) on hundreds of new releases. My personal initiative was to bring each release up to a respectable level of professionalism. Whether the fonts were usable was almost inconsequential. I just made sure they were built well. I learn by taking things apart, and that was basically my job: to take apart some really inventive, unique fonts and make them as solid and complete as they could be. I even reworked some of the classic selections from the library, fixing PostScript errors and fleshing out kerning tables. (The funny coincidence was that I had already been doing this back at Whole Foods Market… fixing old T-26 fonts that wouldn't print.)

I collaborated with designers that were submitting their first (and sometimes only) typefaces. More importantly, I worked with a prolific handful who were really dedicated to building a business of their creativity: Rian Hughes of Device; Peter Bruhn of Fountain; Gareth Hague of Alias; Nick and Adam Hayes of Identikal; Gabór Kóthay and Amondó Szegi of Fontana; Anuthin Wongsunkakon; Charles Anderson a.k.a. Charles Andermack a.k.a. Chank Diesel; and my current TypeTrust business partner, Neil Summerour of Positype. They all made me see the long-term potential of type design and inspired me to give it a go myself.

All in all, I learned that I could run a type foundry on my own. I taught myself the technical side of font production, I learned the legal ropes of EULAS,* I saw what would sell. I came out of the experience with respectable chops and a versatile eye, ready to pursue my own vision.

* EULA: End User Licence Agreement

Quiet Hybrid
[Magnetic Propulsion]
HARVEST SOLAR & WIND ENERGY FOR YOUR HOME

fuel-efficient

$12,345,678.90

Petroleum & Fossil Fuels

{alternative fuel initiatives}

"Just go ride a bike!"

Public transport

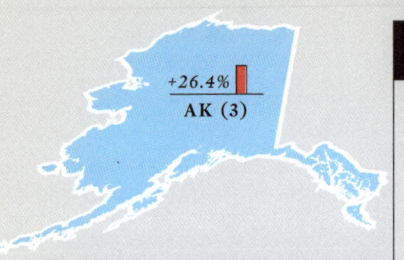

POPULATION

2005 POPULATION:

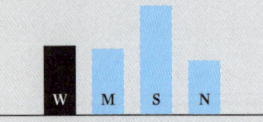

70,096,950
(23.2% OF TOTAL)

JULY 2000 – JULY 2007 PERCENT CHANGE:

3.6% ABOVE NATIONAL AVERAGE

+10.5%

JULY 2000 – JULY 2007 TOTAL CHANGE:

+6,634,913

JULY 2000 – JULY 2007 PECENT CHANGE RELATIVE TO NATIONAL POPULATION:

+0.7%

INCOME

2007 AVERAGE INCOME:

+$3,905 OVER NAT'L AVERAGE

$54,138

POVERTY

2007 POVERTY RATE:
(-0.5% BELOW NATIONAL AVERAGE)

WEST | NAT'L AVG.

12%
(2-PARENT, 2-CHILD HOUSEHOLDS BELOW $21,027/YEAR)

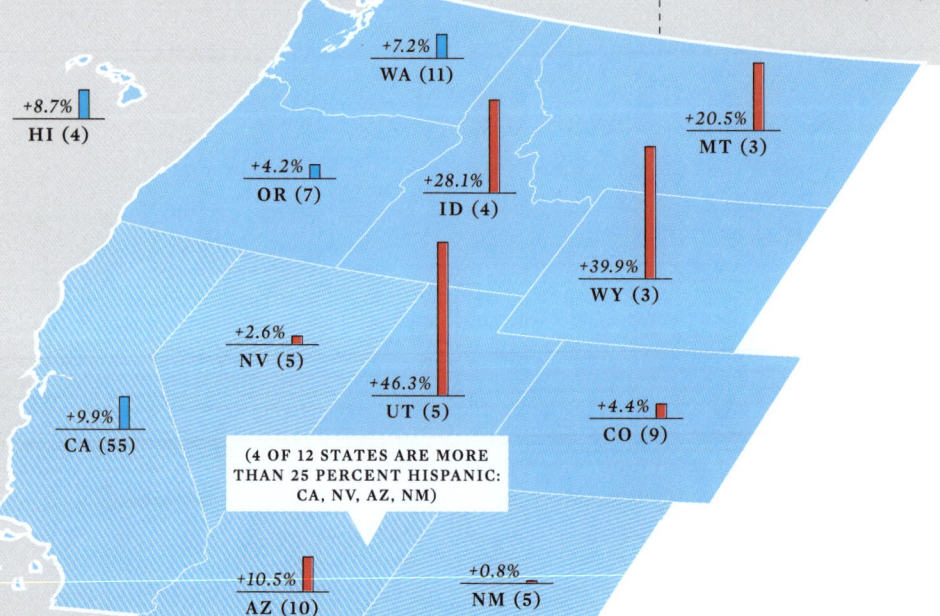

(ONE OF 12 STATES HAD POVERTY RATE ABOVE 15 PERCENT: NM)

+26.4% AK (3)

+8.7% HI (4)
+4.2% OR (7)
+7.2% WA (11)
+28.1% ID (4)
+20.5% MT (3)
+39.9% WY (3)
+2.6% NV (5)
+9.9% CA (55)
+46.3% UT (5)
+4.4% CO (9)
+10.5% AZ (10)
+0.8% NM (5)

(4 OF 12 STATES ARE MORE THAN 25 PERCENT HISPANIC: CA, NV, AZ, NM)

RACE

2007 RACIAL MAKEUP:

- 55.1% WHITE ALONE:
- 27.5% HISPANIC/LATINO:
- 8.6% ASIAN:
- 4.6% BLACK/AFRICAN AMERICAN:
- 2.2% TWO OR MORE:
- 1.5% AMERICAN INDIAN/ ALASKA NATIVE:
- 0.04% NATIVE HAWAIIAN/ PACIFIC ISLANDER:

RELIGION

2000 DOMINANT RELIGION:

CATHOLIC
(HEAVILY INFLUENCED BY LARGE HISPANIC POPULATION IN CA, NV, AZ, NM)

POLITICAL TRENDS/ DISJUNCTIONS:

Democrats picked up 5 house seats in the west in 2006, as well as Montana's senate seat. In 2008, the major races are for senate in Colorado and New Mexico. New Mexico is expected to switch to Democrat Tom Udall; Colorado is polling strongly in favor of democrat Mark Udall.

Tell us about the ideas behind your TypeTrust portal and foundry.
TypeTrust essentially came about because I wanted a direct outlet for my typefaces. I wanted to do it all on my own at first, but I realized that a partnership would be more fun, educational, rewarding, and a little less work. I started bouncing some ideas back and forth with Neil Summerour in early 2005 while I collected my T-26 unemployment and taught myself web development. Neil began releasing his first typefaces through T-26 around the same time I started there. In a way, we grew up in the business together and had a good rapport. Between the two of us, we had everything to start an online shop. I brought the technical and practical experience of running a foundry and organizing the website, while Neil brought the business savvy, boundless creativity, and endless optimism it takes to start a new business.

We steered TypeTrust toward a distribution model rather than a foundry to build a brand. We had both started our own companies, so we kept TypeTrust as a neutral zone. Neil used some rusty Portuguese and invited Dino dos Santos of DSType aboard, and I extended invitations to a handful of others to get the ball rolling. We're still not sure how far to take it in this direction because we want to balance the reseller role with a recognizable brand. It's a rather loose affiliation, but it's intentionally the foundation for a long-term operation. I don't believe in retirement, and I'm looking forward to designing type on into my old age. Neil jokes about early retirement so he can kick back in his home office, design type full-time, and enjoy his family. We're on slightly different tracks to the same destination, but TypeTrust is the common goal.

When you began taking type design more seriously, were there any specific aspects of this activity that surprised, confused or worried you?
Nope. I really felt quite comfortable from the beginning. Type design is a very forgiving activity. You're still allowed to make huge mistakes because the majority of your blunders will go completely unnoticed or even be praised for "breaking the mold."

As you said earlier, type design is as much about practical constraints as it is about expression. Many of those constraints result from the fact that type depends on conventions. Some of your fonts seem to play with the edge of what is still recognizable and legible. Are you attracted by extremity? By transgression?
I don't think any of my work is truly transgressive. It's certainly not my mission. I'm always very concerned with legibility and making things recognizable. I don't want my typefaces to confuse anyone. If they lean toward extremity, there has to be an inner logic across the character set to justify it. That's also part of the charm of decorative typefaces. You can get pretty wild with the overall design, but there's a world within it that has to achieve some semblance of order and respect for convention.

It don't matter
Spudboy
The Smart Patrol
Mister DNA
Supply & Demand
This monkey wants a word with you

Heroic Condensed

▲ Many condensed or compressed grotesques are spin-offs of existing text families. Heroic Condensed is different. The family was conceived from scratch with a structural logic of its own: a fusion of pure geometry and optical balance. There's a simple geometric skeleton at its core, but the forms have been polished and fined-tuned to obtain even color and visual neutrality across its impressive range of eight weights. With obliques and small caps for each weight, Heroic Condensed is a versatile headline family for a wide array of uses.

> "Whenever I get tired of taming Bézier curves, I can hit the twisties up the Angeles Crest Highway or re-grease half a dozen roller bearings."
>
> RESERVATION WIDE BOLD

◀ Detail of an informational graphic designed by Nicholas Felton (of *The Feltron Report* fame) making prominent use of Dilworth's Heroic Condensed. Courtesy of Nicholas Felton.

1. Bananas
2. Eggs
3. Berries
4. Cereal
5. PB&J

Sansarah

▲ Sansarah is based on the handwriting of Sarah Faust, a photographer and designer at Columbia College, Chicago. At the time the font was commissioned, her handwriting style was part of the school's graphic identity. When the time came for Mrs Faust to take maternity leave, Silas Dilworth was asked to recreate the alphabet as a font, so that the school's brand could be maintained consistently "sans-Sarah." For this retail release, the original fonts were expanded to include a full character set, including six alternates for the most common lowercase letters. In OpenType-savvy applications, the stylistic alternates feature will automatically cycle through the alternates for a more varied, natural appearance.

▼ Graphics designed by Nicholas Felton for the New York Times, making prominent use of Heroic Condensed. Courtesy of Nicholas Felton.

People sometimes say that in type design, everything has been done. Do you find it difficult to come up with ideas for new typefaces? How do you decide whether an idea is worth pursuing – is it pure intuition, or is some degree of calculation involved? Do you do market research or informal surveys?

It's a balance of intuition and casual research. I listen to what my designer friends have to say about type. They usually have greater insight into what works for them and for their clients because they get to actually use fonts more than I ever do. I keep an eye on what's popular, but I keep a closer eye on what doesn't work. I design type because I have an opinion on how things might be better or simply more appealing to the end user. I'll quit type design when every fashion is perfected. I haven't begun an ambitious serif or script yet because there are so many good ones already. I'm not sure I could improve on Jonathan Hoefler's eponymous gem, or Peter Matthias Noordzij's PMN Caecilia, or Nick Shinn's Scotch Modern, or Alejandro Paul's advanced OpenType script faces, but I do see a lot of opportunity for new sans-serifs simply because I can never seem to find a favorite.

Is there any type designer whom you admire, or even envy?

I've always idolized Adrian Frutiger and Matthew Carter for their humble sensibility – their designs are always quite practical and usable. Envy is a sinister word, but I might confess to coveting H&FJ's or Jim Parkinson's client lists. I often wish I had started designing type 100 years earlier so I could work with Morris Fuller Benton at ATF. I've been really lucky to work with Rian Hughes. He's a prolific designer, an astute businessman, a knowledgeable academic, and a creative perfectionist.

Outside type design, which are the activities you enjoy most? In what ways do they influence your work as a designer?

I ride a Kawasaki KLR650... a big ol' street-legal dirtbike. It's a simple, grotesque machine and has a supportive fanbase. I burned out my motor on I-90 returning to Chicago from TypeCon in Buffalo last summer. After a 120 mile ride home in the cab of a flatbed tow truck, I rebuilt the engine myself in my driveway with salvaged parts

11/10 **CHUCK CLOSE** honored at Christopher and Dana Reeve Foundation gala at the Marriot Marquis.

11/11 **VETERANS DAY:** parade on Fifth Avenue.

11/12 "MUSEUM OF THE MOVING IMAGE SALUTES BEN STILLER" at Cipriani 42nd Street.

11/13 Panel at the TimesCenter on "GENDER, POLITICS, AND MEDIA," including Ariana Huffington and Geraldine Ferraro.

11/12–11/13 **AC/DC** shakes the Garden all night long.

11/14 **DANIEL CRAIG** returns as James Bond in Quantum of Solace.

that some guy sold me through KLR650.net. It's a true DIY motorcycle – really simple to maintain and modify. Good for tinkerers. Good for learning about the incredible internal combustion engine. Most importantly, it provides a sensory escape from the computer desk. Whenever I get tired of taming Bézier curves or endlessly adjusting the side bearings of a twelve-weight font family, I can hit the twisties up the Angeles Crest Highway or re-grease half a dozen roller bearings.

What do you think will be the most significant development in type design in the next few years?
I'm not one to make predictions or foster great expectations, but I'm rooting for more consistent application support for the progress that the font biz has made in the past ten years. OpenType has such amazing potential, and I'd like to see it stick around for another decade. So many of us type designers have poured a lot of energy into its promises.

I would love to see more work done in the intellectual property arena too. It's upsetting to read the colophon of a best selling novel or the masthead of a major publication and find no typographic information whatsoever. I'm quite skeptical of centralized power and even unionization, but the font world is sometimes like the Wild West. I hope we find a balance between cooperation and independence so we can establish the sort of rights granted to musicians or photographers. This is another reason I wanted to start my own foundry. I can state the terms of use that I believe are fair and begin to claim the reward for what is very difficult, thoughtful, and valuable work.

As a type designer and co-owner of a small font foundry, what has the collaboration with MyFonts meant to you so far?
The MyFonts business model has been a huge inspiration to my entrepreneurial activities and a boon to my bank account. I've never read any Ayn Rand, but I'm sure we'd all make her proud.

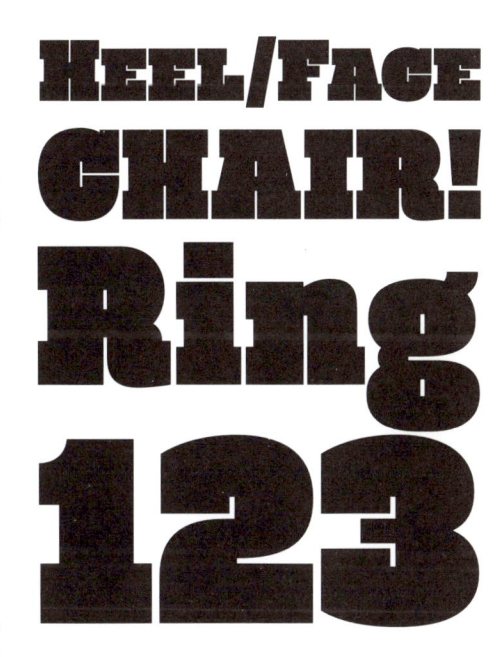

HEEL/FACE CHAIR! Ring 123

Facebuster
▲ This single-weight bold face does two things at the same time: it draws attention to the message, and it makes you smile by doing so in such an outrageous manner. The negative space (the "white" of the letters) is minimal, so you have to make sure you're using it big enough. If you do, the effect is unique – loud yet playful, a striking typeface for posters, book covers and magazine headlines. Facebuster comes equipped with OpenType small caps.

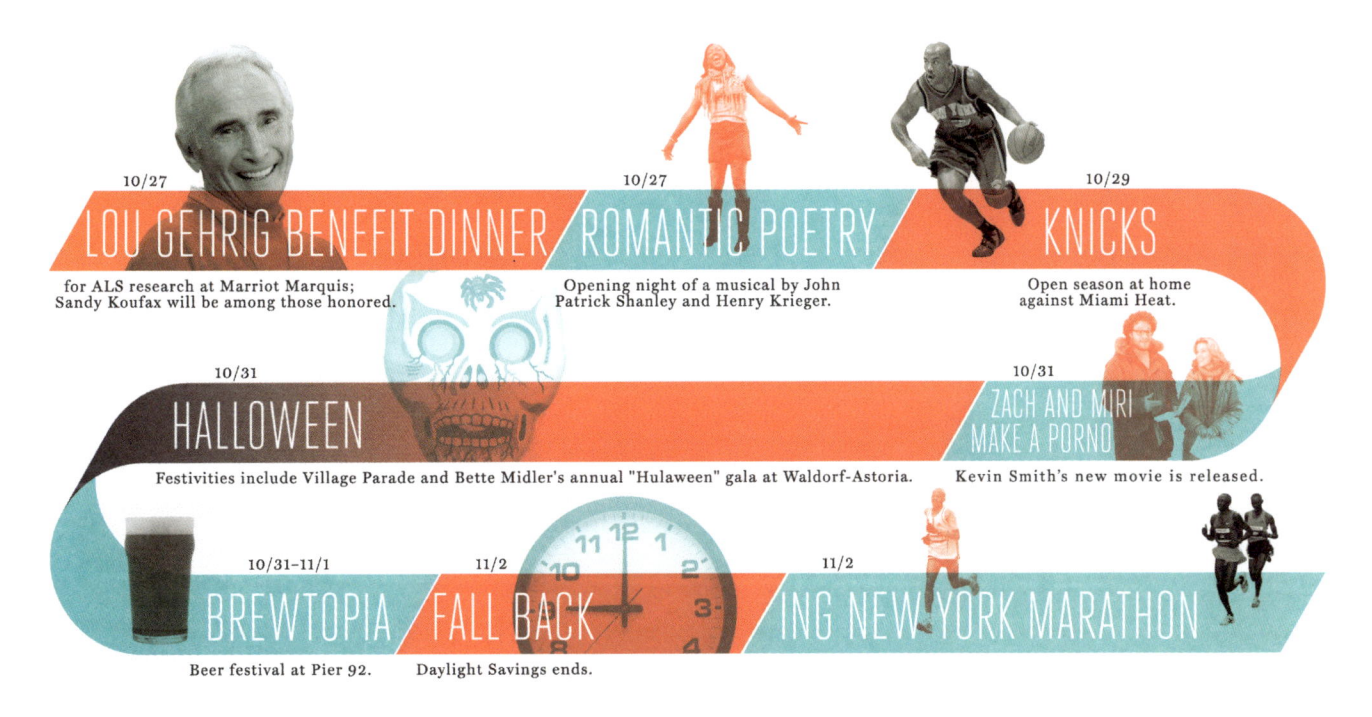

10/27 LOU GEHRIG BENEFIT DINNER — for ALS research at Marriot Marquis; Sandy Koufax will be among those honored.

10/27 ROMANTIC POETRY — Opening night of a musical by John Patrick Shanley and Henry Krieger.

10/29 KNICKS — Open season at home against Miami Heat.

10/31 HALLOWEEN — Festivities include Village Parade and Bette Midler's annual "Hulaween" gala at Waldorf-Astoria.

10/31 ZACH AND MIRI MAKE A PORNO — Kevin Smith's new movie is released.

10/31–11/1 BREWTOPIA — Beer festival at Pier 92.

11/2 FALL BACK — Daylight Savings ends.

11/2 ING NEW YORK MARATHON

Rian Hughes

SLACK CASUAL MEDIUM

SEPTEMBER MEDIUM

In the 1980s, Londoner Rian Hughes was one of the brightest young artists on the British comics scene. He went on to become a versatile designer, illustrator and lettering artist working for clients in the fields of publishing, music, sports, telecommunications, fashion and more. He is also the creator of an ever-growing library of typefaces – hundreds of them, in an amazing array of styles and atmospheres. Most of these have been published by his own type foundry, Device. Besides that, he is a writer and editor, and will be publishing two huge books later this year. Meet Rian Hughes, a designer who wants to do it all. *April 2009*

PARALUCENT MEDIUM

Rian, what are you working on at the moment?
There are always several projects in various stages of completion. At the moment, the main deadlines that are looming are: Finishing the final layouts on two books I've edited and designed; *Custom Lettering of the '60s and '70s* and *Lifestyle Illustration of the '60s*. Both are 576-page doorstops, and represent the culmination of a good few years' work. Watch out for them later in the year.

Other than that: Logo designs for two *Wolverine* comic launches; the rebooted *New Mutants*, and a logo for a new *Batman* series from DC; a logo for Archaia Studios, an independent publisher; a series of illustrations for new ranges from Clairefontaine, a French stationery company; a CD for the Priors, a French band; the cover design for the *Fat Freddy's Cat Omnibus* – this will be stylistically in keeping with last year's Freak Brothers Omnibus – in other words, a hippy feast.

Converting the Device library to OpenType (this one has been pending for four or five years, but I'm getting there! It'd be faster if I didn't keep adding new ligatures and other OpenType fanciness). I have a couple of people – Silas Dilworth, whom you

▲ Cover image for *Custom Lettering of the '60s & '70s*, edited and designed by Hughes, and published by Fiell Publishing.

recently interviewed, for one — helping out. 500+ font conversions, plus additions, is quite a project…

Bubbling underneath; a return to drawing comics; a collaboration with old mucker Grant Morrison; another with *American Virgin* Steve Seagle; and a book for Fluide Glacial that will probably be a collection of pin-up images.

That's quite an impressive to-do list. Of all the things you do, is there a particular thing you like best, or do best?
I have a low boredom threshold, so really variety is what keeps me interested. Almost any commission can be interesting if you look at it the right way (if the client allows you to look at it the right way!).

▲ Poster for the Device Saintbride typeface

ROOM Nº 43
Quizical
OUTBOUND
Roast
Going gaga

Regulator

▲ In much the same way as Paralucent is an alternative Akzidenz Grotesk, and English Grotesque explores the Gill/Johnston idea-space, Regulator ventures into the realm of the geometric sans, the land where Futura is king, Avenir a lofty queen and AvantGarde a wayward prince. Regulator is definitely the non-royalist newcomer, with its unapologetic simplicity, wide body and drastic solutions (look at that 'g'!). Now here comes the twist: it is surprisingly legible. Even at very small point sizes, Regulator performs better than you'd expect from such a geometric character.

You're probably as close to stardom as a type designer and illustrator is likely to get. What are the advantages and disadvantages of that position? Do you often have to refuse work because it simply gets to be too much?

I'm sure I'm not up there in the stellar firmament – there are so many more capable designers with a lifetime of work behind them. Type design can occupy a large or a small chunk of my time, depending on which projects come in. Up until recently when we started on the OpenType conversions, I had not touched type design for almost a year. I have sketchbooks and doodles though, and these will get developed when time allows. Really, rather than having a great plan, what so often happens is the phone rings, or an e-mail comes in with an interesting proposition, and off I go… it's quite often reactive rather than proactive, though I have been trying to change that with the new books and other more authorial projects. I'm pointing myself in a certain direction…

Your roots are in comics. Has there been a moment in your life when you thought you were going to be a full-time comic strip artist for the rest of your life? What is it that is so attractive about comics?

I was pretty much a full-time comic strip artist for six years. After hitting weekly deadlines for so long, I felt it was time for a break and to explore other creative avenues. But comics are in my blood – there's something about the form, the authorial control, that appeals to me. I need to clone myself, and then I could do everything I'd like to do, right now. I'm impatient like that.

You're a brilliant draftsman, and an able user of computer software like Adobe Illustrator. But do you ever miss the pre-digital era?

Thank you – I did draw four new illustrations and endpapers using brush and ink for the Yesterday's Tomorrows book last year. It's a collection of my comic strips – collaborations with writers like Raymond Chandler and Grant Morrison – and I did really enjoy it. It was very quick, strangely – I think though I'm fast with Illustrator, I'm faster with a brush. I was commissioned by a French stationery company to produce four duotone illustrations using brush and ink for a range of items recently – waste bins, folders, binders, that kind of thing, and it was a bit of a nostalgia trip. I then overlaid the images with digital elements and color, something I'd not have been able to do before, so in the final analysis the images were very much hybrids.

As an illustrator, you master several different styles. However, in most cases there is a reference to the atmospheres and styles of the 1950s and early 1960s. What is it – fascination, admiration? Nostalgia perhaps for an era when things seem to be less complicated, and when commercial art was more naive?

I think that it's not an attempt to be knowingly retro – it's more that the colors and shapes, the juxtapositions and motifs that appeal to me tend to be angular, brash and colorful – "graphic", perhaps – so the periods in design and illustration where those concerns were to the fore will appeal to me more, sing in tune with my visual heart. I'm not so lit up by Art Nouveau noodlings, even though it's great fun to work on. I'm sure you could analyze someone's worldview by looking at their preferences for certain curves or angles, colors and shapes. Are you a yellow circle or a blue square?

"A bad typeface is an unresolved typeface, one that doesn't know what it's trying to convey." <small>PARALUCENT EXTRA LIGHT</small>

Or typefaces. Are you a Space Cadet or an English Grotesque?
I'm a Slack Casual. With contextual ligatures.

The range of genres and styles represented in your font library is huge. What is it that inspires you to draw new typefaces?
All manner of things. Like design in general, if there's a cohesive internal structure, an idea expressed through every character, it works for me. Sometimes I'll purposefully set myself up to work against familiar approaches, just to make things difficult and interesting. I currently have a few loose scripts on the drawing board, and am playing with the possibilities of contextual ligatures. I'll probably find a way to make the technology do something other than what it was intended for.

Most of your typefaces capture a certain style or atmosphere without copying a specific model. Do you feel you're a "character actor" in some way? Which of your typefaces come closest to being "you"?
Ministry is the only straight revival I've done, though I'm working on a new, unrelated, American revival. Rather than pastiche, I'd say "essence" is what I'm after. Paralucent and Blackcurrant are very "me." The rough wood types are less "me" but have been hugely popular. Give the public what it craves!

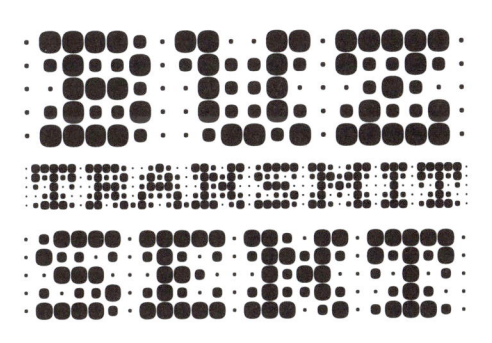

Monitor
▲ Our type designer goes retro-techno in this early experiment – a celebration of TV wall pixeldom. Built with squarish elements in various sizes, the characters have a kind of built-in blur. This results in an interesting property: text set in Monitor becomes easier to read the further away one gets.

▲ Cover for Hughes' book *Industrial Romantic*, a collection of personal photographs of industrial and urban landscapes.

Drinking games
Is this taken?
Seated
BARTOWN
I'M GOOD. REALLY.

Paralucent

▲ Hughes has created a kind of parallel universe of forms and characters that somehow look familiar, but are wholly his own. Paralucent, for instance, is Rian's take on the Helvetica/Akzidenz model – a sans-serif inspired by the industrial types of the late nineteenth century – but it is much more personal and lively. While the forms and counterforms of each letter were carefully balanced to obtain an even image, the result is neither cold nor uniform.

Your English Grotesque clearly refers to the Johnston Underground/Gill Sans model. What was your motivation to design something in that direction?
Again, I was after the "essence" – that clunky Englishness, that ruler-and-compass sans that was derived from earlier serif proportions. I took it back to the sources before Gill to see if I could distil the characteristics further, get at the real evocative heart of that style.

When designing type, are your decisions purely intuitive, or are they in some way function-driven?
They are rarely driven by function if you define that as designing for a specific technical use – but they do need to function as clear expressions of an idea. A bad typeface is an unresolved typeface, one that doesn't know what it's trying to convey. Font design is a curious mix of the technical and the aesthetic, the left and right brain.

As a designer working in digital media, you don't really depend on being in a metropolis like London for making a living. Ever thought of leaving the city?
Geographical proximity to clients is much less of an issue than it used to be, especially as many of them are in the US and Japan. Every time we move studio, it seems to be a bit further out of London. We've moved from Wardour Street to Clerkenwell to Bayswater to Portobello to Kew, which means I now actually travel out from the centre instead of in. It's nice here, though – mellow atmosphere, trees, Kew Gardens and a traditional pie shop. (Wednesday in the studio is Mushy Peas and Pie Day) However, London is a cultural hub, an inspirational resource that always refuels the inspiration – "When one is tired of London, one is tired of life, for there is in London all that life can afford." (Samuel Johnson).

▶ *Batgirl* masthead for DC Comics

"Almost any commission can be interesting if you look at it the right way."

PARALUCENT EXTRA LIGHT

To conclude the interview, we asked Rian to free associate from a list of references and influences. Take it away, Rian...

Pop music? Pop in general. Approachable, hookline design with depth. Grab them with immediacy, keep them with the detail. On iTunes in our studio we are currently playing The Smiths, Electroclash, Ultravox, Heaven 17, Royksopp, Goldfrapp, Kylie, James Brown, Bobby Womack, Steely Dan. The Carpenters, Simon and Garfunkel. Motorhead, Public Enemy. Wasn't into the Spice Girls that much – sorry Geri. I was drawing comics rather than watching Kids from Fame. You do know way more about hip-hop trainers than I do, though.

Bad movies? *Out of Africa* ... zzzzzzz ... Not enough spaceships and explosions for me. I did cry in *Titanic*, though. And *Dead Poets Society*. I'm a big softie.

The Flintstones? "Wehey, Barney..." Barney had the sexier wife, don't you think? The chap who designed a great deal of Hanna-Barbera's output at this time, and drew some of the best of the Dell comics (even though they never carried credits) was Harvey Eisenberg. He was a huge influence on me as a teenager. I've met his son, who works at Warner Animation now. Eisenberg is why I like Serge Clerc so much – Clerc channelled that brushy angularity through a hip adult sensibility.

Thunderbirds? I have a cabinet of Thunderbirds toys. It's a bloke thing. Girls just think we're strange.

Comedy? Flight of the Conchords: "It's business time..."; Flanders and Swan: "A Song of Patriotic Prejudice". (Check it out on YouTube.) The first season of *My Name is Earl*. Monty Python showed us not just comedy, but how to mess with the expected structure of a given thing, in their case a 30 minute TV show. I vividly recall one episode that began with the end credits and ended with the title sequence. No one messes with format and the basic structure like that, except perhaps Alan Moore. And maybe Peter Saville. Moore, Saville and Python. The structural triumvirate!

Playboy cartoons? Not that into *Playboy* cartoons – Annie Fannie was always a bit dumb blonde for my tastes, though beautifully drawn by Harvey Kurtzman. The competition had "TV21" veteran Ron Embleton: he drew Wicked Wanda for *Penthouse*. I rescued several Embleton originals from a skip behind the offices of 2000AD many years ago. This skip was so full of original art that I was actually standing in it, on the art, in order to go through it. I've just discovered the work of Arthur Ferrier. He could draw, yessir.

Flea markets? Let me at them! Junk shops full of mouldy books, mid century modern furniture, paperback SF novels, magazines... The smell of yellowing paper. Mmm.

Pop art? Well, if you know Lichtenstein's references, or are familiar with the Foss/Brown debate, you know who the better artists really are.
The fine art world can be culturally myopic. It's obvious that in music, if you're a DJ, playing something obscure and forgotten loud in a new context like a club, does not make you the author. The art world equivalent – redrawing something big and hanging it in a gallery – should not make you the author either. If you fiddle with it a bit, that's called a remix or a cover version. It still does not make you the author. Never mistake an act of curation for an act of creation.

popgod

Nick Curtis

RUNAROUND SUE

JAUNTY GENT

As soon as the first Creative Characters interview had been published, requests began pouring in to interview the man behind Nick's Fonts, one of the most successful microfoundries at MyFonts. "Please interview the prolific Nick Curtis!" wrote one user. "He really seems to have his finger on the pulse of popular culture. I'm a fan, can you tell?" She is not the only one: Nick Curtis has many admirers, and it's easy to see why. His fonts are charming, witty and often subtly nostalgic. Plus, there's an awful lot of them, and their variety is baffling. How does he do it? May 2008   DAFFADOWNDILLY

On your MyFonts bio page, we can read about the precise moment your "love affair with typefaces" began: when you were about 14, you found a fat green binder filled with type specimens from a Dallas printing shop. What made those alphabets so alluring to you? Did you start copying letterforms – or drawing your own – then and there?

When we learn to read and write, the process is vitally dependent on letterforms – learning to distinguish one from another, learning their sounds and their shapes – but the act of "appreciating" the diverse forms is practical, rather than aesthetic. Thus, at some point in the process of learning to read and write, the medium fades into the background, and the message becomes the focus of our attention. Or, put another way, we are taught to pay attention to what is being said in print, but not how it's being said.

As I leafed through the two hundred-plus pages in my found binder, reading "Matchless in power among the arts of men is the art of typography" in typeface after typeface, it gradually dawned on me that each one was different, some in very obvious ways, some in very subtle ways. Perhaps more important, I began to get a sense of the

Curly Shuffle

▲ Curly Sue visual by Curtis.

▼ Old lettering samples provide Curtis with much of his source material.

differences in tone – or attitude – conveyed by the different designs. This was a kind of epiphany for me: the letterforms themselves began to assume a new meaning, and I began to understand what this oft-repeated sentence meant. So, yes, I began copying the letterforms first, so I could understand – at least approximately – what it was that made each alphabet different from the others, and each letter within each alphabet the same as its brothers and sisters. It was the beginning of a learning process that still continues today.

That binder seems to have helped you decide to go to art college. With hindsight, is it important to have had formal education? What were the most important things you learned?

Actually, I enrolled as a commercial art major at a liberal arts college. The discipline was directed by Walter Ender, who was a recognized eminence in the Dallas commercial art community. He did absolutely gorgeous work, but he tended to achieve his ends by sparing no expense in the printing of his designs.

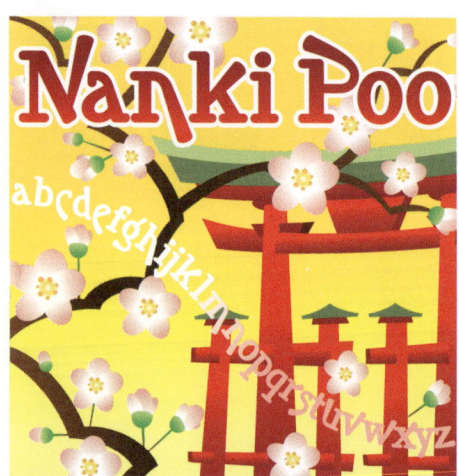

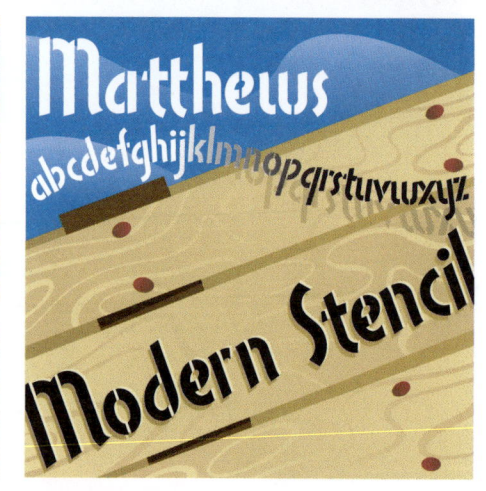

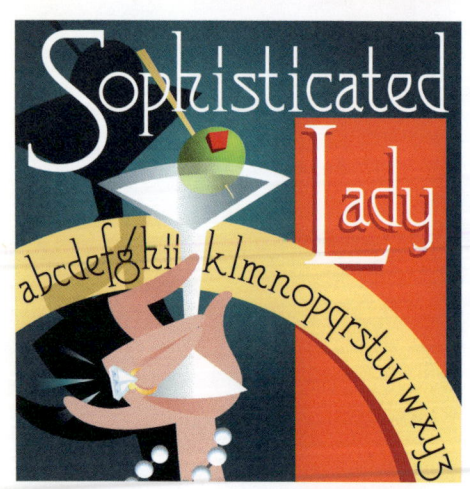

▲ A selection of Nick's "font flags", FROM TOP LEFT: Londonderry Air; Whoa Nelly; Mexia; Nanki Poo; Maloja Palace; Matthews Modern Stencil; Sophisticated Lady; My Dear Watson; Picture Postcard

My first two years in the program were devoted to basic art courses – drawing, anatomy, painting and printmaking – with specialization in one's major occurring in the third and fourth years. As it turned out, by the time I reached my junior year, the college had decided it could no longer afford to print the exquisite pieces that Mr. Ender designed, and the commercial art major was terminated. So, for reasons too Byzantine to recount, I switched my major to English.

The most important thing I learned from my art courses was, to quote my printmaking teacher: "Technique, technique, technique." As it happens, technique is to art what grammar is to English. If you want to express yourself clearly, you need to master the grammar of your chosen medium and, at least in my experience, formal education is the best way to learn that grammar.

In a recent Rising Stars newsletter, we referred to you as a typographic time traveler. What makes letterforms from the past so fascinating to you? Would you describe yourself as nostalgic?
The typography of a particular point in time is as unique as many other aspects of popular culture at any particular point in time. What I find exciting about discovering and reviving these particular letterforms is that doing so not only allows me to be a typographic time traveler, but it allows me to take other people along on the journey.

I'm not sure that "nostalgic" is the right word; all things considered, the "good old days" weren't necessarily uniformly good, but it can be comforting to remember them fondly from time to time.

STARRING MICHAEL McDOWELL
DIRECTED BY CHRISTOPHER PAL
MUSIC BY LEANNE REMINGTON

CC DVD DOLBY SURROUND PG-13

Major Production
▲ Ever wondered where movie poster designers find those compressed fonts to set the credits? Well, here is one that some of the pros actually use. Major Production offers two all-caps alphabets: the uppercase letters are ultra condensed, the lowercase are approximately a third the size of the uppercase. Also included are various logos and symbols suited for real (or fake) film posters or media packaging.

"Every now and then you need to let go of stuff so as not to be possessed by your possessions" MCKENNAHANDLETTERNF

Where do you find your sources of inspiration? Flea markets? Libraries? Travels around the world? Do you collect precious samples of lettering?
Inspiration can be found in the most mundane and unexpected places: I found the inspiration for Quigley Wiggly, one of my early freeware fonts (which mysteriously showed up on a new HP computer that I bought last year), on a toothpick wrapper. Many other typefaces were inspired by vintage posters, which can be found on numerous sites on the internet. I have taken advantage of my close proximity to Washington, DC, the past ten years and have become a registered researcher at the Library of Congress, and I have yet to tap the Maurice Annenberg Collection of type specimen books located nearby in College Park, MD.

As far as collecting goes, over the course of the last three or four years I've trawled websites like eBay and Alibris to amass a collection of over 400 type-related books, from handlettering chapbooks to vintage type specimen books, and also have a small collection of vintage wood type and electrotypes. However, as much as I would like to hold onto all of these goodies, every now and then you need to let go of stuff so as not

French King
Doily Quest
Beauties

Calamity Jane
▲ One of Curtis' most popular fonts, Calamity Jane is not easily overlooked. Its lowercase letters come from a turn-of-the-twentieth-century typeface named Amsterdam, and the uppercase letterforms are based on a 1930s logotype for the Théâtre Moderne in Paris.

Toasted 1984 Brawny

Edgewise

▲ Curtis calls Edgewise a "gentle giant" – which is a fitting way to describe this strikingly bold font. Based on a typeface named Ryter Night, Edgewise is hefty yet playful; its combination of clean lines and whimsical details make it one of the most idiosyncratic alphabets in Curtis' collection.

IMPERIAL Kingdom

Smart Frocks

▲ The most successful of Curtis' recent offerings, Smart Frocks was inspired by a sign in a 1930s London storefront, describing it as "singularly stylish, hip and haughty and decidedly Deco."

Automatic QUICK! Sprinkle

Mikey Likes It Corpulent

▲ Fat and sassy, this ultra bold brush font is based on the works of lettering legend Mike Stevens as seen in his book, *Mastering Layout*. Pick it when in need of a can't-miss headline, or try it to set a short introductory text in magazines or brochures.

---

to be possessed by your possessions… if you know what I mean. So, as I digitally capture the images that interest me, I plan to "repatriate" the major portion of my library through my website in the coming months.

With more than 300 fonts on sale, you're among the most prolific type designers working today. Your range of styles is amazing: from Art Deco to psychedelia, from circus to surf. Is there a particular style you find yourself most at ease with, an era where you feel most at home?

As I was growing up in the 1950s, commercial television was growing as well, and was nowhere nearly as neatly packaged and programmed as it is today. Broadcasters with hours to fill relied heavily on movies and cartoons from the 1930s and '40s, and so I was exposed to a lot of the popular culture from generations preceding mine. It wasn't until several years later that I realized the beginnings of my love of Art Deco began with the Warner Brothers cartoons and Marx Brothers movies I saw as a child. Then the '50s developed its own style, reflected in influences as diverse as Saul Bass and Soupy Sales (to say nothing of Jay Ward and Bill Scott). When Push Pin Studios, among others, reintroduced Art Deco to mainstream advertising in the mid-'60s, it felt like a kind of homecoming to me.

Some of your fonts, like Jaunty Gent and Engels Stabenschrift, are faithful revivals, some are reinterpretations, others are new variations on a familiar theme. Do you prefer one way of working over others? Is one more difficult than the other?

I routinely apply the Goldilocks principle: If an original design seems "just right," I go with what I have at hand and translate it into Bézier curves as faithfully as I am able. In a sense, this approach is more demanding because it requires matching an objective standard. On the other hand – metaphorically speaking – sometimes the porridge is too hot or too cold, so I make changes in some or all of the letterforms as I see fit. In the end, I suppose it all boils down to a matter of personal taste. Thankfully, more often than not, it appears that enough people accept my decisions to make my efforts worthwhile.

You seem to have produced a lot of your lettering work in the pre-digital era. What has the advent of the computer changed for you? Do you still draw by hand when you begin working on a new typeface?

In the pre-digital era, "Undo" meant erasing, painting out or trashing the whole project and starting over. Likewise, testing subtle variations meant starting over, working to a certain point, then trying a different tack at some point in the process. So, in purely economic terms, the personal computer's impact has been tremendous: not only has its use virtually eliminated the expense of art supplies, but it has also reduced the amount of effort necessary to explore different options. So, most of the time I work exclusively on the computer – although, from time to time, I do break out the trusty old pencil and paper to try out some quick variations, especially if those variations are radically different from one another.

When you choose the next typeface to work on, is that a purely intuitive decision? Or do you have marketing plans, clients that want particular styles?
I suppose that, in addition to the Goldilocks principle, I also work by the Garden Party principle, first postulated by Rick Nelson: you can't please everybody, so you've got to please yourself. I tend to pursue projects that interest me, and hope that they will interest other people, as well. Of course, I don't ignore the vox populi, especially since MyFonts makes it so easy for me to gauge public acceptance. If a particular font proves to be a particular favorite among buyers, I try to analyze its appeal and generate offerings that are conceptually, but not necessarily stylistically, similar. Sometimes it works, sometimes it doesn't.

Here's a question some of your colleagues may want to ask you: how do you manage to be so productive?
Two reasons, probably. First, I'm very comfortable with my tools. I draw my outlines exclusively in CorelDraw, which I've been using since version 1. Version 9 is my favorite, perhaps because I served as a Tier 1 beta tester and was intimately involved in its development. This familiarity allows me to knock out the basic shapes very quickly, leaving ample time for fine-tuning later.

Second, I try to keep things interesting by juggling a lot of balls at once. Typically, at any one time I probably have a dozen or more projects in the works. I'll open a project and work on it for as long as it doesn't seem like work; then I'll save it and move onto another project, applying the same criterion. This approach tends to keep each project fresh, and keeps the wheels of industry churning effortlessly.

Zinger Youth

Jaunty Gent
▲ Pre-1940 German script and display fonts are a never-ending source of delight. One of those forgotten treasures is Rheinhold Kräftig by Erich Mollowitz, published by the Hamburg foundry of J. D. Tennert & Sohn in 1936. Curtis subtly reworked the original letterforms, extending them and beefing them up a bit. The result: Jaunty Gent, a script that struts across the page with a determined stride.

▼ Some of Curtis' hand rendered lettering and sketches, FROM LEFT: gig posters in ballpoint pen on notepaper; Pilcrow Morgue; Yelmo, a work in progress.

"If you want to express yourself clearly you need to master the grammar of your chosen medium." MCKENNAHANDLETTERNF

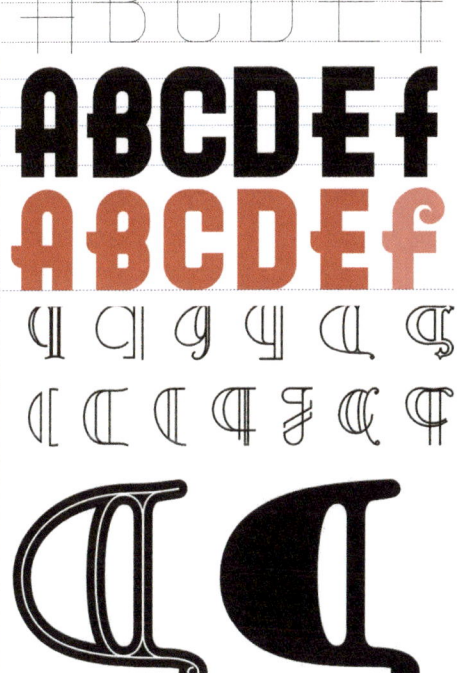

Patrick Griffin

TREASURY

GATOR

When Toronto's Canada Type font foundry made their first appearance in 2004, they could have been just another microfoundry producing nicely made display and script fonts. Over the years, it became clear that they were much more. Although they're just two people – Rebecca Alaccari and Patrick Griffin – their output has been phenomenal, and of consistently high quality. When they do a revival, they go for the "more is more" approach, investing old letterforms with unseen possibilities. When they design a new typeface, the result can be as luxurious as Memoriam or as modestly practical as Informa. Meet Patrick Griffin, the passionate font guy in the leather hat.
June 2009

CLARENDON TEXT PRO

Patrick, Canada Type has risen to prominence in only a few years' time. As type designers, you and Rebecca emerged out of nowhere, so to speak, about five years ago. What is your background, and how did you get into type design?
My background is design in general, and set design in particular. Designing props, sets and collaterals for dramatized documentaries and commercials, that sort of thing. I did that for about sixteen years, and there were my first exposures to type. A few months into my rookie year, colleagues began calling me a type freak. Most of them could not relate to the obsession, even those who were doing the exact same things I was. So I think it's the other way around. You don't get into type. Type gets into you.

Rebecca also has a design background. She was a designer for a couple of big agencies here in Toronto, as well as a freelancer. Her focus was mostly typographic stuff as well. We were both quite happy with our jobs, and did custom font work whenever we could. After Canada Type became popular, the custom font work became a priority. Soon it was full time Canada Type, and the retail operation grew alongside the custom work.

What made you decide to start your own foundry, instead of submitting fonts to other companies?

For a long time, I was against the idea of publishing our fonts. The type publishing model of the second half of the twentieth century was very similar to the book publishing model. The author of the work would submit it to the publisher, who would take time to consider it, wrap it with legalese, and keep the considerable majority of its revenue in the name of editing, printing, marketing, etc. That was an obviously unfair model. Books enjoy global household appeal while typefaces are specialty products with very limited markets. But it was the only option, so type designers could agree to it and make peanuts from their own work while the non-designers raked it in, or stay out of the game.

It really took just the right time, with the right resources and the right distribution model for us to publish our first few fonts. By then, MyFonts had pretty much laid the old publishing model to rest and established a fair, sensible and designer-friendly distribution system. We dipped our toes, and the water was fine. Live long and prosper, Mr. Ying! *

* Charles Ying is the initiator of MyFonts

Ambassador Script

▲ Ambassador Script is a spectacular revival of Aldo Novarese's Juliet, released by Nebiolo in 1955. The Italians called it a "tipo inglese" as it is a reworking of an English roundhand. Juliet became the point of departure for a remarkable labor of love, on which Alaccari and Griffin spent an estimated (and mind-boggling) one thousand hours. Equipped with a huge number of alternates, swashes, flourishes, beginning and ending forms, as well as snap-on strokes, Ambassador Script is typical of a new generation of script fonts that use the possibilities of OpenType technology to the max.

Mystify the office
DISC◯VER
How can I not help you?
Little Secret
Refill Armadillo, Jan 20
CABINET
FROZEN CRANE

Ronaldson

▲ Ronaldson is the outcome of a discussion that took place three years ago on our WhatTheFont forum. A typeface from a 1970s Italian gardening book was identified as the American classic Ronaldson Old Style, a MacKellar, Smiths & Jordan metal type dating back to 1884. The typeface was the magnum opus of Alexander Kay, a first generation Scottish-American punchcutter with an impressive résumé. Having realized that Ronaldson Old Style had never been digitized, Alaccari and Griffin set out on a great 22-month adventure in type history, the result of which is this digital version of what was a best selling American text face of the nineteenth and early twentieth centuries.

How would you describe Canada Type's policy?
It's more of a common sense approach really. Customer convenience is key. We come from design backgrounds, and we've been around the block a few times, so we know what a font user wants and, just as importantly, doesn't want a font to do. So our approach is to try as best as possible to introduce our fonts into people's workflows as transparently and conveniently as possible. No legal hooks or small print money pits in the EULA. Keep things affordable so that everyone can consider your work. Infinite customer support and give-and-take. Sensible customer request consideration. Focus on type, not pillows. From five years of customer response, it seems that people appreciate what we're doing and find our stuff useful, I'm happy to say.

How did you manage to create such a huge number of fonts in a mere five years?
Hard work, constant learning and good scheduling help a lot, but I think it's mostly the love of it. When you love what you do, you are willing to put long hours into it every day. I can't speak for every type designer here, but I found that after a while of doing this stuff, type becomes a constant preoccupation of the mind, always running somewhere in the background while I'm doing other stuff, like the tune in your head that doesn't go away for days. Sometimes it worms itself into daily life in general. Like instead of being angry at a parking ticket, I find myself checking out its design and the fonts used on it. When something has a hold on you like that, it becomes your second skin and comes out of you in spades. It's one of those things that can be a gift or a curse, depending on the situation.

Funny. If I said these same things about a drug, one would be totally justified in considering me a junkie.

Many of your typefaces are based on sources from the past. How do you go about selecting these sources? What are the qualities you find most attractive in a piece of lettering or a font from the past?
Many of our selections for revival or reinterpretation were faces we consider very meaningful historically. It's a strange wonder that we were the first people to bring to the digital world, so late in the game, some of Hermann Ihlenburg's, Aldo Novarese's and Imre Reiner's most important faces, or Ronaldson, or some of the ATF faces.

The digital revolution, in all its past-effacing glory, has not been kind to the history of type. I'm a bit of a design history freak, and inaccurate or made up history gets under my skin. It took me about a month of wading through web search engines and type publisher blurbs before I realized that type history was being reinvented, en masse, which made it incredibly difficult to find what part of the real history was accurately covered in digital form and by whom. Digital copies of old typefaces, hacked or uncredited or poorly sourced, were all over the place. One way out of that mess would be for everyone to give better credit to revivals. We can complain about how the type industry has been unfair to its designers and workers over the centuries. But unless we use the available opportunity to make our product an educational tool as well as a functional one, we're bound to repeat the mistakes made a long time ago and we'll just keep trashing the joint for those who come after us.

What are the steps you take to develop a usable digital typeface from a given model?
It really depends on the model. With most display faces, if we have a good printed specimen of the original, a scan and digital trace is a good enough start. Then comes the cleaning, measuring, tweaking, fitting, character set expansion, kerning, etc. That's the straightforward production model which we used a lot early on. But it has certain limitations. When confronted with an original that is badly printed due to cheap paper or ink spread or broken type, it's better to redraw from scratch. With faces intended for use at less than about 24 points, it's always best to draw from scratch. It takes more time but the final product contains more accurate math and is much more reliable than a font started from a scan.

A typeface produced by Canada Type may be a literal revival or a reinterpretation of an old typeface; it may be a new design inspired by a limited number of characters in a piece of lettering. Sometimes the letterforms are completely your own invention. Are any of those methods simpler than others? More satisfying?
Literal revivals are the simplest. They're good for a mental workout now and then but I'm not too crazy about them. While it's relatively easy to observe an old typeface from two different time perspectives, it's almost impossible to ignore the technological

▲ Griffin: "These sketches were Philip Bouwsma's initial study for the enormous Maestro project that was released late in 2009. Before I saw those sketches I was skeptical about the commercial viability of a new chancery script, but as soon as I saw what he was doing there, I became a complete believer in the project."

"It took me about a month of wading through web search engines and type publisher blurbs before I realized that type history was being reinvented en masse." CLARENDON TEXT PRO

Bouwsma Text

▶ Bouwsma Text is one of the high points in the collaboration between American calligrapher Philip Bouwsma and Canada Type. Bouwsma Text is what Roman type would look like if it had been designed by calligraphers instead of metalworkers. It evokes the formal harmony of the Roman capitals, with tapered stems, graduated curves and serifs that are natural entrances and exits for the broad pen. The lowercase reflects history in a seamless web from the uncial and half-uncial to the Carolingian book script and its profusion of styles. The moving calligraphic stroke brings life and instant familiarity to the letters, combining classical legibility and proportion with the warmth and presence of a manuscript.

Type *instead* of Gutenberg:
this is what
would have developed if
FORMAL
mass-produced   letters had evolved
naturally
from calligraphy
without metal

Calm & Collected
lovers in a dangerous time
Flowers for Anna
jasmines are her favorite
She Looked Back
and saw his heart breaking
Springtime in Vienna
we live to survive our paradoxes

Serena

▲ Working in close collaboration with Alaccari and Griffin, Dutch writer and type enthusiast Hans van Maanen produced a series of revivals of early twentieth century masterpieces in type design. Serena was based on pencil drawings from the early 1940s by Austrian-born Stefan Schlesinger, whose work on the typeface was never completed due to his untimely death in a Nazi prison camp.

limitations inherent in it. The majority of those limitations are now gone, so it's not too hard to synchronize old faces with current technologies. So that's what I try to do with most revivals. Adding extra features to a font makes it more versatile and expands its functionality, so why not? Takes more time, sure, but any quality product needs to take its time. There is no magic pony in type.

Original fonts are more satisfying to make, but some revivals are high up there as well. There is nothing that matches the feeling I had when Ronaldson was finally finished. Same with Clarendon Text. Fonts done at the end of long and enlightening research are quite satisfying as well. Taboo, for instance.

Over the years, you've struck up a fruitful working relationship with two designers in particular: American calligrapher Philip Bouwsma, and Dutchman Hans van Maanen who, amazingly, is a science writer. How did these collaborations come about — and how do you work together?

We're really fortunate to be working with both these guys. They come from two entirely different backgrounds and have entirely different sets of skills and interests — they really are on opposite sides of the type spectrum. So working with both of them is one of those rare parallel experiences that make you have a deeper appreciation for human creativity, watching the ways one interest moves and grows differently through different people.

Hans is the perfect example of what happens when someone is determinedly passionate about something. As you mentioned, his profession is totally unrelated to type.

Big Love

Memoriam

▲ Each December, the last issue of *New York Times Magazine* is dedicated to the people who passed away during the year. For the 2008 issue, art director Nancy Harris Rouemy commissioned Griffin to design a typeface for that project. Based on ideas found in Canada Type's Jezebel and Treasury, Memoriam takes an even more luscious approach, resulting in an opulent contrast-rich calligraphic display face. Memoriam is recommended for use at large display sizes. ▼ Detail from the issue's title page.

Sunny von Bülow b.1932
Studs Terkel b.1912 Bettie Page b.1923
Sydney Pollack b.1934
Dick Martin b.1922 Suharto b.1921
Aleksandr Solzhenitsyn b.1918
Cyd Charisse b.1921 Heath Ledger b.1979
Suzanne Pleshette b.1937
William F. Buckley Jr. b.1925
Odetta b.1930 Henry Z. Steinway b.1915

Treasury

▲ The Treasury script waited over 130 years to be digitized. It took Canada Type seven months of meticulous work – "the most ambitious, educational and enjoyable type journey we've embarked upon," as Griffin wrote at the time.

Based on one of the most fascinating lettering styles in American history, Treasury goes beyond being a mere revival of a typeface. It has been brought into the computer age with more style and functionality than just another lost script becoming digital. The Treasury System takes advantage of one of the most commonly used features of today's design software: layering. With half a dozen different varieties of each letter, Treasury offers limitless possibilities for multi-colored lettering.

Yet because of that passion he has for typefaces, he taught himself the ins and outs of font software in a relatively short time, and ended up digitizing some of the best, and most overlooked, historic Dutch and German fonts around. It's a point of pride at Canada Type that Dutch Mediaeval was the very first text face we ever published. I also love his Serena. Given its beauty and the heart-wrenching story behind it, it's a wonder nobody had brought it to the digital world before he did. But he's that kind of guy, a pearl diver. His research is impeccable, and when he finds a lost gem, he's certainly capable of planning it out and bringing it home in style.

Philip is a very special guy, a real giant in his field. I've always been a fan of his work, long before he came on board. But after working with him for the past few years, he's grown so much as a person in my perspective. I'm not sure whether to call him a type designer or a calligrapher – I tend to think of him more like an alphabet philosopher. It's very natural for him to view any alphabet from multiple angles simultaneously and fluidly, and place it in its exact place historically. Whenever I feel uninspired, all it takes is a phone call to him, and purpose is found again. This past winter I went to visit him at his house in Napa Valley. There was a moment when he was demonstrating a theory to me. He absent-mindedly reached for the shelf, grabbed two pencils and held them between thumb and index like mere mortals normally hold one pencil, and in an instant he had a gorgeous outlined 'a' drawn on his notepad, and he just went on explaining to me about calligraphic stroke stress and what have you. The whole thing took one surreal moment. You can't pay to experience this kind of magic.

Ever since your Clarendon Text came out, some of us have been really curious to see when Canada Type would bring out another fully-fledged text type family. You've now brought out Informa, your first humanist sans-serif. How did it come about? I hear you had some assistance from Europe.

Informa was a project-specific face at first. When we were working on the Canada Type fourth anniversary specimen book in the winter of 2008, we soon realized that we needed a sans-serif text face for intros, captions, descriptions, summaries, footnotes, etc. It was around then that something Erik Spiekermann says in the Helvetica documentary resonated with me. He said a real typeface's rhythm and contrast must come from handwriting, and Helvetica doesn't have any of that. From the ensuing introspective debate emerged the thought that my sans-serif face should be closely based on handwriting.

I fiddled around with basing a few sans-serif letters on a modern classic flare-serif, a film type from 1978 called Signa (by Team 77 from Switzerland), adjusting rhythm and contrast, and I was surprised by how well they worked together. So I decided to keep going in that direction. I put together enough of Informa to make the book. It turned out great and we decided to make a decent family out of it. But my workload was huge so I definitely needed some assistance with the production. Enter Elena Albertoni, who has done design and production work for Luc(as) de Groot. She's great. Very knowledgeable and systematic, with a lot of attention to the most microscopic of details. She saved me months of work. The Informa family would certainly not have been the same without her.

◀ Treasury t-shirt by Nick Sherman, from Oath Threadline, photography by Gennessy Martinez

Although all the Canada Type fonts are available at MyFonts, there are quite a few typefaces you made that we haven't seen here yet, and perhaps never will. These were custom fonts made for specific clients – and some high-profile ones at that. Can you say something about recent custom jobs?

I can say a lot about custom work, but I'm afraid I can't name most of our clients. This is one of those catch-22 situations. We'd love to brag about the fonts we made for the major upcoming athletic event we cannot name, or the ones we did for the international bank we cannot mention, or the work we did for a few major TV broadcasters, or certain global cosmetics and fashion houses – but we just can't, because of all the non-disclosure agreements and legal stuff we've signed. It's great when there are no NDAs. I can certainly say that we've done work for the New York Times, Pixar, Jacquin's, University of Toronto, and the Montreal Airport, among others.

Custom work is really our bread and butter. It's nice to be popular on the retail side as well, but we've been first and foremost a custom design studio since day one. It's really an entirely different gig. With retail fonts, your customers are all over the typographic proficiency scale – from professional experts to the ones who'll letterspace connected scripts. With custom work, you mostly get the typographically sophisticated minds, looking for purpose and perfection in their projects. Working with such people is always a fascinating experience, where you can see the ideas come to life while communication is being exchanged. And when the type work is done and is successfully used within the design it was made for, it's really the ultimate professional gratification on both ends of the working relationship.

Clarendon Text

▲ In the days of metal type, every foundry had its own Clarendon: indestructible romans with sturdy, slab-like serifs. Cutting-edge designers rediscovered Clarendon in the 1990s as a timeless, unaffected industrial style of type. Yet most of the available digital versions performed disappointingly in text setting. This is what Clarendon Text was designed to redeem. It's a radical but respectful makeover of a classic, with elegant italics inspired by Aldo Novarese's 1955 Egizio Italic. The new typeface slightly departs from the original Clarendon to make it better suited for immersive reading.

Gala, Miedinger

◀ Two type families based on Griffin's research of mid twentieth century type design. Gala (left) is the digitization of the one of the most significant Italian contributions to modernist type design: G. da Milano's 1935 Neon, made for the Nebiolo foundry under the direction of Alessandro Butti. Miedinger (right) was based on Horizontal, a forgotten display typeface by Max Miedinger, the designer of Neue Haas Grotesk (aka Helvetica). Miedinger's extended bold typeface became the starting point of a five-weight digital family.

P22
RICHARD KEGLER &
CARIMA EL-BEHAIRY

P22 ZANER

P22 ARTS AND CRAFTS TALL

In the American typographic landscape P22 takes a special place. Having started out as a subversive art project, they morphed into a foundry specializing in typefaces related to art and history. They became known for their spectacular, award-winning packaging. Then a series of unrelated font projects crossed their path, which they decided to accommodate in separate labels: IHOF (International House of Fonts), Lanston Type, Rimmer Type Foundry, and Sherwood Type. They also publish books and music CDs, and co-organized 2008's TypeCon. All of this is accomplished by a surprisingly small staff, led by Richard Kegler and Carima El-Behairy, husband and wife. Meet one of the type world's hardest working couples. *February 2008*

LTC CALIFORNIAN PRO

P22 was originally a somewhat mysterious group of artists. Could you tell us something about those early days, and about that weird and wonderful art form called mail art?

Richard: It was as much a mysterious group as it was my own *nom de plume* for any number of projects that involved not getting a real job. The mail art project started as a way to correspond with a fellow artist who had moved across state. We would send objects through the mail and try to outdo one another. Often objects were sent back and forth with each round adding or subtracting until one of us decided it was "finished" or until the post office lost or destroyed it.

Carima: Our local post office would often display the collaborative pieces that came through. But the mail bombs of the "Unabomber" put an end to irregular mail. A visit from the postal inspector with one of the pieces, extracting a promise never to send objects with electronic components any more, combined with the rise of P22, put an end to the project in the mid-1990s.

Richard, you were also a book artist and a bookbinder. Did that help spark your interest in type?
Richard: 99.9% of the books I made were blank or just sculptural. The truth is I avoided typography in art/design school because the type instructor was notorious for being tough. My general art degree didn't require it, so I did other things.

When you made that first font, did you realize right away: "This is it!" — After all, correcting curves on a computer screen is a far cry from making objects with paper and wire, brushes and cutters…
Richard: The first font was intended only for a minor part of my thesis project installation. It was a mechanical exercise that took Marcel Duchamp's handwriting and randomly selected one of each letter from his notebooks and without adjustment or judgment, assembled the font. It was a specific homage to Duchamp's "ready-made" or found object ethos. It had no intended use other than this one project.

So at the start, it really wasn't about type. The transition from the physical object happened in my graduate studies in Media Study. I was interested in video but quickly fell for the allure of the Amiga, a highly underrated computer system with awful fonts. There was no "Eureka" moment, but years of avoiding getting a real job accumulated a wide range of experience that came in handy for many facets of running a "type foundry." Then, after a couple years of having the P22 type foundry, I was finally able to do a couple of hand made book projects that incorporated our type.

P22 Bifur

▲ Designed as metal type by poster artist A.M. Cassandre in 1929, Bifur was originally available as a single font or as a two-part font in which each letter has been split into two components, to be printed with two colors. In the P22/IHOF version, Cassandre's original all-caps font has been expanded with an inventive lower case. The six-font set offers each alphabet in two grades of hatching. The complementing "half character" fonts can be layered to form multi-tone lettering, offering a wide range of decorative options.

"Part of it is being hell-bent on self survival in our chosen field. Type design is not the most lucrative profession in the world but it is a labor of love." RTF AMYTHEST BOLD ITALIC

In the mid-1990s, when you started out, most designers preferred to submit fonts to existing foundries. Why did you choose to start your own foundry?

Richard: Up to that point the "foundry," like all P22 projects, was a put-on. Using the term foundry was a tongue-in-cheek way to suggest an anachronistic business name. The first font was made available months after the project had been completed. It was offered for sale in packaging (which, at the time, was still undesigned) at the trade show where my blank books were sold to museum gallery gift shops. The P22 distribution system for the first year was solely through museum gift shops via the distribution system that was already in place for my books.

Carima: This distribution allowed P22 national and international exposure without the advertising dollars and within a relatively short span of time. P22 was introduced in August of 1994 and by January of 1995 P22 could count the Guggenheim, The Los Angeles MOCA, SFMOMA in San Francisco, the Art Institute of Chicago, the British Museum, and MoMA New York as customers.

> *"Years of avoiding getting a real job accumulated a wide range of experience that came in handy for many facets of running a 'type foundry'."*
>
> RTF AMYTHEST BOLD ITALIC

P22 Arts and Crafts

Produced in association with The Burchfield-Penney Art Center (Buffalo, New York), the Arts and Crafts font set derives from Roycroft books and periodicals designed by multi-faceted artist, Dard Hunter, in the early 1900s. Arts and Crafts now includes over fifty decorative elements to give your documents a unique and distinguished mission-style appearance. Also included are various ligatures which add even more flair to this distinctive font set.

Many of the early P22 fonts were based on artists' handwriting, and many recent fonts are still inspired by hand-lettering and handwriting. In the originals, every single letter is different. How do you go about transforming them into a font, where there is only one version of each letter, plus maybe a couple of alternates?

Richard: In handwriting every letter is different, but there is always an exemplar or average of most letters. The trick is to digitize letters that work together without jumping out too much. The distinctive swash 't' in Cézanne was an experiment that stuck but we knew it was too much so we included an alternate in the original PostScript version. The advent of OpenType made us re-examine the "must choose one" approach, and thus Cézanne Pro was a logical choice for us.

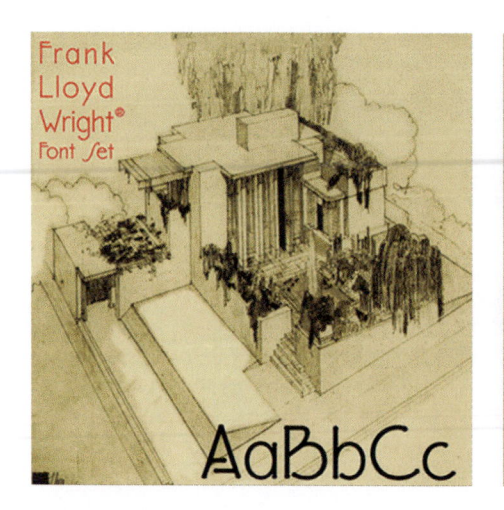

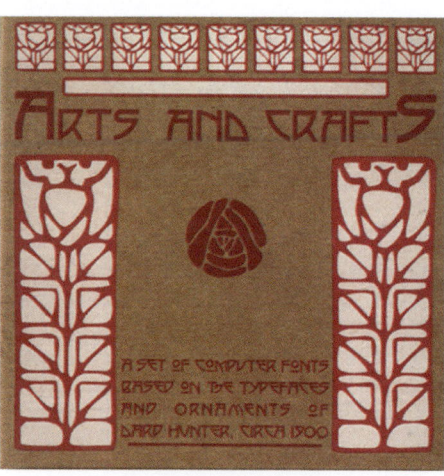

▲ CD-ROM covers for P22 font sets.

French Toast
French Maids
French Fries

King Arthur was at Caerlleon upon Usk; and one day he sat in his chamber; and with him were Owain the son of Urien, and Kynon the son of Clydno, and Kai the son of Kyner; and Gwenhwyvar and her handmaidens at needlework by the window. And if it should be said that there was a porter at Arthur's palace, there was none. Glewlwyd Gavaelvawr was there, acting as porter, to welcome guests and strangers, and to receive them with honour, and to inform them of the manners and customs of the Court; and to direct those who came to the Hall or to the presence-chamber, and those who came to take up their lodging.

P22 Cézanne

◀ Cézanne is one of P22's classic handwriting fonts. Based on the handwriting of the French artist Paul Cézanne, it was originally created in 1996 for the Philadelphia Museum of Art. However, it didn't reveal its full potential until the recent Pro version, one of the most complete fonts of its kind. When using programs that support full OpenType functionality, type a text in Cézanne Pro and watch how the characters adapt to the context, forming ligatures and words in a lively rendition of Cézanne's handwriting. The font comes with some fine skulls, but for a full set of drawings by the great artist, try Cézanne Sketches.

P22 has grown into a multi-foundry conglomerate: besides the P22 mothership, it includes IHOF, Lanston Type, the Sherwood Collection, and the Rimmer Type Foundry. Why so many different labels? And how do they relate to each other?
Richard: The growth of the P22 empire was somewhat organic and definitely not part of a five-year plan. International House of Fonts (IHOF) was created because P22 was at the time strictly defined by packaged discs (first floppies, then CDs) that had specific art themes. We had no way to deal with submissions from freelancers, or our odd designs that didn't fit the P22 model. So IHOF was made to be what P22 was not: online only, a wide scope of styles, freelance submissions. Without a large investment in packaging and disc duplication costs, we could take more risks with unusual releases.

Carima: All of these labels have one thing in common: they are all historically based or have historical references. At the time, hardly anyone was releasing historical faces. Each one of the foundries evolved to meet a need expressed by our customers or a need that came out of the foundries themselves. For example: Sherwood evolved out of Ted Staunton's vision and expertise in historical typefaces. He came to us with one face and then when that went well, he asked if we would be interested in a couple of others he had. Well, there were more than a couple, it was more like 25. And Sherwood was born.

Each label has its own personality, and it wouldn't be fair to lump them all together and expect them to act, or look like the other labels or foundries. Much like family members, they look similar but each are individuals.

There has been an incredible boom in script fonts lately. Did that have an impact at P22 as well? Why do you think these fonts have become so popular?
Carima: We probably could have ridden the Script wave a bit better, but in some ways we already had our script fonts released and we had moved onto other things. Cézanne, Zaner and Corinthia are very different types of scripts, but they continue to do well for us. Meanwhile, we have spent the last couple years focusing on the Lanston and Rimmer Collections. We do have a couple of new scripts in the works, though. Even with everything out there, we still see voids that we would like to fill.

Richard: Why are scripts so popular? I still think part of it is the backlash against technology. The ability to be geometric and perfect is still dehumanizing to many. The natural or flawed script fonts evoke a real human element. Very few people can actually write like these fonts, so to some it is also an aspiration to have such writing oneself.

As for the stuff that people create with our handwriting fonts – we have seen just about everything. Cézanne in particular went through a coffee phase where at least five major coffee purveyors were using it. Recently there has been a chocolate glut using Cézanne. Food packaging seems like a constant, while invitations are another perennial favorite.

The Lanston Type Company is a continuation of the legendary Lanston-Monotype company. How did you come to acquire Lanston – why was it so interesting to you?
Richard: Gerald Giampa approached us because we had digitized a Goudy face and linked to his web site for reference. He also liked our font collection. My first reaction when he posed the question was to laugh and say we were flattered but we were in no position to acquire a company. I was always confused and intrigued by the distinction between Lanston and Lanston Monotype and Monotype so I decided to at least hear him out. We talked to our bank and the numbers made sense. As the library was very complementary to the P22 collection, with no real overlap in styles, it became a separate label.

P22 Zaner
▼▲ While there's a spontaneous and irregular edge to handwriting fonts like Cézanne and Roanoke, P22 Zaner is clean, smooth, flawless elegance. The font's shapes are based on ornamental penmanship as taught by Charles Paxton Zaner at the turn of the twentieth century. The font family's possibilities are almost endless, thanks to the availability of four complementing fonts. The best package of all is the Super Pro set that contains a staggering 3,000+ characters. It uses the OpenType Stylistic Sets feature to great effect. If you want your script to look impressive, posh and/or classy but are bored by the usual roundhands, try Zaner.

▲ Wood blocks from the original typeface.

P22 Underground Pro

P22 UNDERGROUND PRO TITLING

EDWARD

Johnston's typeface for the London Underground is an icon in graphic design and typography. Commissioned in 1916 by First Chief Executive of London Transport, Frank Pick, Johnston's design was intended to be distinctly legible and functional. It can be argued that Johnston's design defined a new category of typefaces: the humanistic sans serif. Although there is much of the ruler and compass to be found in the design, the influence of the pen and of the calligrapher's touch is felt in every letter. Before designing his "sans", Johnston was best known as a teacher of calligraphy and lettering; he wrote a seminal book on the subject.

Part of the charm of Johnston's Underground type is the imperfect nature of the type. The strict unmodulated stroke, the overabundance of charismatic glyphs, the great width of the characters are all features that could be considered detrimental to the design but ultimately, these are the same aspects that make the typeface accessible and endearing, as well as enduring.

In extending the typeface to create a type system, designer Paul D. Hunt took great care to try to retain the characteristics that make the Underground typeface what it is. The essence of the original has been infused into a range of weights for usage with additional scripts, notably Greek and Cyrillic, making Johnston's original typeface more applicable to new environments and increasing its versatility while remaining true to the type's basic character.

▲ Johnston's original paste-ups for Underground.

P22 UNDERGROUND PRO BOOK

With thanks to Paul Hunt

▼ Stills from Richard Kegler's film of Jim Rimmer working on the Stern typeface

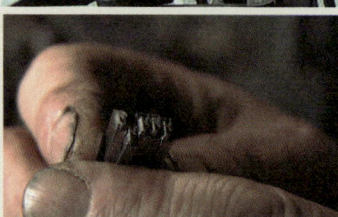

Stern
Named in memory of Christopher Stern
1950–2006
Letterpress
Artist
Printer

Canadian designer and craftsman Jim Rimmer worked for almost six decades as a pressman, typesetter, designer, lithographer, illustrator, bookbinder and teacher. Rimmer, who died in January 2010, also ran the prolific one-man venture Pie Tree Press, which published limited edition books of which Rimmer designed all aspects. Yet what probably represents his most important legacy to the typographic world is his output as a type designer. Rimmer created dozens of digital typefaces, plus ten that were cut by hand and cast in metal. During the last decade, he struck up a fruitful working relationship with P22 for the distribution of his fonts.

One of Rimmer's final achievements was the creation of Stern, the first typeface in history that was simultaneously released digitally and in metal. Its creation process illustrates his remarkable approach to type design. Using the same process for decades, all of Rimmer's rough work was done by hand before being translated into digital form by means of a plotting pen, using the Ikarus program. The characters then were output to a laser printer. While there is nothing new about this part of the process, Rimmer's application took it a step further by using the result as the basis for metal type design and casting. From the paper master pattern a lead working pattern was created and scaled to a brass matrix (16 point, in the case of Stern); from the matrix or mould individual letters were cast one piece of type at a time. Working for metal is very different from working directly to digital. Through his unique process, Jim Rimmer managed to cross over a century of printing technology using digital as an intermediate step.

The making of the Stern typeface at Rimmer's studio was documented in HD video. A trailer for a feature video documentary was distributed, but production was delayed by Richard Kegler's efforts to start up a new book arts center in his city, Buffalo, NY. In March 2010 he launched an internet pledge for funding, hoping to collect $3,000 by June. Instead, he collected around $7,000 in less than 24 hours.

Big Man
FELL 230 TREES
Ox Bro
50 axehandles or so
TIMBER
That's an amazing beard.

You do a lot more than just publish typefaces. You've co-edited and published the wonderful *Indie Fonts* books, you're active members of the Society of Typographic Aficionados and this year you'll be hosting their annual TypeCon conference… so you seem to be hell-bent on keeping typographic culture alive!
Richard: Part of it is being hell-bent on self-survival in our chosen field. Type design is not the most lucrative profession in the world but it is a labor of love. *Indie Fonts* came about as a promotional vehicle more than anything else and with the non-competitive nature of most indie foundries, making the books a co-operative venture was actually quite easy. The camaraderie of attending a type conference makes them memorable events on so many levels, so when we were asked to host TypeCon for 2008, we looked at each other and said… sure. This is not a 9-to-5 job. As much as many people want to leave their job behind and look forward to Fridays, I actually look forward to going to work. There aren't enough hours in the day to do what we want, so we do as much as we can.

P22 is also a music label. Could you say something about your relationship to music and, perhaps, about the link between type and music?
We tried, on and off, to make the record label a true companion of the foundry. Emigre did it for a while, and the recent TypoBerlin conference with music as the theme shows there is more than a passing synergy between type and music. It seems many type designers are also musicians. We have four releases that have a font along with audio on a CD, but this usually just confuses people looking for just music or fonts. I guess I just still regret selling my Rickenbacker guitar years ago, and releasing other people's music is my vicarious way to stay involved with music without having to actually practice or perform.

Apart from being the heart and soul of P22, you're also a married couple. Do you somehow manage to separate business from private life?
We try. It is difficult. Our offices are on opposite sides of the building. We don't recommend couples sharing businesses together. It is a true test of a relationship.

Californian
▲ Frederic Goudy was associated with Lanston Monotype for 27 years as art director and art counselor. So it's only fair that revivals of that great communicator's typefaces take center stage in P22's Lanston Type Company.
Californian is considered by many to be Goudy's most restrained, most balanced typeface. It was designed in 1938 for the University of California Press. Twenty years later, it was commercially released by Lanston Monotype.
The LTC version is a beauty. True to the original, it does not have a bold weight – but it has great typographic sophistication, thanks to its separate cut of Display fonts, its small caps and swashes. The OpenType version has a huge range of numerals – including small caps and tabular oldstyle – and lots of extra ligatures.

▲ Patterns from the metal cutting of Californian

Nick Shinn

HANDSOME THIN

BEAUFORT HEAVY

Usually the Creative Characters interviews are conducted by e-mail, in a series of back-and-forth exchanges. Nick Shinn, an Englishman in Canada, prefers the old-fashioned way: the immediacy and natural flow of a real conversation. This approach seems to relate to how he makes type. Not that the type designs in the ShinnType collection are old-fashioned… they are simply different. And yet, as Shinn would say, all are wickedly usable. *September 2008*

PRATT PRO

You came to type design through a series of other activities. Most notably, you were an art director in a number of Toronto advertising agencies. How did one thing lead to another?

First of all, I went to art school. But I soon decided I didn't want to be an artist. Then I thought, "what will I do to make a living?"… and dry transfer lettering was something that appealed to me. I thought I might be able to make a living designing dry transfer typefaces and live off the royalties. I was always interested in doing graphic art as part of my fine art and I've always liked working in black and white. I did printing and sculpture, I tried everything, but from an early age I particularly liked drawing in black and white. I was pretty much interested in the whole spectrum of culture: writing, music, film, art… I thought that typography combined a lot of things, especially writing and art. So I started submitting type designs to Letraset, but none were accepted.

Then after I'd moved to Canada, I got into advertising. I thought that if you wanted to understand the modern world, you had to understand advertising, and the only way to understand it was to get inside it and become involved in doing it in a practi-

◀ Sleeman Breweries packaging by Dossier Creative featuring Shinn's Beaufort (inline detailing by the agency), complemented nicely by Goudy's Copperplate Gothic

Beaufort

▼ There are not many typefaces today that look like Beaufort. It is a near-sans, with tiny, pointed serifs that help enhance legibility at small sizes, and add finesse at display size. It has a 1900s look and feel, recalling the kind of "spur serif" style that was popular in the early twentieth century, while its proportions are those of the classic oldstyle types, from Granjon to Times. Yet Beaufort is contemporary, made to take advantage of the way that sharp points in digital type are infinitely scalable and always crisp, their sharpness limited only by output resolution.
Designed for clarity and word count, Shinn's most successful text face is both even and powerful – "beau" as well as "fort."

Székely fighter
Alma Mater — Scholomance
Dracul
3 beautiful brides
Borgo Pass
Land beyond the forest

cal sense. In those days, when starting at the bottom in advertising you did a lot of manual things, like paste-up and mechanical assembly, and especially comps that would be rendered with a marker pen on paper, showing how an ad would turn out once it had been photographed and typeset. Doing that, I acquired a certain amount of knowledge of typography and the hand skills to draw type. So when I eventually came to design my first digital typeface, Fontesque, it expressed a lot of those skills, and the looseness of that comp drawing.

Some of your lectures and articles present a kind of visual history of advertising typography, much of it done by hand. Were you always interested in hand-lettering?
Not particularly hand-lettering, I was just interested in the way advertising was made in the past. Some of it was typography – printing types – and a lot of it was handmade. Looking at the relationship between the technology available and the hand skills at any particular time, I just wanted to understand that; to find out how things were done.

Perhaps another reason why I was interested in hand-lettering was that I had studied calligraphy, because I thought it would help me understand the structure of type. This in turn would be helpful in designing typefaces, given that type evolved from the manuscript hand. So I thought I could learn about it by doing it rather than just reading about it. That's a big principle of my approach to art and design: just do it, don't think about what will work or what other people have done. Just work with these tools, with the ideas that currently happen to be floating around in my head, and see what comes out.

So as a designer of digital type you are totally self-taught. Nobody showed you how to do it.
Yes. I started when Fontographer was relatively fresh. Type design is taught in schools now, but then it was something you just had to figure out. The drawing tools were very similar to Adobe Illustrator, which I was familiar with. In the early 1990s, Fontographer had a very intuitive, Mac-centric interface, which I immediately felt comfortable with.

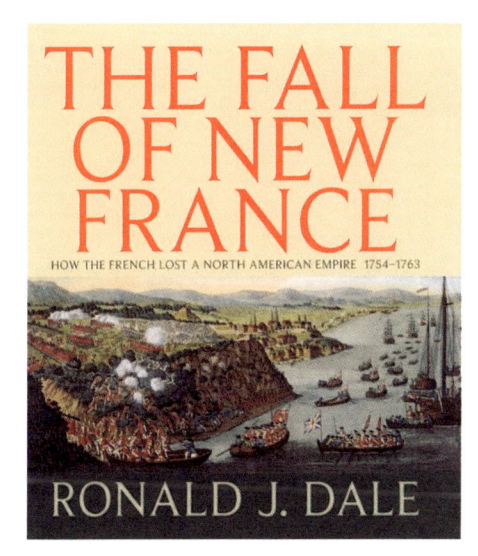

▲ *The Fall of New France* by Ronald J. Dale, designed by Nick Shinn using Beaufort, published by James Lorimer & Company Ltd

Sweet waffles
NORTHERN
Summer snow storms
Bed & Breakfast

Duffy Script

ShinnType's latest script is an interpretation of the lettering of contemporary Canadian illustrator Amanda Duffy. Amanda uses this style of script to accompany the hilarious celebrity cartoons she has produced for many major publications, drawn in a style that is "two-thirds Renaissance, and a sixth each of Twenties' Deco, Beat Generation Cool and postmodern Punk." Her writing is more like post-punk scribble, though, and Shinn has converted it into a bouncy set of fonts. OpenType coding is used to randomly choose different versions of each glyph for a subtle, natural effect.

What prompted you to abandon advertising work and concentrate fully on type design?

One of the things that appealed to me about doing type full-time was: the final cut. It's like, you're the boss. I worked in advertising for many years. And you know how it goes, you do great work and it might not get produced. Or it just might go wrong for a number of other reasons. I liked the idea that with type I would be the total boss. If I wanted to do a certain type of work and publish it, I could do so, even if it didn't make any sense. I could still do it because it would be my idea. That was one reason why I wanted to get into it. The other reason was I realized that e-commerce would make it possible. I had designed other typefaces before that had been published by other companies – this goes back as far as 1980 – but as a designer you always got a very small percentage. Once you're able to become your own publisher, the percentage is much higher. So that's when I realized that I could start a foundry and publicize myself with my own website and work with third-party distributors like MyFonts. My presence on the internet could be just as significant as a very large corporation. The internet is really a great leveler of perception.

There are many type designers who are also writers, but you're one of the few who write about type and design in a way that is not purely historical or technical. You tend to tackle social and philosophical aspects of visual culture.

As I said, one of the reasons I went into advertising was that you get to work with words and images. I was working in an ad agency in the mid-eighties, and an account executive who thought I was very opinionated said: "You should write your opinions in a magazine." That was when I started writing a column on art direction for *Marketing* magazine. So I wrote a lot of magazine articles, in particular for the Canadian computer arts magazine *Graphic Exchange*. Now when you are a regular columnist you quickly run out of things to say about your specialty, so I started writing about … anything, trying to get under the skin of it and try to see it from a deeper perspective.

In what way is type design an expression or a symptom of cultural change?

It's very complex. I do think there are sociopolitical aspects to it. Take the script phenomenon. Scripts have become immensely popular. In America, there is a kind of retro-ironic nostalgia, and I can't decide whether it's a backlash to the freedom and experimentation of the '60s and '70s – very conservative – or whether it's a reaction to the high-tech world we live in being so hard-edge that people want something softer and more human. Also, people aren't writing by hand any more because it's not necessary, and we kind of miss that in our culture. So there are all these different reasons that script fonts are interesting and people want to use them and design them. And there are other reasons too. With OpenType we have a technology that does a much better job of simulating handwriting and script than has been possible in the past. That's something I like to explore: the potential of new technologies. I've done that in Handsome Pro and the new Duffy Script.

◂ Nick Shinn by Amanda Duffy

"In America, there is a kind of retro-ironic nostalgia. I can't decide whether it's a conservative backlash to the freedom of the '60s, or whether it's a reaction to the high-tech world we live in being so hard-edged." BODONI EGYPTIAN LIGHT

When you make a script like Handsome, there must be a kind of triple joy in it for you: commenting on a cultural trend, pulling a great virtuoso technical trick, and producing something that people may be interested in (which might result in a certain commercial success). Are you aware of all these levels as you're working?
The trick is like solving a puzzle. If you make every character work with every other character, when you're done there may be the same sense of completion as when finishing a jigsaw puzzle or, for a mathematician, solving an equation; everything just drops into place. Or maybe collectors have the same feeling when they obtain the final piece of a set, the piece that was missing. So when a new technology comes along, you think, how can I use this to make a font? And then you work towards completing the solution that the new technology is suggesting when it's applied to the old question of completing an alphabet… and… what were the other levels you mentioned?

The commercial aspect.
I wouldn't say I want to be commercial by being trendy. I'm interested in the idea of scripts as a contemporary phenomenon, not because they're "in." Type design can last a long time. People are still using typefaces that were designed centuries ago, or fifty years ago – they have longevity. You don't have to make it faddish to make it useful and functional. As long as you design something that is unique and original, because the global market for fonts is so huge, and people in different countries are so different, you never know how people are going to use fonts.

I don't think you can predict what will sell. Of course you can say, "scripts are popular," and you can predict that your script will be more popular than a text font. But if you design an original text font or whatever, there'll always be a market for it. It's the Long Tail theory of marketing. I designed Panoptica for a very specific use, which was constraint-based concrete poetry where every character had to have the same width. Now there's not a huge market for that but there will always be someone somewhere who's interested in it, so it addresses that minority usage, or anything else that people can think up for a novel font.

Constantly Lost & Eventually FOUND

Softmachine

▲ Softmachine is another Shinn font made for a specific use. It is a display font designed for use with standard outline strokes as provided by most drawing and layout programs. In most typefaces, abrupt joints and sharp corners result in awkward clashes and spiky points when applying outline strokes. Not Softmachine! Thanks to its even thickness and smooth curves, making Softmachine glow by adding outline strokes is a breeze; the process is further smoothed by the spacing and kerning of letters.

◀ ABC Paper cups by I Am Design, with Softmachine

Modern Suite

▼ With the Modern Suite, Shinn revisits the place and time where the modernity of the machine age began – London in the early 1800s. Typography went through a phase of unprecedented experimentation, with fat face, slab serif, sans-serif and decorated faces developed by type foundries like Caslon, Fry and Figgins. Shinn conceived a convincing reinterpretation of Figgins' famous sans-serifs, combining it with that iconic nineteenth century type style, the Scotch Modern. Shinn achieved authenticity by redrawing the typeface by eye (with the aid of a loupe). "No scans, no tracing." Not just a romantic notion, but also a practical way of bridging the gap between metal type and the digital realm.

▶ Invitation to a lecture designed by Nick Sherman.

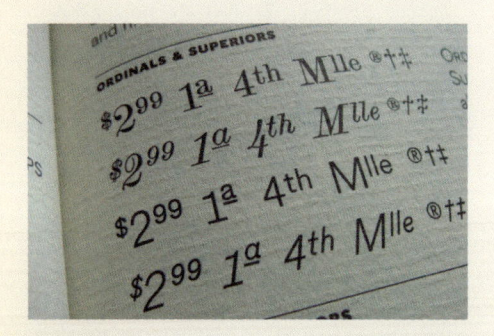

A Rebuke of the MODERNIST MYTH.

A talk by type designer Nick Shinn.

7:00 PM—April 30th, 2009

For all the design profession's infatuation with it, Modernism was a marginal influence on the typography of 20th century mass media, where the dominant force was Historicism. In fact, the most radical and sweeping changes in type design occurred in the early 19th century.

In a process of critical design, Nick Shinn has explored this phenomenon through the revival of two types from that era—Scotch Modern and Figgins Sans—recently published as the Modern Suite. This presentation follows his work from a critique of conventional wisdom to the discovery of new relationships between culture, technology, and designed form. Following the talk, Nick will be signing copies of his book, *"The Modern Suite"*.

the URBAN GALLERY
☞ #401 Richmond Street (*beside Swipe Books*), Toronto

SCOTCH MODERN ITALIC
SWASH CAPITALS & SMALL CAPS

You seem to be somewhat of a natural rebel.
I would say I'm a contrarian, yeah. I look at what everybody else is doing and I say: "I don't want to do that, it's too obvious. Or too conformist."

How is that expressed in your typefaces?
Choose a face.

The latest family: the Modern Suite.
A lot of people don't like the nineteenth century Scotch Moderns. They are said to have poor legibility and too much "sparkle" due to the contrast between the thin hairlines and the heavy verticals. But the modern face was the main face used in all kinds of publications in the late nineteenth century when mass literacy arrived in the United States. So how can you say that it doesn't have good readability when it was instrumental in promoting mass literacy?! That's how the contrarian in me looks at it, and it's why I would do a revival of that face. Another thing is, I didn't scan it; I drew it by eye, with a loupe. It's a kind of romantic notion that you can draw a revival typeface like that.

How about Alphaville?
Alphaville is my techno typeface – as I'm very eclectic, I want to have an example of every genre in my catalog. I designed it at a time when I liked techno music a lot. I also happened to be writing an article about square typefaces and it occurred to me that I had not designed a square font myself. Now the problem with square alphabets is the letter 'V.' Every other letter in the alphabet you can square up with a vertical stroke. There's no confusion. But if you do that with 'V' you can't distinguish it from 'U.' So you have to have at least a minimal diagonal element in your design. As I wanted to keep it absolutely consistent, I introduced these scribal diagonals throughout the alphabet, all with the same angle as the letter 'V.' I find that if you set yourself a set of constraints and follow that in a design, it might not look pretty or trendy, but it has an integrity because it is a designed solution.

One of your latest fonts is Duffy Script. A script font based on another designer's lettering, it is an exception in your catalog. How did it come about?
When I was an art director, Amanda Duffy was one of the illustrators from whom I frequently commissioned work. She would do celebrity illustrations with big heads and little stick bodies, and I always kidded her saying: "You should do a picture of me like that." One day she did – which was very nice of her – and I said: "In return, I'll turn your lettering into a font." Hence the Duffy Script typeface.

To tell the truth, I don't find scripts as complex and meaningful as text faces. Maybe that is a bit snobbish or academic, but… there had to be something else to interest me in a script, and that was this personal aspect – that she is someone I know. It took me years to get around to it. In fact it was the development of OpenType that led me to a new McGuffin, as Hitchcock would have said; a new gadget that pushed me to interpret her lettering. Her writing is so quirky, it's all over the place, it dances. How do you get that level of spontaneity into something as rigid as type? Eventually, because I participate on Typophile.com, where a lot of ideas about how to use OpenType's contextual alternates to animate typefaces are discussed, it occurred to me that I could use those ideas to address her lettering and put it all together.

Handsome

▲ Shinn's remarkable skill as a draftsman is illustrated by this gem of a script font. Handsome was drawn freehand with a digital drawing tablet to connect seamlessly. What makes the family really special is its choice of writing instruments, from a fineliner to a broad-nibbed pen. Letters subtly jump up and down along the baseline, creating a deceptively natural flow. For the look of real handwriting, Handsome is most convincing at around 15 points. Used bigger, it can be made to look like hand-painted sign lettering, or neon.

▲ Book jacket by Nick Shinn featuring Handsome, for *Let Them Eat Prozac* by Dr. David Healy

Alphaville

▲ Its name borrowed from a Godard movie, its shapes simplified and strictly geometric: within the ShinnType universe, Alphaville represents the subtly retro-futurist, techno state of mind. Read the designer's comments in the main text.

"I would say I'm a contrarian, yeah. I look at what everybody else is doing and I say: I don't want to do that, it's too obvious. Or too conformist."

BODONI EGYPTIAN LIGHT

Panoptica

▲ Panoptica was made for a special occasion: a book of concrete poetry by Christian Bök for which the author needed a monospaced font to obtain a grid of vertical as well as horizontal lines. Shinn found that ordinary monowidth type had too many connotations of the office, as well as being uneven in color (compare 'm' and 'i'). His solution: a font family that is unicase (mixing upper- and lowercase forms) as well as monospaced. He then applied the principle to a wide range of styles. Besides the roman, italic and sans versions, Panoptica comes in hand-written, pixelated and octagonal varieties. Finally, there's Panoptica Doesburg, an homage to the 1920s Dutch artist's experimental alphabets. Weird, yet surprisingly usable.

Is it important to feel part of an online community, to take part in those discussions?
Absolutely! The other alternative is to go to school. But the thing is, if you really want to stay on top of things, you have to be online and kicking ideas around with other people. And we're very fortunate to have a genuine online typographic community – Typophile – where people from different areas of typography exchange ideas. So you get artists talking to programmers, those are the two extremes: on the one hand you've got the glyphs which have to be beautiful, on the other hand you've got the programming and coding, which has to make a functional font. When you're trying to make these work together to max out the beauty and functionality and you discuss it online… I got ideas for the alternate encoding, three or four people that I talked to contributed ideas, and I too contributed, so hopefully we can all use these ideas we came up with together.

When you spend part of your professional life in an online community, the place where you are physically becomes less significant. How important is it for you to be in Canada, in Toronto?
It influenced me more when I was an art director. But we do have a type club in Toronto that meets several times a year, and there is a small typographic community, and I like to collaborate with my competitors. I'm great friends with Patrick Griffin of Canada Type; we feel that rather than being jealous of each other, we can help each other. We'll all get further ahead by collaborating. We get together, eat sushi, talk type. It helps that we have separate marketing positions… we don't compete in creating the same kind of type. But then who does really?

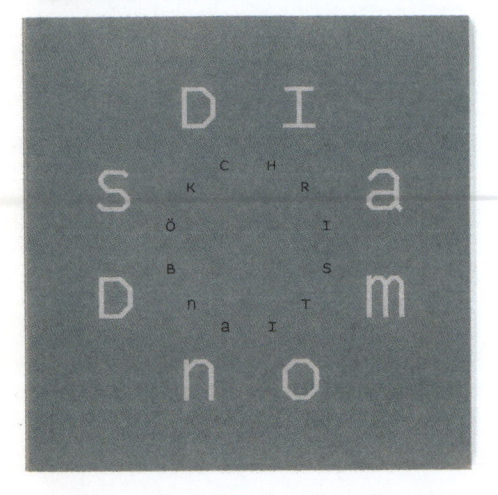

▲ Cover and spread of *Diamonds* by Christian Bök, the book that Panoptica was originally made for.

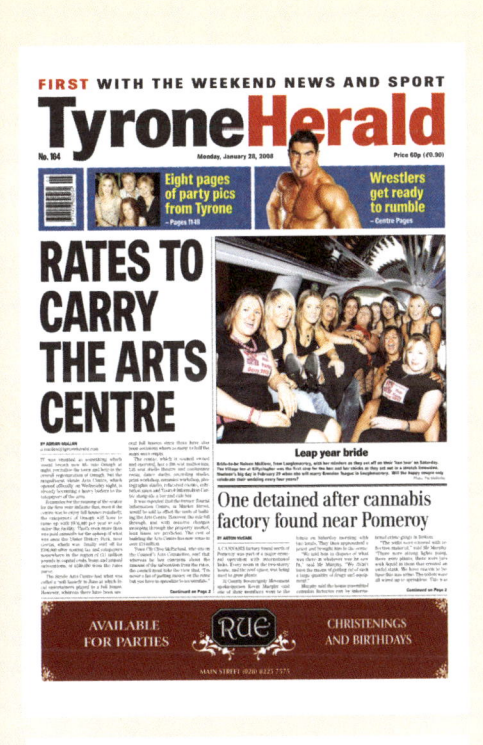

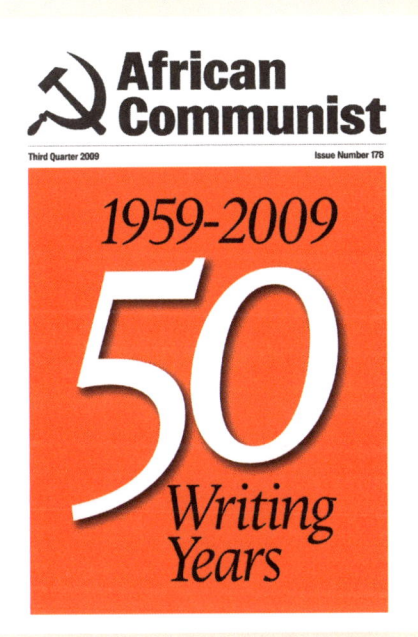

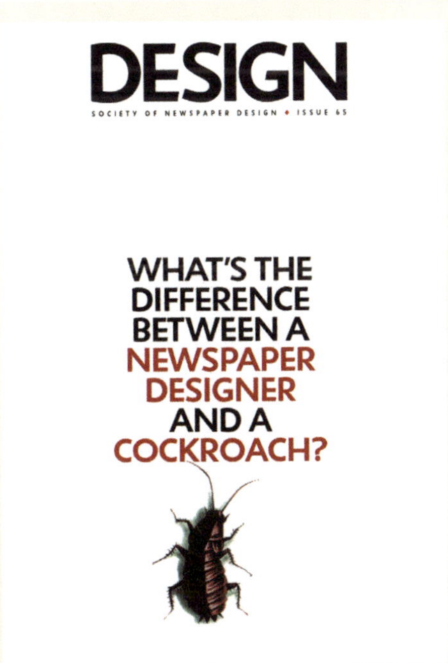

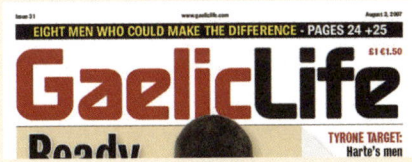

Publications designed by News Design Associates, (Tony Sutton) using Shinn's font families to suit a broad range of editorial design styles.

◀▲ FROM TOP LEFT: *Tyrone Herald*, featuring Worldwide and Brown Gothic; *Weekend Post* masthead (Worldwide Bold Condensed and DIN, with skybox headers in Brown Black); *African Woman* (Brown and Worldwide); *African Communist* (Brown, Goodchild and Nicholas); *Journal of Society of Newspaper Designs* (Shinn typeface for masthead and headlines); *Sunday Focus* masthead (Worldwide Headline Bold); the custom font Kickoff used for the headlines in *Soccer Week*; *Tweed Daily News* (masthead in Nicholas Bold, headlines in Brown); *Gaelic Life* (masthead based on Alphaville).

Hans Samuelson

COLIN SAMUELS BOLD

VICTORIA SAMUELS

Hans Samuelson of Stockholm, Sweden, is a freelance graphic designer specializing in package design and typography. His packaging assignments for food products such as cider and chocolate naturally led to the design of typefaces evoking class and taste. Out of his passion to create the right font for each project grew Samuelstype – a one-man foundry that joined MyFonts in early 2007. Although Hans' typefaces are quite varied in style, they can be recognized immediately – they are all called 'Samuels'. We asked him why. *July* 2007

REBECCA SAMUELS

Could you tell us something about your background as a graphic designer? When and how did you begin specializing in type?

In my late teens my school years interest in drawing shifted towards a fascination for calligraphy, an interest which deepened and lasted for many years. Probably because it is a very controlled form of design; an area where you gain a lot from attempting and finally mastering shapes of letters. To become a professional calligrapher would never have been a realistic aim, though, and I found work as an assistant graphic designer at an industrial design studio in Stockholm. From there I went to the Berghs School of Communication to study graphic design. The division between design and advertising was not so clear in Sweden back then as it was, for example, in the UK. I wanted to create beautiful things and so I went for graphic design rather than advertising since aesthetics is not a top priority there (I mean, an ad campaign can be extremely successful and still no one knows they've actually seen it).

After Berghs my interest in letterforms had become a passion for typography, but although I had done a few type designs, I had no means to produce them for commercial purposes.

It wasn't until the mid-1990s that I took it to the level of actually producing fonts. I was now the co-owner of a major design studio, Embrink in Stockholm, doing package design for many of Sweden's large companies and brands. Anyone who has worked at a studio or agency knows the appeal in the idea of designing for your own pleasure and still produce saleable objects. I started drawing letters as a side business.

In 2004 I became a freelance designer and have since spent more and more time on type-related projects.

Did you receive any formal training in type design?
Not really, other than the few classes that were given at Berghs. But then classic typography was really big around 1990 (before the Mac revolution) with a huge interest in letterpress among ad people. At least in Stockholm so I did pick up a few somethings.

Although your typefaces cover a wide range of styles and genres, they all belong to the same family – the Samuels family. Only their "first names" are different. That's not exactly how we would normally define a type family. Is there something that connects them – other than having been drawn by the same designer?
Using personal first names for my fonts is a result of my relation to them. As soon as they are named they also have a face and a personal character. I am not the first to do it but possibly the first to do it consistently. A type family would usually be a group of fonts based on the same cut. I have simply broadened the definition.

For Maya, my latest design, I considered leaving the concept, but in the end I felt it had a certain relevance. It does tie together, as you call it, "a wide range of styles". And it does have a marketing advantage as it links any specific font directly to me.

▼ Victoria Samuels on chocolate packaging

Opulent
Women of Mayfair
Quills
Chocolatiers

Victoria Samuels

▲ Victoria began life as a custom font for a chocolate box design project, so it breathes a sense of quality and luxury. Not only does Victoria have airy, open capitals, it also comes with a very nice set of alternate capitals with luscious swashes.

▼ Victoria Samuels includes a range of swashed alternates.

Nothing more to add
ACTUALLY
Demonstrations and tastings available

Rarefied

in whisps, hanging in the air

Bottled 1956

Allowing for a universal approach seems unlikely

Not without my cheese

Persuasive

Let it out. Slowly!

one can taste the seaweed

Maya Samuels

▶ Originally intended for magazine use, Maya Samuels was drawn to be soft on the eye without losing character in details. The capitals' angled terminals and chiseled cross-strokes lend Maya an unusual flexibility. It works well as a contemporary, lucid text face, and when used in large sizes and/or all caps it radiates luxury and elegance.

▲ Reimersholms Aquavit bottles, front and back labels, featuring April Samuels (adapted in the logo) and Maya Samuels.

▼ Maya Samuels in a promotional booklet for Reimersholms.

Could you say something about your method in designing type? Do you start with hand-rendered drawings? Or do you construct fonts directly on the screen?
I am old school in the sense that I always start on paper. I need to isolate the basic idea or shape on an independent medium to keep the idea separated from the process. This way it works better as a reference when the work is under way. Also, I find that the pen gives more freedom in finding and exploring shapes. This, of course, applies in particular to work with calligraphic shapes.

The major design work is done in Adobe Illustrator, testing shapes and thicknesses and building the basic system. The basis is often a semi-bold, and from that I make an ultra-thin. Any other weight is drawn within the frames constituted by these two.

Andrew Samuels and Rosemary Samuels are both original and interesting sans-serifs. Could you tell us a little more about the ideas behind these fonts and the purposes you had in mind when making them?
Andrew Samuels is one of my older designs and was drawn to work as a headline as well as a text font. I think it has a healthy amount of pent-up frustration to give it a certain flavor. As with many designs, the starting point here was the 'a'. The somewhat crude cut is meant to provide interesting details when used at a large size and to help connect the letters when used in smaller sizes. Andrew was developed as a custom font for the Nocom Software Company.

Rosemary Samuels dates back to a holiday drive in Scotland, where I was inspired by road sign type. It has much smoother and friendlier shapes; someone called it humanistic and I think that description fits well. It was intended as a text font rather than for headlines and I have found it to be one of my most useful designs. Rosemary became a supporting corporate font for Spendrups Breweries.

As for Maya Samuels, the shapes and basic idea of this face came to me over a long period of time. I felt it had to be a very useful and allround font. The first roughs sat for a long time in the back of my head before it all started unravelling. I think this process worked well and I am very pleased with the result. When it was nearing completion I was assigned a makeover of the identity of Sweden's largest selection of Aquavits (Reimersholms) and decided to use Maya. This was a great incentive to finish the production.

Your serifed typefaces, April and Rebecca Samuels, are rather small families. Do you have plans for extending them?
I agree that they are not as extensive as they have potential for. It is simply a matter of priorities. April is first in line to be extended with a light version and possibly a bold.

Rebecca's main feature is that it's designed to need a minimum of kerning (to perform well in applications that do not handle kerning). It is a complete set in the traditional sense and has been met with some interest. Rather than extending it further I would go for a sans serif version.

One of your specializations is package design, and several of your alphabets were originally made for packaging. What makes you decide to design a custom font for a project? Is that done a lot in Sweden?
When working with package design in the food and drink area (which is my specialty) you are creating personalities; identities that you want people to relate to, come back

---

1951: Polar Expedition #6
Anchorage, AK
Under Ice
intellectual carrot
blueberry muffins
KEEP WATCHING THE SKIES!

Andrew Samuels
▲ Originally designed as a custom font for a software company, Andrew Samuels has become the most widely used of Samuelson's fonts. Andrew is an all-purpose sans-serif with powerful, idiosyncratic shapes that make it stand out from the crowd. Thanks to its open shapes, it remains eminently legible even at small point sizes.

OVERTIME
EXCEPT MONDAYS AND FRIDAYS
PUNCH-IN
10 MINUTES, 15 AT MOST

Bradley S
▲ Bradley S is not as well-behaved as most members of the Samuels family. Its rowdy behavior recalls the misdeeds of 1980s and early 1990s dot matrix printers. When used in small sizes, though, its legibility is surprisingly good. Interesting geometrical shapes show up when blown up.

"Using personal first names for my fonts is a result of my relation to them. As soon as they are named they also have a face and a personal character."

ROSEMARY SAMUELS BOLD

to and recognize as their choice. To me this means text, image and color are free to interact in order to create a unique expression. Usually, this means I draw the name or logo for the product in question. If this results in lettershapes worth developing further I do that, and if this results in a font I go back and apply it to the product or project. This goes back and forth until the result is either an applied font or an independent one.

I find that more and more often agencies incorporate custom fonts (or tweak existing ones) in corporate design projects or major campaigns.

Would you say there is a specific Swedish or Scandinavian style in type design?
I really couldn't say. We have a reputation for a design style that is airy, blond, minimalist and functional, but whether this applies to type design as well I am not sure. I do find we have a preference for plain and straightforward styles rather than more flourished or decorated ones.

Who are your typographic heroes?
I would say Eric Gill or perhaps Edward Johnston among the classics. Both true artists with groundbreaking achievements in treatment of letterforms. Among the living it would be Gerard Unger. All his designs bear his unquestionable characteristics and I find that brave.

What are you plans for the near future, type-wise?
Apart from the extensions mentioned above, I am following my calligraphic heritage and exploring lettershapes to that end. Also, I try to diversify as much as possible and go into new regions. Hence I recently released Arnold Samuels, a headline face unlike any of my others, inspired by 1920s Art Deco-shapes.

Hill Valley, California
FLUX
1.21 Gigawatts
chicken

Colin Samuels
▲ Colin Samuels is wide, straightforward and confident. It's the perfect voice for headlines and slogans that want immediate attention. Colin is a contemporary grotesque with retro influences.

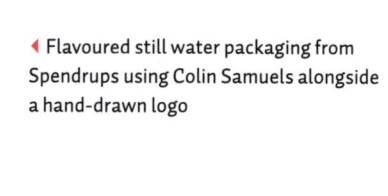

◀ Flavoured still water packaging from Spendrups using Colin Samuels alongside a hand-drawn logo

Bar Italia Orlando Jungle Crew

Orlando Samuels

Hans Samuelson on Orlando: "Another trip back to my calligraphic roots. A companion to Victoria in the more extravagant category, Orlando lends itself well to dramatic headlines or luxurious invitations."

Ellinor Maria Rapp

FG JENNIFER

FG ADAM

One of the special things about the MyFonts sales model is its openness. Like a good local bookshop, MyFonts offers products from big companies as well as one-person outfits. Some success stories are truly remarkable. Take Font Garden from Sweden: they arrived at MyFonts in 2007 with a basketful of spirited handwriting fonts — and those began selling like crazy, making them the most successful new foundry on the website. To Ellinor Maria Rapp, the person behind Font Garden, the success came as a very nice surprise. But for now, she has no intention to give up her day job. *December 2007*

FG REBECCA

You seem to have a long-time love affair with handwriting fonts. How did it start?
It was probably some weird experience in my childhood, as it usually is… but it really started with me getting an internet connection in 1997. Fonts were fascinating and beautiful, and still hard to find then. So I started collecting them, and built an online collection of free fonts, which I still have and work on. It has changed names quite a few times, but now it's Font Garden. And to me, the best and most beautiful fonts were always the handwritten fonts.

I had, and still have, major problems writing anything on the computer without changing the font a hundred times, then not getting the essay, letter or whatever finished on time because I was busy changing fonts all the time.

Later on I got curious to see if it was possible to make my own fonts, and after experimenting with quite a few programs, I ended up with the application I still use today – ScanFont. Then after I had digitized all possible variants of my own boring handwriting, I started to make fonts of other people's handwriting. First in my neighborhood, then over the internet, for free. When it grew more popular, it developed into an online business. That's where I am today.

Have you had any formal training as a graphic designer or type designer? If not, would you have liked to?
No, I don't have an education as a graphic or type designer. I would have loved to, but I didn't realize I could work as one, so I chose a laboratory education instead. But it's never too late, right?

On your website you mention that you can be reached after working hours. Does that mean you have a day job as well?
I work at Örebro University Hospital at the microbiological laboratory as a biomedical scientist. I work part-time to try to keep up with the font jobs and my other online sites and hopefully I will be able to keep on doing that.

On the Font Garden website, many fonts and dingbats are given away for free. Is that out of idealism or is there some kind of plan behind it?
When I started collecting the fonts and redistributing them, it was pure love and obsession. I wanted to share them with the world and also point Font Garden's visitors to the font foundries where they could buy more fonts, so I could help the font foundries get some business.

Now that you're "in business" yourself, you're free to determine your own prices. Font Garden fonts are among the most affordable fonts on the MyFonts website. What's the reason for that?
I think type should not be that expensive, it leads to piracy and redistribution of commercial fonts. I also determine the price on the amount of time spent on the font, and compare the font to the competition. I think everyone should be able to afford buying ten Font Garden fonts to have a few to chose between – that's more fun than to spend a fortune on one font and realize it doesn't work for the project.

It sounds as if you have two jobs at once. You're also a home maker and a mother, aren't you? How do you manage to combine all these activities?
Yes, it's actually three jobs… I have a hard time finding the time to manage everything. The kids take up most of the time and they should! But often the fonting gets behind, so I have a bunch to do when I get to it. Then I sit up all night and work – it's the time when I am most likely to get something done. It's rather cozy sitting up all alone in the dark making fonts, drinking tea and listening to some good music.

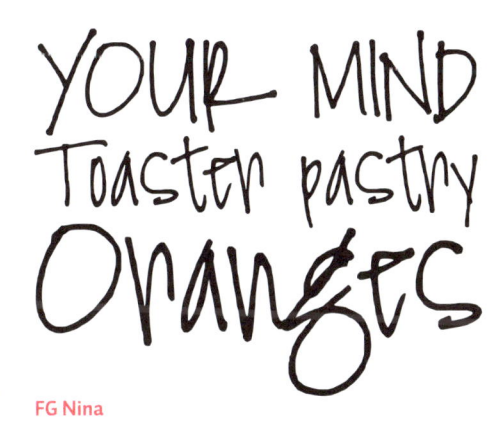

FG Nina

▲ Nina is cheerful and cheeky. The handwriting it was based on is pretty interesting: although the letters lean backward a bit, it still has a forward-pushing energy. The alphabet was drawn at Ellinor Rapp's request by a Font Garden customer for whom she'd "fonted" another sample of handwriting: Amanda. Nina's best feature is its lowercase 'g'. It looks like a cartoon character about to make a witty remark.

FG April

▲ April is based on a hand-drawn alphabet by Ellinor. Although it looks informal and nonchalant, it is reminiscent of the kind of elaborate lettering that could have been done for a book cover or invitation in the 1950s. The double strokes of the capitals combined with the curly single strokes of the lowercase create a colorful visual rhythm.

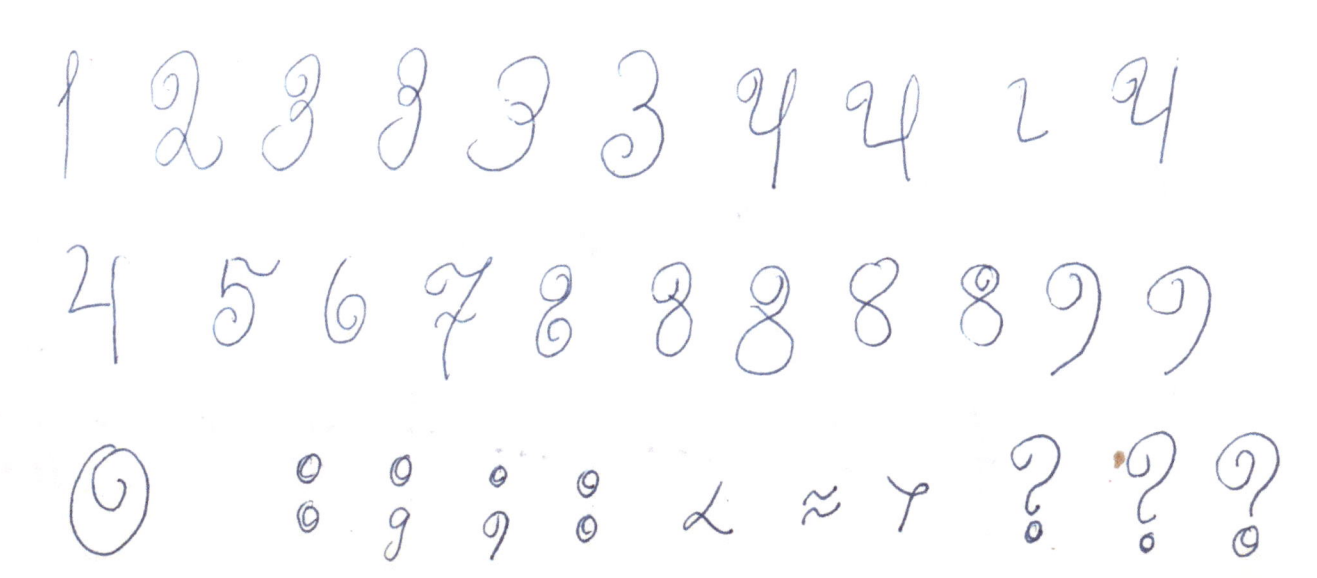

"It's rather cozy sitting up all alone in the dark making fonts, drinking tea and listening to some good music."

FG MATILDA

Digital clocks SAY WHA? Tie your shoe

FG Saga

▲ Saga has power and pace. It has a strong personality, but some quirky features as well. Some letters, notably the capital 'K' and 'R', may be hard to recognize in certain contexts – but as long as that doesn't create any confusion, Saga is a great choice if you want a script face that has a kind of nervous energy about it.

colorful beaks ON THE HILL Feathery friends

FG Rebecca

▲ Rebecca is what they call a "steady seller": since the original interview was published, it has continuously been on MyFonts' bestseller list. Apart from its pricing there must be a special quality about it that attracts font users. It may simply be that it looks so normal – natural, no-frills handwriting that is not particularly sloppy or elaborate and therefore extremely usable.

Do you see any overlap or similarity between your work as a scientist and your font-making endeavors?

I get to see lots of doctors' handwriting on the clinical data slips, and I'm quite good at deciphering their cryptic scrawls. (Not all doctors have bad handwriting; there are a few doctors who have readable writing actually.) I get a lot of good ideas for new fonts from nurses' handwriting, which tends to be beautiful and neat – although there are exceptions there as well, of course. Characters here and there can sometimes turn into a complete font – like FG Ellinor, which is partly based on a receipt written by a nurse.

Do you think you would ever consider giving up your job to work only on fonts?

I think I would be alone too much if I didn't have my job at the laboratory and I simply love that work too much to let it go – even if I probably could make a living making fonts. I also have wonderful colleagues to chat with at work but when I make fonts, I only have myself to talk to and that's rather scary sometimes.

One of your services is to make people's handwriting into fonts. Do you get a lot of requests? Is this also how you collect samples of handwriting for your retail fonts?

I do get a lot of requests, and they usually arrive all at once. So I have a full schedule making fonts during the weekends. I promise to deliver within ten days and I manage to do that most of the time. I sometimes have a rush order – then I let go of everything to create the font. I let the customer decide whether or not they think it's a good idea to make money off their handwriting or get it exclusively made just for them. Many agree to let me sell them online and they get a commission on each sale – at the moment it's 25% of the revenue. But the most fun part is when someone sends in scans of old letters or recipes or diary notes from their great-grandmother or from an old uncle who has lost his writing abilities. Then I extract the font from those notes and create the missing characters to complete the character set. It's very time-consuming, but really fun.

How about the names of the fonts – do they usually refer to the people whose handwriting you used?

Sometimes. Other times it's just a name that suits the font. I started out with Swedish names during my first years of business, now I'm at English names. I don't know if I will change the naming to something different. I thought of naming fonts after viruses and bacteria – but who would ever want to use a font named "FG Staphylococcus" or "FG Porphyromonas"?

Which type designers or graphic designers inspire you?
Early on I got most of my inspiration from the Astigmatic One Eye font foundry, Font Diner and Chank Diesel. Ray Larabie is someone I am in awe of. How can he produce so many typefaces?

Now there are so many foundries to get inspiration from. For one, Ronna Penner produces lovely, whimsical, useful fonts. Perhaps one day I'll get that good at it! I could probably do it, but I lack the amount of patience it takes, so the handwritten font arena suits me better.

Have you ever considered designing a larger family of display or text fonts?
As stated above, I have to admit I am a bit impatient. I want things to be done quickly, and to design a family will probably take three months. When I get that much time on my hands I'm going to give it a go. For now I think it's more fun making fonts directly for people — they get really excited when they see the result and it gives so much feedback. The closest I got to designing a font family is with Norah and Jacky.

You signed up with MyFonts in 2007, but Font Garden had been running for almost ten years by that point. Had you thought of joining before? And were you surprised with the success?
I first requested the forms to fill out in February 2004, but didn't complete them, and tried one more time in 2006, but didn't get around to doing it then either. I just did not think there was an interest in handwritten fonts. Was I wrong! To my surprise several fonts hit the best selling list. That certainly proves there is a market for these fonts. Several ad agencies use them for personal advertising. In Sweden I find handwriting fonts on milk cartons, TV commercials, potato chip bags, greeting cards — they are everywhere!

FG Jennifer

▲ With its regular flow and connected, supple strokes, Jennifer appears to be a script from an "older generation." The original handwriting came from another of Font Garden's visitors who order custom fonts for their own use. This one required a little more "fonting" work than usual, says Ellinor, as the alphabet had to be carefully modified in order to connect the letters.

Alejandro Paul

AFFAIR

WHOMP

Buenos Aires, the capital of Argentina, has been at the forefront of graphic design in Latin America for decades. Today, one of that city's most prominent forces in type design is Sudtipos, a remarkable type collective founded in 2001 by four experienced designers from the world of corporate and packaging design. This chapter's interviewee is Sudtipos' spokesman, who became famous for drawing and programming some of the most intricate script fonts ever digitized. Meet Alejandro 'Ale' Paul, a man who likes to raise bars - and we don't just mean chocolate bars. August 2009

GROVER SLAB REGULAR

Sudtipos was founded by a group of Argentine designers who have all worked with major studios. What were your reasons for starting up your own foundry? How did you get together?

Much of the entire Sudtipos partnership was really a kind of "survivor grouping." In December of 2001, Argentina's economy collapsed, which caused a far-reaching crisis throughout the country. Everyone was affected both personally and professionally. Naturally there was much less demand for graphic design. I lost my job as an art director and began doing freelance packaging work for some of the few agencies that somehow managed to survive the collapse.

Along the way, I had met other graphic designers who had a particular appreciation for type. The foundry, or collective as we prefer to designate it, started because of that – packaging, editorial or brand designers making fonts for other designers. The first time we seriously spoke about founding Sudtipos was at a Buenos Aires event organized in 2001 by Rubén Fontana.

To what extent is your work as type designers linked to your practice as graphic designers?

The type link first became evident in design school. As a student I had to make my designs unique in order to stand out. Type is a design element that helps accomplish that in a big way. At first it was just things like applying type effects, or slightly modifying a letter here or there to make the design more personal. After graduation, real-world packaging design was an eye-opening experience as it implied looking at type very closely. For example, when you have to design the front of an ice cream container, common "fashion" fonts almost never work exactly the way you want them right out of the box. There are millions of containers that use the word "light," and the last thing you want as a packaging designer is your design to be plain or impersonal or look like someone else's.

That original link is still there. Our aim is to always be graphic designers making typefaces for graphic designers. We try not to lose that particular focus. We're always thinking about how to make a graphic designer's work easier when it comes to using the type element in his or her design. Personally, I really like the idea of a graphic designer consciously choosing the perfect alternate character that fits a specific design project. It shows aesthetic sophistication and professional maturity. Whenever I manage to get a graphic designer to consciously choose an OpenType feature in one of my fonts, I'm happy.

Cigars * *New York* * *Shine* *

Ministry Script
▲▼ Ministry Script is one of Alejandro Paul's best known and most elaborate script fonts. It is also one of those OpenType-programmed scripts that (when used with contemporary layout software) magically help you select the ideal version of each cleverly particular combination. With Ministry Script, you have amazing headlines and logos at your fingertips. A single face with over 1,000 glyphs, Ministry Script comes with a galaxy of alternates, swash characters and ligatures to explore.

Ministry Script

All Night Jam-out

Best Swingers

SUDTIPOS PRESENTS

The Real Sign Painting

Lettering with Open Type

SWASHES
ALTERNATES
LIGATURES

Based on calligraphy by A. Becker

ARGUABLY THE GREATEST AMERICAN SIGN LETTERING ARTIST OF ALL TIME

One of your creative partners when designing fonts for Sudtipos is lettering artist Angel Koziupa. How did this collaboration come about? Could you describe the process of working together?

I met Angel through one of the agencies I worked for as a freelancer and was asked to art-direct a project with him. He had been doing lettering and logo retouching for design agencies for decades, but never a complete alphabet. I told him about Sudtipos and offered to help him turn one of his popular logotypes into a complete font. He picked up quite quickly on my instructions, and our first collaboration went very smoothly. Our working process evolved into something that was a lot like New York City in the 1930s: art director and lettering guy working jointly to create a design. But now of course it's all digital, so the tasks of each team member usually have something to do with computers and software.

At first we were envisioning a collaboration that produces fonts representing South American cultures in general, and Argentine culture in particular. Many graphic designers in Argentina, even long before the economic collapse, were dreaming of exporting our design style to the world at low cost. So there's some of that dream in the first few projects Angel and I did. They were basic and very personal, and they contributed in a major way to shaping Sudtipos as a packaging-oriented type collective. Angel's experience with lettering was a very good complement to mine with type. We used that dynamic to produce alternates and subtle digital variations to bring the type closer to real lettering. Most packaging designers work under the tightest deadlines —so the less work they have to do with a font, the better for them. The fonts that Angel and I produced seemed to strike a chord with exactly that kind of professional, which was very encouraging and gave us incentive to keep going.

Our working process varies with the project. How it starts is usually the defining element. Sometimes it starts with one of us noticing a particular market need, or a gap to fill. Sometimes Angel simply sends me some ideas and we take it from there. Sometimes I try to provide inspiration by showing him new trends and ideas. We've been at it for a few years now, and we've learned a lot from each other. These collaborations have helped both of us in defining and making the most of our individual roles in the collective.

Are many of the Sudtipos fonts based on typefaces that were originally developed as corporate fonts or packaging type for a specific client?

A few of our fonts have their roots in custom logo work we've done for high profile clients. Habano ST, for example, was based on one of the most famous logos in Argentina, the Quilmes beer logo, drawn by Angel Koziupa long before the font existed. But the majority of the Sudtipos fonts are really reflective of ideas we've had for something graphic designers would need to help make a difference in their design, especially in packaging.

Buffet Script

▲ Buffet Script is one of a series of wonderfully complex script fonts that made Ale Paul's name as a master in this field. Like the exuberant Whomp, it is based on fantastic calligraphy by Alf Becker, arguably the greatest American sign lettering artist of all time.

In 1941, *Signs of the Times* magazine published an anthology of the alphabets Becker had drawn for the magazine on a monthly basis. In the late 1990s and early 2000s many of these alphabets were digitized, but no one dared touch the one alphabet that eventually became Buffet. It's easy to see why: that particular page shows a jungle of letters running into each other and swashes intertwining – almost impossible to "fontify." Ale Paul finally pulled it off. Using his trademark OpenType wizardry he turned that single page into a fascinating collection of letters, flourishes, alternates and ligatures. When using an OpenType-savvy program, all these alternates interact to allow the composition of just the right word or phrase. Spectacular.

> "Argentines put all of our being into our work, and it comes out looking more innocent and more human - less of a machine base."

GROVER SLAB BOLD ITALIC

◂ Buffet promo specimen by Ale Paul.

Roundabout Vacation Cannot get left BIG BEN Parliament 362 times

Grover

▲ For those who know Alejandro Paul as the king of scripts, Grover may seem out of character. But a simple search will demonstrate that Ale (and please pronounce that Aah-Leh) is a designer who masters a broad range of styles. Named after Grover Washington, Jr., the jazz saxophone player, Grover is one of his personal favorites for everyday use – a readable display-and-text face that comes in a sans and a slab serif version. Grover unites two very different styles of typeface: the European grotesque of the late nineteenth century and the rounded style found in 1960s America. The result is a clear, friendly face: geometrically constructed, yet very human in appearance.

CANDY Please?

Mati

▲ The story of how Mati came about is one of those heartwarming father-and-son stories that are only too rare in the digital font world. The alphabet that it is based on was originally given to Ale by his son Matias as a Father's Day present. Ale lovingly digitized it, and lo and behold: the result was a cheerful, cheeky, usable *and* commercially successful 3D font drawn by an eleven-year-old. Matias has grown up since then, so even bigger things may be expected from him soon.

In Argentine graphic design and advertising, is it difficult to convince clients to order custom-made type?
It almost never happens here actually. Local agencies don't recognize the value of type in general. This is mostly an education problem, since design schools here don't provide adequate focus on type. Designers graduate and begin working for local agencies, and the type-ignorant mentality spreads.

But there are some international agencies here that understand the value of customization, and they consult with us for some special work. We've done some custom fonts for local children's books, banks and TV commercials. Those were mostly commissioned by international agencies. The majority of our custom work is for major American and European agencies.

There has been an incredible boom of type design and typography in Latin America, and especially in Argentina. What do you think are the main reasons for this? Why has Argentina – and notably Buenos Aires – become such an important center?
I think the curiosity and experimentation were always there, but not so conspicuously. Graphic designers are always looking for ways to differentiate themselves from the crowd, and type was still officially uncharted territory in 1990s South America. Then came the internet, which brought it all to the surface. Hence the overwhelming exposure of a lot of South American work all at once. And it persisted because the internet suddenly made the whole world an open market for us, instead of the almost non-existent market we'd had here all along.

There is also something to be said about the Argentine design process, which is part of the appeal to the world markets. Argentina doesn't have the European design history, but we do put all of our being into our work, and sometimes because of that it comes out looking more innocent, more real, more human, with less of a machine base.

Could you tell us something about type design education in Argentina?
Until recently, type design education in Argentina was quite poor. Most of our universities didn't even have a typography class as part of their graphic design curriculum. Designers interested in type usually just went to a series of talks we started a few years ago, an event called T-Convoca, where we just learned from each other's experiences. In 2009, typography in Argentina took an enormous progressive step when the first Masters of Typography was created at the University of Buenos Aires. It's an extensive course that lasts a year and a half, given by a team of some 25 teachers, lead by Rubén Fontana, the man who introduced typography as a mainstream design class in Argentina more than 20 years ago.

Much of your work was inspired by twentieth century lettering and type design. So do you have any heroes in this field?
My heroes are the American lettering guys from the days before photo composition. People like Charles Bluemlein or Alf Becker amaze me with their ability to branch their work out in so many directions for the same project. These days I find myself in love with the Zanerian school of calligraphy, but that's the way I've always been when doing my research for the projects I'm working on at the moment. Pre-tech American lettering has a fantastic history that is mostly overlooked by academics, so whenever my research reveals something new, it feels like I've discovered a treasure.

Casa en Lote

Moutard de Dijon

My Beautiful

Champignon

Frozen Night

Mother's Day

Tango Passion

Pure Real Jazz

Rue de la Paix

Bakers Delight

1930's

Charles Bluemlein

SCRIPT COLLECTION

The Charles Bluemlein Collection

◀ The Charles Bluemlein Collection is based on a 1940s catalog from the Brooklyn-based Higgins Ink Co., which contained a portfolio of script alphabets credited to lettering artist Charles Bluemlein. Whether Mr. Bluemlein was a real person or an invention of the Higgins company's editor may never be certain; he is not mentioned anywhere outside the booklet. The original scripts were assembled in an unusual way — by collecting signatures (real or fake? — again, we'll never know) that were then expanded into complete alphabets. Ale Paul took extreme care to render the original scripts authentically, keeping the names that were originally assigned to each alphabet.

Kiwi by the pound
Dietetica
Organic Season
Best prices guaranteed
Supermarket

Amorinda

▲ One of the best-loved script fonts from the Angel Koziupa and Ale Paul team, Amorinda is a connected script that manages to be capricious and disciplined at the same time. It can scream wildly within a design or smoothly blend in to make it more human. With its versatile character and a complete set of alternates, Amorinda is a display face for everything from product branding to signage.

▲ Packaging using Amorinda by Ale Paul and Angel Koziupa

As far as metal type goes, my favorite faces are the ones by Barnhart Brothers & Spindler, from the late 1900s. I also like the timeless work of Hermann Zapf and Ed Benguiat.

Some years ago, you put together the lovely Bluemlein Collection. Could you tell something about your research into the work of Charles Bluemlein?
After working with Angel on a few projects, I became very interested in the lettering tools and methods he uses. I began researching where all this stuff came from. I remember he once showed me an old lettering book he kept. It was from the 1940s. I wanted to see and learn much more. So I became a library regular, a bookworm and an old book collector. The subject of lettering started spilling over in conversations with my friends. Then a friend of mine showed me a Higgins catalog and told me that I should digitize all 32 specimens there, because they are a great representation of the golden age of American commercial lettering at a time when many calligraphers-letterers like Charles Bluemlein were still trying their best to say no to the new film type technology that was doing a hell of a job mechanically emulating their skills and competing with their livelihood. I felt a solid connection with that last point, because I started designing type for a living when I lost my original job as an art director.

The Bluemlein collection was a lot of work, and it took a long time to complete. It was also quite meaningful, at least to me personally, as the point after which I began designing more elaborate and overloaded scripts. And of course, the Bluemlein collection was a golden moment for my subsequent research and discoveries. It put me on the way to discovering old sign painting masters, showcard letterers and calligraphy artists from all over the world.

Script typefaces are one of the strengths of the Sudtipos collection. Would you say this has to do with Argentine graphic culture – or is it more of a personal thing?
It's more of a personal thing. Outside of common product packaging, Argentine graphic culture is more European and modernist in character, rather than personalized with scripts. My experience in branding product packaging was a natural catalyst for me to be interested in scripts and seek like-minded people for the collective. Since then, my passion for early twentieth century American lettering was the main drive for most of the scripts we produced. Sometimes you can find a rhythm expressive of our culture in some of our fonts, like Candombe or Murga, but for the most part our work is done for international users rather than motivated by local culture.

What constitutes a good script font?
A good script should, just like any other typeface really, perform well in the task for which it was made. This has to happen on many levels, like readability and visual stroke consistency. The relationship between characters should be visually balanced. In connected scripts the connections should be perfect, and in disconnected scripts the spacing should provide the visual balance. Technically speaking, the script should be made with the least amount of Bézier nodes possible, overlapping strokes should be crisp and simple where needed, and the counter of the script's overall setting should harmonize as much as possible. A script can have a billion swashes, but it will be visually appalling if everything doesn't fit together in visual harmony.

▶ Composition by Ale Paul made with Affair.
▶ Poster for the Brazilian theater show *Valsa No. 6* designed by Mopa, Brasilia, using Affair as well as Underware's Sauna.

Affair

▲ Affair is an enormous, intricate OpenType font based on a 9x9 inch photocopy of a page from a 1950s lettering book. This is how Ale Paul's Affair began: "Tourists don't go to libraries in foreign cities. So I walked into one. Two hours later I wasn't in New York anymore. I wasn't anywhere substantial. I was the crazy type designer at the apex of insanity. Alphabet heaven, curves and twirls and loops and swashes ... To this day I can't decide if I actually found the worn book, or if the book itself called for me. Its spine was nothing special, sitting on a shelf, tightly flanked by similar spines on either side. Yet it was the only one I picked off that shelf. And I looked at only one page in it before walking to the photocopier and cheating it with an Argentine coin, since I didn't have the American quarter it wanted. That was the beginning. It was an Affair to remember. I am not exaggerating when I say that the letters themselves told me how to extend them. I was exploited by an alphabet, and it felt great."

Many of your fonts are based on pieces of lettering showing only a limited number of letters or a partial alphabet. Do you have a method for expanding such an incomplete alphabet into a full set of characters?

I usually begin working with words. I try to keep it real. ABC and AaBbCc sequences are not real. I realize that sometimes a single glyph shown attractively can sell a font, but I'm more interested in how an alphabet works in its totality, in real words and sentences. I always look for new possibilities of mixing letters, as long as those possibilities are real. In the beginning the mix is just pairs of letters randomly falling together, just to see what works within the concept I have in mind for that particular project, what is needed to fix the original structure, and what kind of limitations I will have to play within. There I said it: Play. I do play a lot with words and letter combinations. It's really more like a puzzle that I'm putting together, a kind of game.

Is there a particular project in type design that you hope to be able to work on in the near or distant future?

Perhaps one of these days I'll try my hand at a serious text font, but for now I'm quite content with the projects I have lined up.

> "Our aim is to always be graphic designers making typefaces for graphic designers."

GROVER SLAB BOLD ITALIC

Mark SIMONSON

KINESCOPE

MOSTRA

He's one of those designers who live and breathe letterforms, whose hand-lettered titles and brand names look as if they've always been there. Based in Saint Paul, Minnesota, Mark Simonson worked as an art director and lettering artist for many years before being able to fulfill a lifelong dream: to become a full-time type designer. Having started out in the pen-and-ink, cut-and-paste era, he has made the transition to digital design with flying colors. Meet Mark Simonson, a contemporary craftsman. *January 2009*

PROXIMA NOVA REGULAR

Mark, you founded your own company as an independent graphic designer and lettering artist in 2000. What did you do before you decided to go solo?
I did a couple stints at advertising art studios in Minneapolis as a graphic designer, but my main thing for the first 15 or 20 years of my career was as an art director for magazines and other publications such as *Metropolis*, a weekly tabloid in Minneapolis, *Minnesota Monthly*, Minnesota Public Radio's program guide and regional magazine, TWA *Ambassador* and *Utne Reader*.

Lettering was something I had been doing since high school, and I always looked for ways I could apply that skill in redrawing or redesigning the logo or doing lettering for a feature story when it was called for, and later on when I was doing packaging and product designs for Minnesota Public Radio.

During all this time, when I was working as an art director or graphic designer, even back in college, I dreamed of designing typefaces. An ambitious early effort was submitting a design to ITC in 1978, but it was rejected.

When I got my first Mac in 1984, I found out how to make bitmap fonts for it using a developer tool from Apple called Font Editor and, later, a commercial program called Fontastic by a company called Altsys. In 1986, Altsys released Fontographer, a program for creating PostScript fonts. I thought I could use it to design fonts to submit to ITC, where they would be turned into "real" fonts for typesetting machines. Drawing a typeface by hand with paper and ink was laborious and time-consuming, and I thought Fontographer would be kind of a short cut. While I was playing around with this idea, the typesetting industry was turning upside down, and these PostScript fonts were starting to take the place of "real" typesetting.

By the late '80s, this stuff had almost completely taken over, and all these new companies and people were making fonts and selling them directly to users on floppy disks and CDs. I was freelancing at the time and put some effort into creating fonts for this new market. In 1992, I submitted what I was working on to Mark Solsburg at FontHaus and he picked Felt Tip Roman, Proxima Sans, and Kandal. Felt Tip Roman was closest to being done and only took a couple of months to finish, but the other two were multi-font families and took another two years to complete. During that time, my partner and I had a baby, bought a house, and I got a full-time job again, so it was becoming harder to find time to work on fonts. And once these fonts were released, the small amount of income they brought in – even though one of them, Felt Tip Roman, was a minor hit – didn't seem to justify the time and effort it took to make them. I set the dream aside for a while.

COIN-OPERATED
It's an old machine
O-Matic
They don't make 'em like they used to
ICY & COLD

Refrigerator Deluxe

◂ Refrigerator Deluxe is the enhanced version of the original Refrigerator, a condensed, geometric sans-serif inspired by mid twentieth century lettering styles. Refrigerator is perfect for evoking the era that produced huge, humming fridges, but also graces the covers of books on contemporary politics or urban culture.

"I never really decided to become a full-time type designer. I had hoped it would happen, but I didn't really expect it to." PROXIMA NOVA BOLD

◂ During Simonson's time as Art Director at Minnesota Public Radio, he created audio packages for Garrison Keillor's Lake Wobegon series, as well as *Minnesota Monthly*, the network's programme guide and regional magazine.

STRONGBOX
Certified
Class TL-30
Put it under lock & key
Combo: 6-32-14
Kling klang
GRANTED

Proxima Nova

▲ Proxima Nova is an impressive tour-de-force: a sans-serif text family spanning seven weights and three widths – 42 full-featured OpenType fonts in all. Stylistically, Proxima Nova bridges the gap between geometric typefaces like Futura and nineteenth century "industrial" faces such as Akzidenz Grotesk. The result is a very original hybrid that combines the straightforward clarity of the geometric sans with the excellent readability of humanistically inspired faces. Equipped with small caps and multiple figure styles, the basic Proxima Nova fonts provide the demanding typographer with all that they may expect from a professional text font. Nevertheless, supplementary fonts are included to offer those same features to users of programs that do not yet support all OpenType features, such as Microsoft Office and Flash.

Both Proxima Sans and Kandal were very accomplished typefaces and respectful of tradition, especially by early 1990s standards. Who taught you how to do it?
Unless you count a couple of lettering classes I took in college, I'm completely self-taught when it comes to type design. Ever since I can remember, I've been drawing letters, often out of boredom or when I was supposed to be doing something else. It's the default thing I do when I'm doodling. I fell in love with type while working on the newspaper and yearbook in high school. By the time I was in college, this combination of love for type and obsessively drawing letters led to the idea of designing typefaces. I read everything on the subject I could get my hands on – books by Frederic Goudy and Adrian Frutiger in particular. By the early '80s, I had several typeface ideas going. Proxima Sans and Kandal came out of that period. I made a lot of false starts before any of my fonts were published, and there are many ideas from back then that never made it beyond the drawing board.

Having put your type design career on hold to take care of your young family, what prompted you to change course again and become a full-time type designer?
I never really decided to become a full-time type designer. I had hoped it would happen, but I didn't really expect it to. But then in early 2000, a friend told me about this guy who was looking for fonts to sell at a newspaper trade show, which was to be held in St Paul that year. I looked at what I had and finished four fonts that had been on the shelf from the '90s – Refrigerator, Blakely, Felt Tip Senior, and Sharktooth. Nothing came of the guy at the conference, but now I had four fonts that were ready to sell. I discovered a sort of font consignment web store called Makambo and started selling them there. That did not last long – their parent company pulled the plug – but MyFonts, which had not been around long at the time, contacted all the people selling fonts on Makambo, including me, and I started selling on MyFonts in spring of 2001.

But, to back up a little, something extraordinary happened at the end of 2000. My partner, Pat, was a contestant on Who Wants to Be a Millionaire. She did well enough to enable me to take six months off my freelance design business to work on new fonts. During that break, I created Coquette, Anonymous, and Mostra. I went back to my freelance work, but my font income began to increase and my dream of designing type full-time started looking a little more possible.

▲ Proxima Nova in use. CLOCKWISE FROM TOP LEFT: *Minnesota Environmental Partnership*; *What's on TV*; *Contemporary Design in Detail: Sustainable Environments* by Yenna Chan, published by Rockport; *Kraft Philadelphia* packaging; *What's on TV*; *Minnesota Environmental Partnership*. Photos by Mark Simonson.

▶ Proxima Nova full specimen sheet

PROXIMA NOVA

*3 widths
7 weights*

9/10 PROXIMA NOVA THIN
A BALL OF FIRE said to have knocked out a 30-year-old Scout Master, has sent the Air Force Flying Saucer Investigation Squad to Florida. There it has been told a strange story by ex-marine Scout Master D. S. Desverges, who says he was going home with three scouts when he saw flashes of light in a wo

9/10 PROXIMA NOVA LIGHT
A BALL OF FIRE said to have knocked out a 30-year-old Scout Master, has sent the Air Force Flying Saucer Investigation Squad to Florida. There it has been told a strange story by ex-marine Scout Master D. S. Desverges, who says he was going home with three scouts when he saw flashes of light

9/10 PROXIMA NOVA REGULAR
A BALL OF FIRE said to have knocked out a 30-year-old Scout Master, has sent the Air Force Flying Saucer Investigation Squad to Florida. There it has been told a strange story by ex-marine Scout Master D. S. Desverges, who says he was going home with three scouts when he saw flashes of

9/10 PROXIMA NOVA SEMIBOLD
A BALL OF FIRE said to have knocked out a 30-year-old Scout Master, has sent the Air Force Flying Saucer Investigation Squad to Florida. There it has been told a strange story by ex-marine Scout Master D. S. Desverges, who says he was going home with three scouts when he saw flash

9/10 PROXIMA NOVA BOLD
A BALL OF FIRE said to have knocked out a 30-year-old Scout Master, has sent the Air Force Flying Saucer Investigation Squad to Florida. There it has been told a strange story by ex-marine Scout Master D. S. Desverges, who says he was going home with three scouts when he saw fla

9/10 PROXIMA NOVA EXTRABOLD
A BALL OF FIRE said to have knocked out a 30-year-old Scout Master, has sent the Air Force Flying Saucer Investigation Squad to Florida. There it has been told a strange story by ex-marine Scout Master D. S. Desverges, who says he was going home with three scouts when he sa

9/10 PROXIMA NOVA BLACK
A BALL OF FIRE said to have knocked out a 30-year-old Scout Master, has sent the Air Force Flying Saucer Investigation Squad to Florida. There it has been told a strange story by ex-marine Scout Master D. S. Desverges, who says he was going home with three scouts when

9/10 PROXIMA NOVA CONDENSED THIN
A BALL OF FIRE said to have knocked out a 30-year-old Scout Master, has sent the Air Force Flying Saucer Investigation Squad to Florida. There it has been told a strange story by ex-marine Scout Master D. S. Desverges, who says he was going home with three scouts when he saw flashes of light in a wood. Going to investigate, he saw "an object large enough

9/10 PROXIMA NOVA CONDENSED LIGHT
A BALL OF FIRE said to have knocked out a 30-year-old Scout Master, has sent the Air Force Flying Saucer Investigation Squad to Florida. There it has been told a strange story by ex-marine Scout Master D. S. Desverges, who says he was going home with three scouts when he saw flashes of light in a wood. Going to investigate, he saw "an object

9/10 PROXIMA NOVA CONDENSED REGULAR
A BALL OF FIRE said to have knocked out a 30-year-old Scout Master, has sent the Air Force Flying Saucer Investigation Squad to Florida. There it has been told a strange story by ex-marine Scout Master D. S. Desverges, who says he was going home with three scouts when he saw flashes of light in a wood. Going to investigate, he saw "an

9/10 PROXIMA NOVA CONDENSED SEMIBOLD
A BALL OF FIRE said to have knocked out a 30-year-old Scout Master, has sent the Air Force Flying Saucer Investigation Squad to Florida. There it has been told a strange story by ex-marine Scout Master D. S. Desverges, who says he was going home with three scouts when he saw flashes of light in a wood. Going to investigate,

9/10 PROXIMA NOVA CONDENSED BOLD
A BALL OF FIRE said to have knocked out a 30-year-old Scout Master, has sent the Air Force Flying Saucer Investigation Squad to Florida. There it has been told a strange story by ex-marine Scout Master D. S. Desverges, who says he was going home with three scouts when he saw flashes of light in a wood. Going

9/10 PROXIMA NOVA CONDENSED EXTRABOLD
A BALL OF FIRE said to have knocked out a 30-year-old Scout Master, has sent the Air Force Flying Saucer Investigation Squad to Florida. There it has been told a strange story by ex-marine Scout Master D. S. Desverges, who says he was going home with three scouts when he saw flashes of light in a wood. Go

9/10 PROXIMA NOVA CONDENSED BLACK
A BALL OF FIRE said to have knocked out a 30-year-old Scout Master, has sent the Air Force Flying Saucer Investigation Squad to Florida. There it has been told a strange story by ex-marine Scout Master D. S. Desverges, who says he was going home with three scouts when he saw flashes of light in a wood. Goi

9/10 PROXIMA NOVA EXTRA CONDENSED THIN
A BALL OF FIRE said to have knocked out a 30-year-old Scout Master, has sent the Air Force Flying Saucer Investigation Squad to Florida. There it has been told a strange story by ex-marine Scout Master D. S. Desverges, who says he was going home with three scouts when he saw flashes of light in a wood. Going to investigate, he saw "an object large enough for six or eight men to stand in. It was about ten feet high in the center and about thirty feet in di

9/10 PROXIMA NOVA EXTRA CONDENSED LIGHT
A BALL OF FIRE said to have knocked out a 30-year-old Scout Master, has sent the Air Force Flying Saucer Investigation Squad to Florida. There it has been told a strange story by ex-marine Scout Master D. S. Desverges, who says he was going home with three scouts when he saw flashes of light in a wood. Going to investigate, he saw "an object large enough for six or eight men to stand in. It was about ten feet high in the center

9/10 PROXIMA NOVA EXTRA CONDENSED REGULAR
A BALL OF FIRE said to have knocked out a 30-year-old Scout Master, has sent the Air Force Flying Saucer Investigation Squad to Florida. There it has been told a strange story by ex-marine Scout Master D. S. Desverges, who says he was going home with three scouts when he saw flashes of light in a wood. Going to investigate, he saw "an object large enough for six or eight men to stand in. It was about ten feet high

9/10 PROXIMA NOVA EXTRA CONDENSED SEMIBOLD
A BALL OF FIRE said to have knocked out a 30-year-old Scout Master, has sent the Air Force Flying Saucer Investigation Squad to Florida. There it has been told a strange story by ex-marine Scout Master D. S. Desverges, who says he was going home with three scouts when he saw flashes of light in a wood. Going to investigate, he saw "an object large enough for six or eight men to stand in. It

9/10 PROXIMA NOVA EXTRA CONDENSED BOLD
A BALL OF FIRE said to have knocked out a 30-year-old Scout Master, has sent the Air Force Flying Saucer Investigation Squad to Florida. There it has been told a strange story by ex-marine Scout Master D. S. Desverges, who says he was going home with three scouts when he saw flashes of light in a wood. Going to investigate, he saw "an object large enough for six or eight

9/10 PROXIMA NOVA EXTRA CONDENSED EXTRABOLD
A BALL OF FIRE said to have knocked out a 30-year-old Scout Master, has sent the Air Force Flying Saucer Investigation Squad to Florida. There it has been told a strange story by ex-marine Scout Master D. S. Desverges, who says he was going home with three scouts when he saw flashes of light in a wood. Going to investigate, he saw "an object large enough for six

9/10 PROXIMA NOVA EXTRA CONDENSED BLACK
A BALL OF FIRE said to have knocked out a 30-year-old Scout Master, has sent the Air Force Flying Saucer Investigation Squad to Florida. There it has been told a strange story by ex-marine Scout Master D. S. Desverges, who says he was going home with three scouts when he saw flashes of light in a wood. Going to investigate, he saw "an object large enou

▶ The lettering artist's ultimate dexterity test: designing a *rotational ambigram*, or *flipscript*: a word that when rotated 180 degrees spells the same word as before. In case you have trouble figuring out what Mark's word is, here's the uoıʇɐlǝʌǝɹ.

No Kryptonite It's a bird! Speeding Bullet Justice

Kinescope

▲ This dashing, stylish script was inspired by hand-lettered titles in Fleischer Brothers' Superman cartoon series from the 1940s. This font features advanced OpenType magic to automatically choose the most aesthetically pleasing letter shapes as you type, as well as providing extended language support.

In 2002, I was invited to be part of the second *Indie Fonts* book, which P22's Richard Kegler was then preparing. I felt that the number of fonts I had on the market was too small for the number of pages I had to fill, so I went on a crash program to finish thirty-five new fonts before *Indie Fonts 2* was released in July 2003. I added new weights to existing fonts and introduced Goldenbook, Changeling and several others. But I still wasn't making enough to do type design full time yet.

What made that happen was releasing Proxima Nova in 2005 – a redesign of my earlier Proxima Sans – which nearly doubled the number of fonts (by which I mean single weights) I had on the market. At that point, I was making enough from selling fonts that I didn't need to do web or print design anymore.

You master a wide range of lettering and type designing styles, many of which are rooted in the American visual culture of the near and distant past. Who are your main heroes and examples? What is your favorite style or period?
Most of my influences I can trace back to when I was starting out in the '70s – Push Pin Studio, ITC (Herb Lubalin, Ed Benguiat, Tom Carnase and all those guys), Jim Parkinson's lettering and typefaces for Rolling Stone, Phil Martin's Alphabet Innovations, Michael Doret, and some of the stuff that Letraset was doing back then. I really like the idea of recreating or re-imagining earlier periods through lettering and typography – taking something old and making it new. I tend to gravitate towards '30s and '40s lettering styles, but I also enjoy working in other styles.

> "I personally like to see a mixture of old and new. The world around us is not all new or all old, it's everything all at once."

PROXIMA NOVA BOLD

For a designer, what is the main difference between doing a lettering assignment, say, for branding or packaging, and designing a complete font? Is it different now from what it was like when you started out?

With lettering, each letter only needs to look good within the context of the particular word or phrase you are drawing. With a font, every letter needs to look good with every other letter in the font in any conceivable combination. With lettering, the shapes of the letters are freer, not bound by the requirement to be interchangeable and modular.

There's a general tendency in American type and illustration to refer to shapes and tastes from the past. Do you ever feel trapped by nostalgia? By irony?

Not really. I personally like to see a mixture of old and new. The world around us is not all new or all old, it's everything all at once. The idea of creating only things that look new and different seems limiting. Anything totally new ends up looking hopelessly dated sooner or later anyway. Very few designs are truly timeless and I don't know if it's possible to design something like that intentionally. If I want nostalgia, I'll watch an old movie or look at old photos. When I decide to work in some period style, it's usually because I just like the way it looks. Every era comes and goes, and a lot of beauty goes with it. When I look at old lettering, I try to think what was in the artist's mind, try to bring back lost ideas, things that could be appreciated in the present, although maybe not in the same way. But I enjoy fresh, new things, too. I don't really see a conflict. I enjoy the contrast.

I remember seeing your early work as an illustrator and lettering artist when I became interested in Garrison Keillor's Lake Wobegon stories on Minnesota Public Radio. Tell us about your relationship with Public Radio.

I started working with them in the late '70s as a freelance art director for their program guide. Later, I worked there full-time for about five years; I was responsible for all their design and graphics. This included packaging and products for Garrison Keillor's *A Prairie Home Companion* radio show, and there were lots of opportunities for me to do lettering with that since the show often evoked an earlier time. While I was there, government subsidies for public broadcasting were being taken away. One of the things Minnesota Public Radio did to try to make up the difference was to publish a mail order gift catalog. It was called Wireless. It became so successful it had to be spun off into a separate company, Rivertown Trading, in order to preserve MPR's non-profit status. After I left MPR in 1985, I continued doing projects for both companies, especially anything to do with Garrison Keillor, and eventually agreed to work full-time for Rivertown Trading. In 1999, Target Corporation bought Rivertown Trading, renaming it "target.direct." I stuck around for another year, but by then, the company I'd grown to know and love didn't seem to exist anymore and I left.

Many type designers who evoke past styles are avid collectors. How about you?

I don't know if I'm a collector so much as a pack rat. There are a few things I collect on purpose, like type specimen books and printed ephemera, such as old magazines. Lately, a lot of this "collecting" has been supplanted by digital photos. I carry a small camera with me at all times now. If I see some interesting bit of lettering or typography in an antique store, I take picture. It's not quite as nice as having the real thing, but it sure saves space.

GO ABROAD
Liverpool dockyard
SHIP
HER MAJESTY'S LINER
Atlantic
CRUISE

Mostra Nuova

▲ Mostra Nuova is an expanded and enhanced version of Mostra, a striking display face inspired by Italian posters and advertising of the 1930s. Simonson decided that Mostra's Art Deco concept was a good starting point for a more versatile typeface family. By adding a lowercase to what originally was an all-caps display family, he turned Mostra Nuova into a typeface for many occasions, from posters and advertising to pull quotes and intros in magazines. Mostra Nuova contains many alternate characters, representing commonly found variations in Italian Art Deco lettering. There are six weights, ranging from the almost invisible Thin to the ridiculously bold Black.

I heard a story.
Neighborly
Everybody's talking
WHISPERING

Felt Tip Roman

▲ Mark was ahead of his time in 1989: he was one of the very first designers to realize that his own handwriting could be made into a useful digital font. Felt Tip Roman became a very popular typeface; Bold and Heavy weights were added to broaden its usefulness. Other Simonson fonts based on the same principle include Felt Tip Senior, based on the handwriting of the designer's father, and Felt Tip Woman, modeled on the handwriting of his partner, designer Pat Thompson.

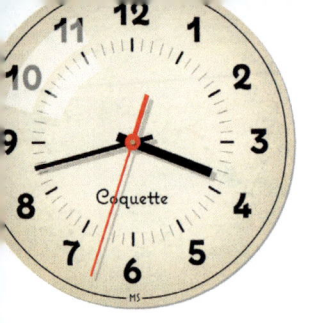

You're also, at times, an outspoken commentator on things typographic. Probably the most linked-to article on your website is a fiercely critical article on Arial. Do you actually get emotional about type? What was the most amusing or striking reaction to that piece?
What upsets me most is simply ignorance about type among graphic designers – about its history or how it's used. But I try not to take it too seriously. There are more important things in life to worry about. And for people who do care about type, thanks to the web it's easier than ever to learn about type.

I like to think my Arial article has contributed to that. Almost all the feedback I've gotten has been positive. One funny story I got was from a designer who said he secretly substituted Helvetica whenever his clients asked for Arial on their jobs. They never noticed.

Of your own fonts, which is your favorite? Why?
Coquette is my favorite. It's one of my more original designs and I learned some important things when I did it. It started out as a logo idea for the Signals mail order catalog. The idea was rejected, but it kind of grabbed hold of my imagination and I sketched out what it might look like as a typeface. It seemed to bubble up from my subconscious fully formed. I can identify things that were probably in the back of my mind, like Typo Upright and Kabel, but I'm not sure where a lot of things came from, such as the little ball on the inside of the 'o'. One thing about it is that even though it's new and original, it has this kind of familiar feeling, as if it's always been around. It's a bit mysterious. The other thing I learned from it was not to rely so much on geometry. My early attempts to digitize it failed because I tried to construct it with perfect circles. Compared to my sketches, it looked stiff and lifeless. Once I let go of the circle, and learned to trust my eye, it all fell into place.

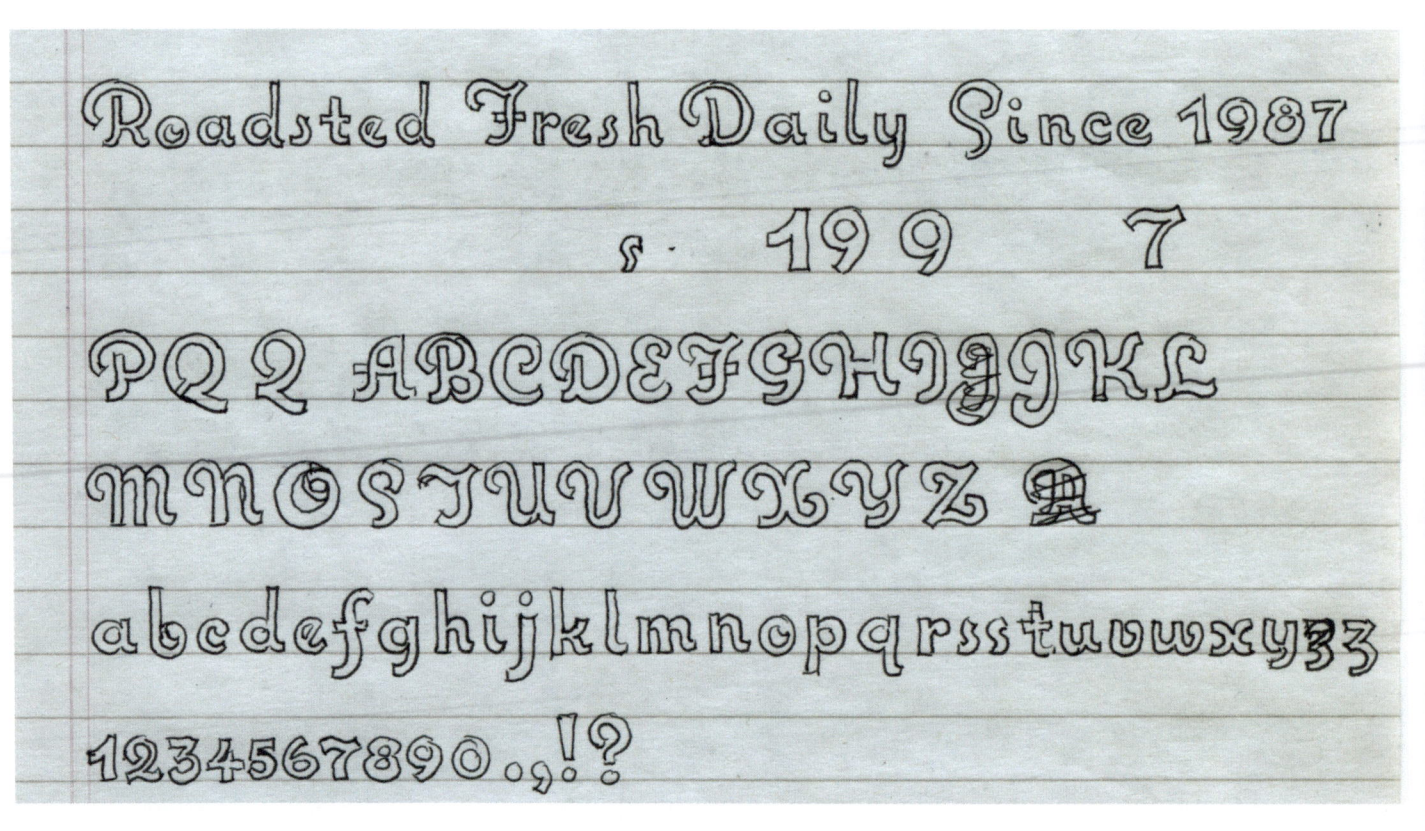

Coquette

▲ Coquette is Mark Simonson's personal favorite. As he explains, this unconnected script was not derived from any specific existing source, yet has something familiar about it. Combining an Art Deco feeling with some elements of geometric sans-serif, Coquette is an interesting hybrid that could have been born to French/American parents in the 1940s or '50s. Coquette has been adopted for a wide range of uses, including packaging, shop displays and book covers. ▲ Mark also designed and programmed a virtual "Coquette Clock" for the computer desktop. ▼ Coquette sketches.

Proxima Nova has been a huge success. Are you working on another major text type family?

Yes. Lately, I've digitized a lot of older fonts that I didn't design. I'll continue to do some of that, but I want to get back to doing my own designs. I'm working on a big family that has both serif and sans-serif members. It's partly a revival, but I don't want to say too much about it. I don't know how long it will take to finish, but I've got the foundation in place. I started working on it a few years ago and set it aside in order to get OpenType versions of some of my other fonts out. Since then, I've been itching to get going on it again. I expect by the time this interview is published I will be working on it again.

Finally, the self-serving question: in what way does your collaboration with My-Fonts influence the way you operate?

MyFonts isn't the only distributor I work with, but it's the only one that sends me an e-mail every time I sell a font. It might not seem important, but those emails help in a funny way. It may sound superstitious, but when I'm not working on fonts, my sales go down. When I'm working on them, sales go up. So, if I have a day when I haven't gotten many MyFonts emails, that means I need to get back to work on fonts. I know it sounds silly, but it works.

Lettering work

▲▼ Before he became a full time type designer, Mark Simonson was a graphic designer, illustrator and lettering artist. Having trained to render letterforms by hand – with pen and ink on paper – he has developed an impressive skill in imagining and drawing nameplates and logos. Witness these examples of logotypes produced during the past decade.

129

Eric Olson

BRYANT PRO BOLD

BRYANT PRO LIGHT

In a relatively short time span Eric Olson's Process Type Foundry has become one of the most successful micro-foundries in the US. His retail fonts, such as a the cool, clean Bryant and the highly fashionable Klavika, enjoy increasing popularity in print as well as on screen. In addition, he has worked on a wide range of assignments for clients ranging from Chevrolet to the Walker Art Center in Minneapolis, his home town. All this is good news for typography, because Olson's typefaces are carefully drawn, well-equipped and original. They're also quite extensive: you might say that Eric Olson is a family man. *November 2008*

KLAVIKA REGULAR

Eric, you've worked in and around Minneapolis during a large part of you career. Is it an attractive city for designers and artists to work in?
It must be, because there are thousands of them here. It doesn't move with the pace of New York or London. And if you've decided to stay, chances are you find that valuable. It seems to follow that, with the slower pace, the room for working naturally opens up and things start to happen.

You're a full-time type designer and the principal of your own foundry. Was this something you envisaged when you designed your first typefaces in the late '90s?
Never. When I designed my first typefaces I was in design school and very focused on becoming a graphic designer so the thought never crossed my mind. At the time my dream was to design magazines and album covers and drawing typefaces was just a way to make my graphic design more original. I think along the way I realized designing type was really satisfying and soon I couldn't stop.

Designing type all day, every day – does it ever get boring?
There is a certain amount of tedium associated with type design because it's exacting work – and maybe that notion is at the root of your question – but the detailed construction and care of every glyph is what really makes a typeface sing. Attempting to get the total system of a font into harmony might be frustrating, annoying, or exasperating but never boring. And of course, when you publish your own typefaces, you become involved with every aspect of running a business and that means there is always something to do besides just drawing letters. Customer questions have to be answered, new website features need to be implemented, ads have to be designed, or whatever the business requires at the moment. In fact, it is often a luxury to be able to focus solely on designing type for hours on end.

You worked as a graphic designer before, taking commissions from clients such as the Walker Art Center. Do you think it is important for type designers to be able to identify with their users, i.e. have first-hand experience of how graphic design works?
It can't hurt. As a type designer one of my challenges is to make work that graphic designers find useful and I find interesting. That's hard to pull off, but there are other disciplines that face similar challenges. Think of jazz fusion! It's music for musicians and only marginally for ordinary listeners. First hand experience of the field is helpful in this respect because it establishes parameters for use (make it durable) and lays out expectations (make it do everything). Obviously perfection isn't possible, but these parameters can be a reality check along the way.

Portuguese Father
Only on the Continent
In just 3 weeks
Marmalade

Lingua
▲ The nearly 200 ligatures for Lingua were built around the most common letter pairs within the English language. Letter combinations once thought mundane like 'th' and 'an' can now be used alongside their more traditional counterparts. As a result, the normally reductive geometric forms of Lingua can be turned into a nearly upright script with the ligatures turned on. Since Lingua is an OpenType font all of the ligatures and special features are contained within a single cross platform file.

▼ *Space for Art cover by Atelier David Smith, Dublin.*

FOREIGN AFFAIRS OF DUTCH DESIGN MVRDV ARCHITECTEN KESSELSKRAMER KOEWEIDEN POSTMA HELLA JONGERIUS GILIAN SCHROFER WAREHOUSE DROOG DESIGN

Exhibition Foreign Affairs of Dutch Design
Cultivate Centre, Temple Bar
6–11 November | 10am–5.30pm daily

Loving Architecture Lecture Winy Maas MVRDV
Gaiety Theatre, Dublin 2
Thursday 9 November | 6pm

Lecture KesselsKramer / Koeweiden Postma
Morrison Hotel, Dublin 1
Wednesday 8 November | 6pm

Showcase Hella Jongerius / DROOG Design
HAUS Outlets, Temple Bar
6–11 November | 10am–5.30pm daily

Seminar/Workshop Gilian Schrofer / Warehouse
IADT Dun Laoghaire / NCAD Thomas St
6–11 November | Education Only

Tickets/Information for Design Week 06
Contact: elaine@icad.ie | idi@indigo.ie
www.icad.ie | www.idi-design.ie

NOVEMBER 06–11 | 2006

DESIGN WEEK 2006
Exhibitions | Lectures | Workshops | Awards

Koninkrijk der Nederlanden | the foreign affairs of dutch design | design week 06 | Premsela Dutch design foundation | Irish Architecture Foundation

Atelier
- Threex3 Internship Programme 2009
- Off the Shelf_Studio Culture
- ICAD 2008 Exhibition & Awards

Projects
- Glenpark Project
- Folio 1_Posters
- FSWS 10_ A Retrospective
- At Sea_Gary Coyle
- Ground Up 2003.2007
- Catherine Delaney_Inside Outside
- More Facts About Irish
- DAA_Annual Report 2007
- Not in Alphabetical Order
- House Projects
- Space For Art_Sligo Arts Plan
- PALLAS Heights
- Year of the Golden Pig
- Elevate
- Umbrella Project
- I NOT I / Beckett, Guston and Nauman
- Stephen Brandes_Klutz Paradiso
- Brendan Earley_Veneer
- Blake & Sons
- Through the Looking Glass
- Isabel Nolan_What it does to you...
- Venice Biennale_Ronan McCrea
- Appassionata Flowers
- Placing Art Colloquium Papers

Studio
- about us
- contact
- newsletter

11.2 km/s
Gravitational slingshot
ENERGY
Breaking free
Achieve escape velocity
Outer Space

Klavika

▲ There have been other squarish sans-serifs before and after Klavika, but Eric Olson's typeface has been recognized as something of a milestone in the genre. It is clean and technical, but has retained a certain friendliness. It is also easier to read in longer texts than other typefaces of its kind. No wonder that Klavika has been used by the likes of Nokia, NBC and the Boston Phoenix. Features like small caps, true italics, extended language support and multiple numeral styles make Klavika an versatile workhorse typeface.

One typeface, one design agency, different projects: Klavika in use by Atelier David Smith, Dublin:
▲ Atelier David Smith's website
◀▲ Klavika used throughout *Through the Looking Glass* for the Lewis Glucksman Gallery
◀◀ Poster for Dutch Design Week 2006 in Dublin

133

MASTER BUILDER 12½
ERECTOR
A fine-tuned robot
Small constuction crew
Machinery
1931 Hudson & Tender
Blueprints on file
The Last of the inventory

Bryant

▲ Bryant's geometric shapes and rounded angles were inspired by the mechanical lettering kits used in pre-digital times by draftsmen and amateur sign makers. Bryant is now an extensive family in three widths, for branding, editorial design, packaging and posters. Bryant Pro, the most extensive and versatile sub-family, has italics for all weights, plus an "Alt" series with interesting alternative shapes. Bryant Condensed, the mid-width member of the series is condensed in name, but its body width is similar to many standard grotesques. It's equally suited for text and display work. For situations where large point sizes and maximum letter count need to coexist, Bryant Compressed is the narrowest of the Bryant sub-families. Sharp stem joins and increased contrast allow this face to keep the Bryant style while maintaining a narrow width.

A large part of the fonts that are released in the USA are revivals and reinterpretations of faces from the past. You are one of the designers who are constantly pushing boundaries, trying to come up with original solutions. Does this make you feel different?

No, I don't feel different, and though it's been relatively limited, I've dabbled in that area a bit. I suspect the revival-based approach in America is coming to an end in terms of impact because the context for using this work is shrinking along with the reasons for creating it.

Do you mean that users are getting more and more interested in contemporary letterforms?

I have a hunch that users have always been interested in contemporary letterforms. I like to think graphic designers are taking their role as messengers of contemporary information more seriously and given that, revivals present a problem. They arrive with historical baggage, conservatism, pre-defined outcomes and an inherent denial of possibility. Unless the goal is to honor these qualities or make light of them, why would a graphic designer use fonts like this when making work reflective of their time?

When designing a new typeface, say a contemporary sans-serif, what are the things that inspire you? The street? Art and architecture? Other designers' work?

It really depends on the situation but I am often inspired by the ways in which graphic designers abuse fonts. It represents a legitimate desire on their part to make a typeface perform a particular function, a function it was probably not designed to perform. That missing function points the way to new designs or possibilities. For example, sans-serifs are often chosen for long passages of text – despite conventional wisdom. Is it possible to design a typeface that meets this requirement? Not all of these questions end up as typefaces (or maybe a series of ideas end up in one typeface), but they open up avenues of exploration I might not have traveled down myself.

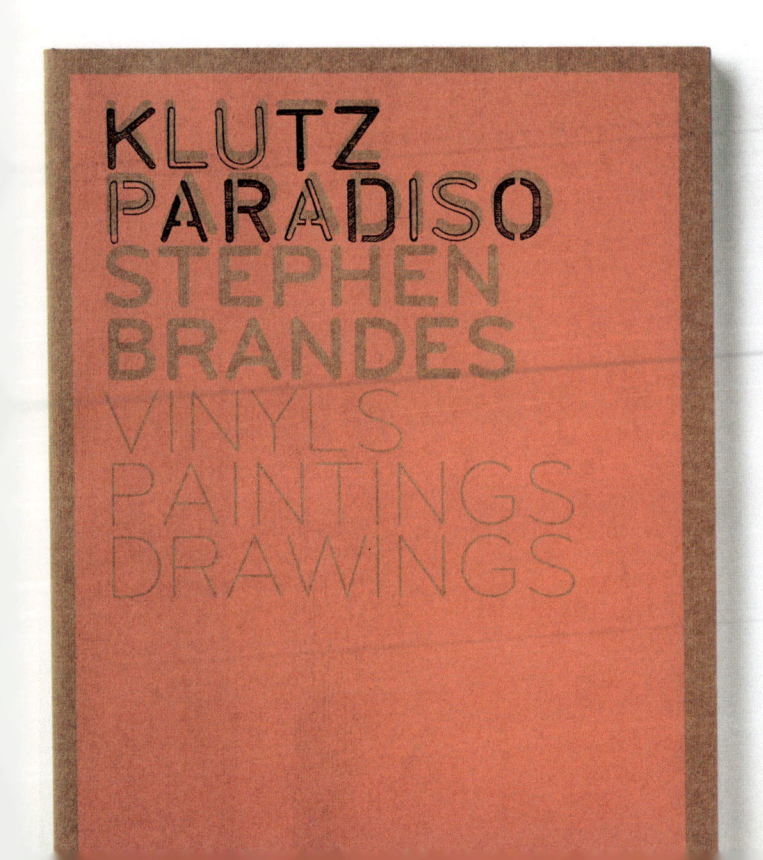

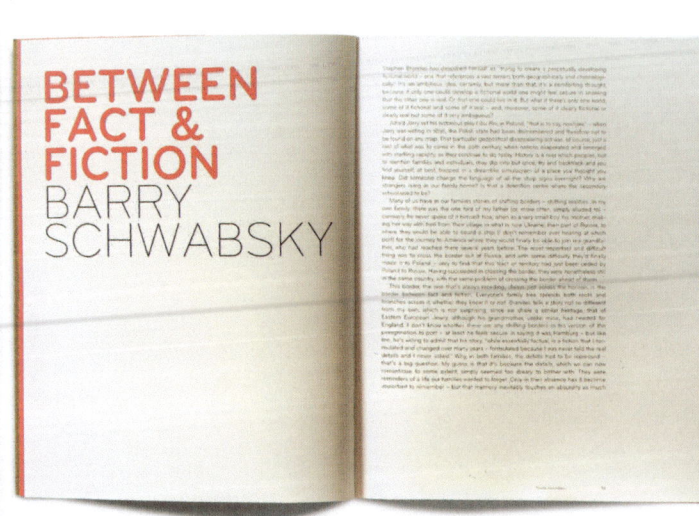

◀▲ Bryant in *Klutz Paradiso* by Atelier David Smith for Stephen Brandes

▲ Bryant in *Crafts* magazine. Editorial design: Marcus Piper for one8one7.com

When you begin designing a new typeface – assuming it is not an assignment with a precise briefing – where do you start? Is there an element of marketing, of trying to find a new niche?

It usually starts with an impulse driven by one of two reasons. One, I have a big idea. For example, "what if a typeface could do this?!". And second, "what if I designed it this way instead?". This is my formal idea. Both of these approaches then fail, every time almost without exception. I then put the results in a folder and file them away being careful to keep them for another time. I have a few hundred of these on various hard drives around the studio gathering dust. It's only years or months later while showering, biking or drawing that the solution will hit me and I'll dig the files out and start again. As you can imagine, my non-client work evolves quite slowly!

Do you do sketches on paper at all, or is all your type designing work done on the computer?

In the very early stages of a design, I like to rough out letterforms by hand but I rarely refine them on paper because they're only skeletal and quite crude. The point, however, is to set the pace and get a rough idea of the proportions of the typeface. From there on out, I work almost entirely on the computer. I am better able to take those initial

"I use the tool that is best for the task at hand and not necessarily the tool one might expect a type designer to use."

MAPLE MEDIUM

135

Find Replace

▲ FontLab, the application that most professional type designers use for making fonts, has a Find and Replace function that is normally used for eliminating unwanted curves or elements throughout a font. Olson used it as a design tool, replacing each of the vector-drawn "pixels" or modules that make up the font's characters by crosses, hatches and other elements. The result is especially interesting because the fonts all share the same widths, and can be layered to dazzling effect.

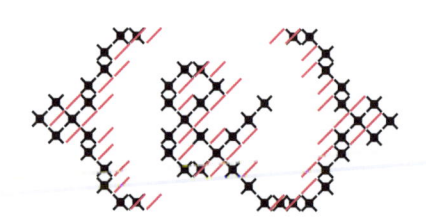

sketches and quickly generate many possible combinations of letterforms or spacing, and most importantly, see how the glyphs work together. This is simply much harder to do on paper. If I'm really stuck, I might use a broad nib pen to emulate the letterforms I'm working on to remind myself of the rhythm of the letterforms. I try not to pick favorites, though, when choosing which way I work. I use the tool that is best for the task at hand and not necessarily the tool one might expect a type designer to use. Better work comes out of possibility and experimentation, rather than expectation.

When designing custom-made fonts, what would your ideal client be like?
Something similar to my relationship with the *New York Times Sunday Magazine* comes closest to an ideal. The art directors Arem Duplessis and Gail Bichler, aside from being talented typographers, planned and expected the project to take many months rather than weeks. Custom jobs almost never go that way. A client may know ahead of time they want a custom typeface, but rarely commit to the idea until they're just eight weeks away from desperately needing the fonts. At that point, any time that could have been used to reflect on the work is completely out of the question. Clients deserve much better, but they have to acknowledge that typeface design follows its own particular schedule. There is simply a lot of raw production work that has to happen and it takes time. But, as with all things, it's much easier said than done.

Having performed a wide array of design-related jobs, how would you describe the role of type design – is it a catalyst, an area for expression and research, or merely the production of modest and practical tools?
At the risk of sounding all inclusive, all of the above. Fortunately for type designers, the field is wide and the possibilities are endless for those willing to find them. When I speak with other type designers or attend conferences, I'm always taken aback by the range of pursuits within the field. We have a lot in common, but for the most part, there is very little overlap between what each of us does when compared with other fields. It feels like there is legitimate room for pursuit in any of the interpretations you list above.

What is your most challenging prospect when thinking of future designs?
Probably the prospect of irrelevance. I've designed many fonts to satisfy my own curiosities and likely always will, but the fonts I release to the public have to be durable. To make something durable, but also fresh and relevant, is terribly difficult and I'm certain I've fallen short of this many times.

"Fortunately for type designers, the field is wide and the possibilities are endless for those willing to find them."

MAPLE MEDIUM

One of your best selling fonts is Klavika. I once read that you almost abandoned it. What happened?

Just the usual I guess. I'm always second guessing myself and after all these years, I've come to think that's just how I work. If I could have one wish in my daily working life, it would be to have automatic objectivity and unfamiliarity. If I could just turn on my computer and look at something I've been working on and be a complete stranger to it. Can you imagine that? That would change everything! But alas…

Klavika has now become so successful that other people are imitating it. What do you think when you see a design that is too close for comfort?

Mostly I find the imitations confusing. It should be said, the difference between influence and imitation is pretty important. With Klavika I was influenced by, amongst other things, Bell Gothic Black and Dave Farey's amazing Cachet. Klavika wears these influences on its sleeve but they're only a starting point or reminder along the way. The goal was to make something new and hopefully that's apparent. The imitations you mention are efforts to get in on something and make a few dollars. Unfortunately there's a long history of this in type design. Have a look at many of the phototype catalogs from the 1970s. I'm not sure why you'd want to repeat this because there must be easier ways to make money.

What's been the biggest thrill in seeing your fonts used by others?

Well, it's just generally seeing my fonts used by others, period. It never gets old.

Maple

This is how fellow type designer Mark Simonson described Maple when he chose it as one of Typographica's typefaces of 2005: "Other type designers have mined the nineteenth century English grotesque, but Eric Olson gives it an energetic crispness which makes earlier attempts seem a bit stuffy. Maple captures the exuberant quirkiness of the grots without slavishly imitating them."

Mário FELICIANO

RONGELOSF ITALIC

MORGAN BG3

He is a unique figure on the international type design scene. Energetic and open-minded, Portuguese Mário Feliciano is part of a new generation of type designers that has put the Iberian peninsula firmly on the map. A self-taught type designer, he initially made experimental and grungy fonts, but his work quickly gained maturity and professionalism. Having run a successful graphic design studio in Lisbon for several years, he gave it up to fully concentrate on the fonts published by the Feliciano Type Foundry (FTF) and on type consultancy for magazines and newspapers. *June 2008*

RONGEL OSF REGULAR

Mário, what is early summer like for a type designer working in Portugal? How do you spend your days?
Strangely, the summer hasn't arrived down here yet. Two weeks ago I was in Denmark giving a lecture at the SND/S annual workshop and it was warmer up there!

Otherwise I keep my work flowing as usual, running the foundry, upgrading old designs and creating new typefaces as well. I also do some consultancy work for special clients, mostly newspapers. Most importantly, I am converting the FTF library to OpenType format. That is a lot of work.

On Typeradio I heard that you're a surfer. During your early career, you designed surf magazines, just like David Carson. Did you experiment as much as he did – and were your graphic explorations picked up outside the surf world?
David Carson had a strong effect on me – I had been aware of him since his early days at *Surfer* magazine. For years, *Surfer* was my favorite magazine. When Carson was hired to do *RayGun* magazine, that was the thing! He was my biggest influence – even

more so than Emigre, which also influenced me a lot. I was lucky to be able to experiment a lot at *Surf Portugal* magazine. Maybe I was able to do in a surf magazine what David Carson was doing in a rock magazine!

My work was influenced by worlds outside surfing as well: art, rock, and pop culture. This was when "type design" came into my life. At the time, the only way to make any graphic design work that remotely looked like David Carson's was to design my own fonts – that's how it all started. Curiously I came to know Carson's work before I knew Neville Brody, let alone Erik Spiekermann or other famous type designers. This was the early 1990s…

Rongel

▼ Rongel is one of the font families that resulted from many years of research of historical Spanish letterforms. It is roughly based on a typeface shown in a Spanish type catalog from 1799. Rongel is a true revival in the sense that it adapts a typeface that only existed in a previous and obsolete technology. However, Feliciano aimed for an interpretation rather than a faithful copy, correcting obvious flaws and introducing new ideas. The result is one of the liveliest recent examples of historically inspired Iberian type.

Cuffley

What were your earliest typefaces like? Are you embarrassed when you look at them now?
No, I'm not embarrassed, even if they look quite bad. There are some I just don't like any more, but I understand why I did them. There are even some that are still on the market! I have done some wild stuff, and quite a few rip-offs as well…

The computer we had at the magazine was a Mac LC II (I think). One guy left some floppy disks with the first version of Fontographer, and two days later I was modifying fonts and generating them directly on the system folder. Then I bought the next version of Fontographer and started some more serious work. My first fonts were done around 1994 and before that I'd already hand-drawn some alphabets with no practical use. Gradually I got to a more interesting level.

You published a number of playful display faces with T-26 and Adobe. Then, rather suddenly, you became very serious about type design and began working on large type systems like Morgan, and historically inspired typefaces like Rongel. How did the change happen?
Of the fonts I designed during my years of experimentation, several were published including one Adobe original, Strumpf. Then in 1997 I went to the ATypI conference in Reading – and it all changed. I was lucky to meet Peter Matthias Noordzij – the first type designer I ever met, and with whom I created a very special bond, personally and professionally – and John Downer, who also became a good friend and advisor over the years, among other people. At the first night in Reading I had dinner with Matthias, John and Fred Smeijers, Robert Bringhurst, and a few other others that I can't recall. I had never heard of any of these people! So, I think that dinner somehow changed my career and my entire life. After that I became interested in the tradition of typography and started studying type history.

&

Good Hope 1785
Navigation
Discovery & Misfortune

3-DIMENSIONAL
Feathered Serpent
MARTIANS!
ADVENTURES
Rocket Ship
My Silver Fiancée

Morgan

▲▼ The Morgan Project is Feliciano's superfamily: a versatile suite of compatible fonts. All family members have a basic visual idea in common, of simple, square shapes with rounded corners, but between the various versions there are notable differences, appropriate to each version's purpose. The fonts in the Morgan Display Kit 1 – Morgan Tower, Poster & Big – have simplified, square counters; the text versions Morgan Sans and Sans Condensed are smoother and rounder.

▶ Morgan interpretation by designer Anthony Noel.

Since then, you've actively sought to establish contacts with colleagues around the globe. Which contemporary type designers have influenced you most, and what have you learned from them?

Several people influenced my work in different ways and at different points in time. In the early days I was lucky to work with Carol Twombly before she left Adobe, and she was very good. I exchanged "mail" (prior to email!) with Rudy Vanderlans, who was very kind to comment on my designs. After that meeting in Reading, more people influenced and helped me. I admire Matthias Noordzij's work; he only published one typeface (Caecilia) but he is a great typographer and knows very well how fonts work. The Dutch tradition has been very important to me; I think of Gerard Unger, Fred Smeijers but above all Bram de Does. His Lexicon is my favorite typeface. Then Christian Schwartz, he is very good, very hard not to be influenced by. And, of course, Matthew Carter.

You started the Feliciano foundry in 2001. What made you decide to publish your own typefaces instead of licensing them though an established foundry?

It was more intuitive than anything else. I had a few interesting proposals but I wanted to do things my own way, taking risks. I had been working as an agent in Portugal and Spain for The Enschedé Font Foundry since 1999 and they have a very peculiar way of running the foundry that I have not found anywhere else. I wanted to bring some of that spirit to my foundry even when working alone. However, when I decided to create the Feliciano Type Foundry I was still doing graphic design work and running a design studio. I could not yet imagine becoming a full-time individual type designer. But in he end, that is what I decided to do.

In many creative areas the general tendency is to become self-publishing. Platforms such as MyFonts make it economically feasible; I also have a special joint venture with Village.

I do think that professional relationships mainly based on digital communication are quite limited in terms of the personal bond you create with those with whom you work. You kind of lose the really good part of collaboration – to be with other people.

"At some point the older designers have always thought that the time for experimenting was over."

STELLA OSF ITALIC

| MORGAN TOWER | MORGAN POSTER | MORGAN BIG 1 | MORGAN BIG 2 | MORGAN BIG 3 | MORGAN SANS OFFICE & CAPS | MORGAN SANS CONDENSED OFFICE & CAPS |

CCTV

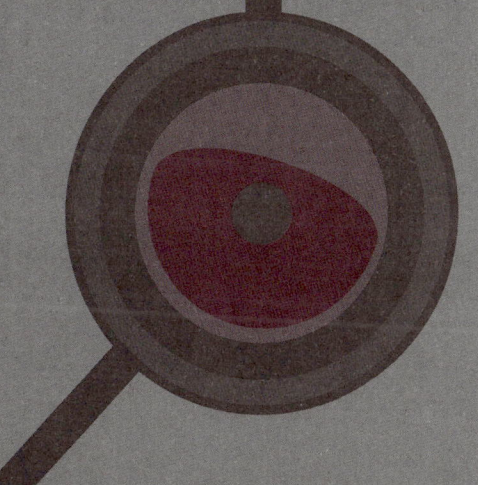

THE CAMERAS ARE RESTLESS

ARDENT MACHINES
TURNING IN
ROLLING OUT
LESSONS UNTAUGHT
BUT ALWAYS HEEDED

"There is one fundamental thing that may help to sustain the work; to bring some sense of history into it. It doesn't matter how."

STELLA OSF ITALIC

Four Dollars
UNITED STATES OF AMERICA
five-pointed star
Double Eagles
PATTERNS FROM THE 1800S
LIBERTY BUST

Stella

▲ Stella is Feliciano's humanist sans, although he tried not to give it too much of a pretty, oldstyle-like flow. It was designed to be used as a text face, and optimized for optimum legibility in small sizes, but its careful detailing makes it suitable for uses in display sizes as well. With its supple, narrow italics, small caps, lining and oldstyle figures – proportional as well as tabular – Stella is a versatile typeface that lends character to classy brochure, book or signage projects.

Among your own typefaces, which is your favorite? Could you tell us something about the way it was conceived?
That's very hard to tell, really. I would say that the favorite part of my work is the work that I've done based on old Spanish types. It comprises a group of six or seven typefaces, not all of them fully finished, including Rongel, which on some days is my favorite. All those typefaces were designed after several years of research on old Spanish books and type specimens, research trips to Spain and a lot of reading about that period. All those fonts went through a long and not very systematic design process, with a lot of trial and error. I do not really make sketches by hand. I did a few in the beginning to please my eye but I found them to be useless. Everything changes (with increments of very small measures!) when you move to the digital world… I really do appreciate other designers who have their sketch books on hand all the time and make all those nice drawings. I can't do that. Nor do I travel with a computer for work purposes. I can only work in my working room. With music, most of time. Many styles of music, depending on the typeface at hand.

The past five to ten years, there's been an impressive upsurge of "Latino" fonts from the Iberian peninsula and Latin America. Do you feel part of the movement, or group?
I don't know if you can call it a movement. But if that's the case, I do want to be part of it. I see it more as a rise of interest and typographic consciousness. And in terms of form, style and visual tradition, I think the "Latinos" have a lot to say.

Young, budding type designers have more role models today than you did 15 years ago. At the same time it may be more difficult for them to experiment, because so much has already been done. What is your message to them?
I think that there is always room for experimentation in typography. It has always been like that: at some point the older designers have always thought that the time for experimenting was over.

I believe that in terms of style one should follow one's instinct. For me there is one fundamental thing that may help to sustain the work: to bring some sense of history into it. It doesn't matter how. The way Matthew Carter does that is quite different from what Jonathan Barnbrook is doing, but they both have a sense of tradition in their work. I guess that helps and gives focus. It is also very important to be up-to-date on the latest relevant technology, both for the use and the design of type.

Not only are your fonts used by dozens of magazines, you've also developed custom type for a number of newspapers, including *Expresso* in Portugal and *El Pais* in Spain. And then there is BesSans, a type family that was custom-made for a large Portuguese bank. I was told it was very rare for a Portuguese organization to commission a typeface – is this changing? And are these assignments influencing the way you work?

I think it is changing but not significantly. I don't get those kind of assignments every month, probably not even once a year. Neither do my colleagues, I think. The market is rather small. Companies do not see a reason to invest in custom type. In publications it happens more often, maybe because the time of exclusivity is normally reduced to one or two years and therefore there the costs are lower when compared to those of corporate type that might include five or ten years of total exclusivity.

Working for these companies influences the way I work because it gives me no room to fail, so I have to be very certain about what I'm doing and why I'm doing it. It's a bigger challenge.

Escrita

Released more than 10 years ago, Escrita is one of Mário Feliciano's earliest published fonts. A pioneer of the distorted formal script genre that has become wildly popular lately, Escrita is still one of Feliciano's best-selling faces. The name means "written." Thanks to extra fonts containing fancy initials and endings, the font does a nice job in imitating handwriting – albeit of a very quirky kind.

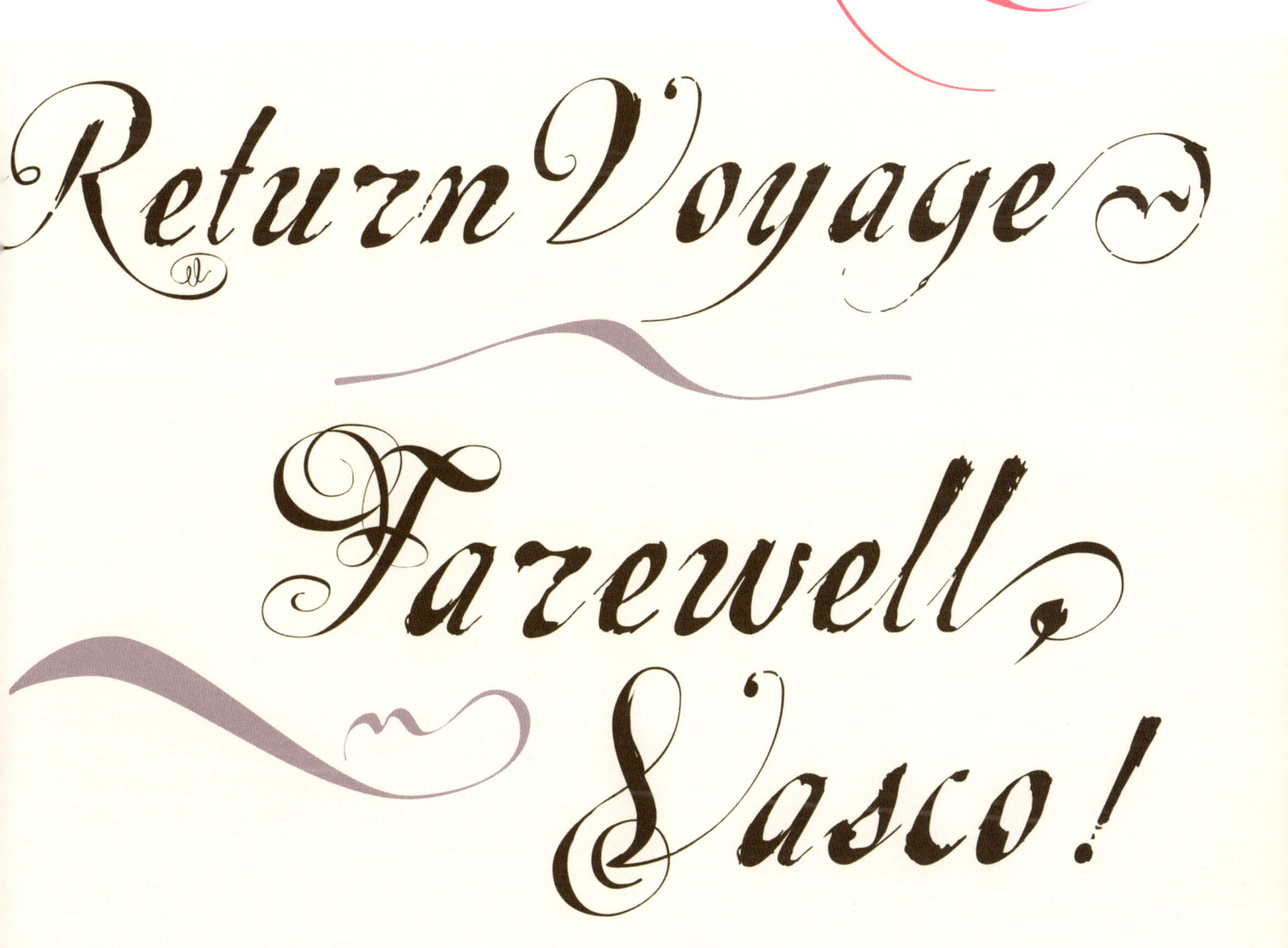

Return Voyage

Farewell, Vasco!

Dino dos Santos

BOLDINA SERIF

ANDRADE SCRIPT PRO

Based in Porto, Portugal, DSType is one of those one-person foundries that have more or less grown up together with MyFonts. Designer Dino dos Santos began designing custom typefaces for magazines and corporations in 1994; he felt confident to start up his own collection of retail fonts after his first experiments with distributing through MyFonts had proved successful. Dino dos Santos is a hard-working designer, and DSType is one of the fastest growing one-man type libraries around. It includes striking experiments, charming display type and, most notably, an amazing collection of well-wrought, extensive text families. *November 2007*

ESTA PRO

When did you start thinking about specializing in type design? Was there a specific occasion that sparked off your type designing activities?

I'm a self-taught type designer; my education is in graphic design. I began designing typefaces in the early '90s because there weren't many typefaces available to us in those days, just the Macintosh system fonts and dry transfer sheets from Letraset and Mecanorma. So I started designing fonts that matched the new typographic experience. To me, graphic design was never about taking a picture and then just choosing one of the available typefaces. I felt the need to design my own stuff – very strange stuff I must admit – and to achieve that, I learned Fontographer. Now I am a full-time type designer. I try hard not to do any graphic design at all. But I do pay attention to what is being done on the international design scene. I need to know if my typefaces are keeping up with the changing circumstances.

You studied at ESAD Art College in Matosinhos, near Porto, Portugal, where you have also taught for more than ten years. What kind of school is ESAD, and how would you describe its position in the Portuguese design landscape?

ESAD was founded in the late '80s, and since its inception played a major role in the development of Portuguese design. Part of ESAD's philosophy was the idea that the school was to establish a close alliance with the industry. It was understood that the client is a very important partner – not a monster that will destroy creativity. ESAD also distinguished between art and design, while in most fine arts institutions the two used to be treated as a single subject. I have taught computer graphics, multimedia projects, and design theory, among other disciplines. In order to face the new challenges ESAD has incorporated a new discipline called typographic studies, which I now teach. Its aim is to provide the students with typographic knowledge, both theoretical and practical, understanding the relevance of type design and typography in the graphic environment.

There is a small group of young, prolific type designers from Portugal who are internationally known – people like Mário Feliciano and yourself – but was there an "older generation" before you? When starting out, where did you look for your role models?

There is not much of a type design history in Portugal. People are now getting more interested and some new type designers have emerged, which is a good thing. When I first started, Emigre was one of my favorite models, and so were the typefaces they published. It seemed very natural that I should start doing something like that – vernacular stuff, blending typefaces from different periods, using them in my own graphic design work. I have since learned about type designers from "older" generations who designed non-digital typefaces, but in those days I wasn't too interested. What I wanted was to do things like those that were shown in books like *Typography Now*. I just wanted to do cool and fashionable stuff, especially things that no one would be able to read (David Carson was an idol then). Now I'm very interested in what has been done in Portugal by older generations of type designers and calligraphers. I want to understand what happened, how things worked back then, and expose the world to some lesser-known work.

Estilo and Estilo Script

▲ Estilo and Estilo Script were inspired by that special style of lettering from the Art Deco period that mixes geometric construction with an eagerness to please. Designer Chris Rugen, who chose Estilo as one of Typographica's Favorite Fonts of 2006, wrote, "Set a few headlines to see Estilo's stylish and classy moves: alternates, ligatures, swashes, Greek, all in a handy contextual OpenType package."

Capsa

▼ Capsa, one of dos Santos' more traditional book faces, is chock full of options and alternate glyphs. Inspired by two faces from the mid eighteenth century specimen of the printer Claude Lamesle, Capsa is not a revival but a contemporary take on an elegant rococo book face. Instead of a large spectrum of weights, it offers only a Regular, plus a Bold version for emphasis. The Regular comes with a wealth of swashed italics, fancy ligatures, and ornaments – plenty of material for the discerning typographer to design page after page of stylishly arranged text.

▲ Typefaces from DSType in use. Clockwise from top left: Estilo; Ventura; Leitura; Estilo; Glosa; Leitura

▶▶ Detail from *Dazed and Confused* magazine, which uses Estilo for headlines
▶▶ The Paris daily newspaper *Le Figaro* using Glosa and Prelo; *Courrier Internacional* magazine using Estilo and Leitura.

In Portuguese cities, the lettering on historical buildings is often stunning. I imagine that this kind of context can be a great source of inspiration to type designers. Has this been the case for you?
Yes! But not only in Portugal. I'm influenced by every country I visit. For example, I started designing Greek typefaces after I had been to Cyprus, and designed Kartago after visiting Tunisia. I find it very important to get the feeling of a particular place – to understand its cultural processes and get in touch with the local lettering. I'm currently developing a typeface inspired by the lettering on one of the most important monuments in Portugal. I was really amazed by that lettering, because it's a block of text mostly composed of ligatures, very vernacular but pretty cool. I'm trying to take those letters out of context in order to provide them a very contemporary and fresh look.

Five years ago, you received a Master's degree in Multimedia Arts with a thesis on Digital Typography in the Multimedia Environment. You designed the Monox type family as part of that project. Could you tell us something about the topic of your thesis – and about the role of the Monox typeface?
Well, my thesis was about legibility in multimedia systems and about how typography, when used dynamically, can present us with different levels of understanding that go far beyond its own meaning. Monox was presented as part of the research on monospaced typefaces and mechanical aspects of readability, but it was also the subject of all the dynamic and interactive interfaces that I developed to present to the jury. Monox was also my first attempt to interpolate two extreme letter shapes in order to generate new weights. That was very useful for some of my latest releases, like the many styles of Leitura.

SPRING/
SUMMER FOR
LOUIS VUITTON
IS ALL ABOUT
CHARISMATIC
OUTSIDERS

PHOTOGRAPHY PHILIPPE &
CESARIE YARD
STYLING STEVEN WESTGARTH

"Students need to enjoy what they do, understand that design is not just a profession but a daily attitude." ESTA PRO

Squeamish

Deal with it

There's no sense in trying

But let her touch, and feel

staunchly

Surprising what comes up

THICK & EVENLY SPREAD

Of utmost importance to create a fresh, clean finish

Another cover

Leitura Type System

◀▼ Leitura is an elegant, versatile type system that comes in four varieties: a crisp roman, a stylish sans serif, a News version specially designed for newspaper body text, the beautifully drawn Leitura Display, and finally Leitura Headline. In addition, there's a clever set of symbols. With its many variants Leitura is a versatile and beautifully designed toolbox for restyling a magazine, designing a corporate identity, or making a complex book.

Bronzed & Taut
Gold Buckle: Weight & Substance
Cancel the milk

Prelo system

◀◀ With Prelo, dos Santos released an extended new family with an interesting structure. The basic typeface is Prelo, a neutral, highly readable typeface for identity, editorial and information design available in nine weights with true italics. Prelo is a versatile typeface with a lot of character that will work well both in text and headline sizes. For compact, space-saving headlines with extra punch there is a narrow version, Prelo Condensed, and an even narrower one, Prelo Compressed. Each of these varieties offers small caps, tabular figures and oldstyle figures, and a Central European character set. Finally, there is Prelo Slab, the slab-serif family that is the perfect companion to Prelo for demanding typographic jobs.

When asked for a piece of "essential type advice" by *Computer Arts* magazine, you wrote: "Link the past to the present. Connect history and technology. History reveals some of the greatest typographers and calligraphers, and in their work it is possible to find the path that leads us to new typefaces. That's why redesigning history is a step towards designing the future". Could you say more about the role of technology in updating or adapting old letterforms?

History is often seen as something that passed away, and that's it. But for me history is one of the most relevant aspects of type design. The modernist movement rejected history as part of the design process, with the results that we know. I believe that we do need to understand history in order to understand ourselves. I believe we are made of history, but I also believe that we should take a step forward by connecting it to the present and the future, and we can do that through technology. With OpenType we can now bring back historical forms, ligatures, swashes and alternate characters into one single file. Since the early days the history of type has always been full of avant-garde ideas, and it is possible to introduce old letterforms to the future generation of readers and designers.

State-of-the-art type production technology is no guarantee that the fonts made with it look contemporary. Would you agree that a lot of type designed today has a touch of nostalgia? Can a font be based on historic sources and still be truly contemporary?

Nostalgia seems to be at the center of the contemporary society and I don't agree with that. In my opinion there are two different ways of seeing this matter. One way is to accept nostalgia as a kind of post-modern condition (that seems easy: we are not obliged to think about it and just accept it). The other way is to research history, in order to interpret our own era, redefining it and redesigning it. I believe I achieved a very Art Deco feeling with Estilo and Estilo Script without doing a revival and without making it look too dated. I also didn't design Andrade or Ventura out of nostalgia, but because I felt the need to open people's eyes to two amazing calligraphers, and Portuguese calligraphy in general.

Ventura
– a revival

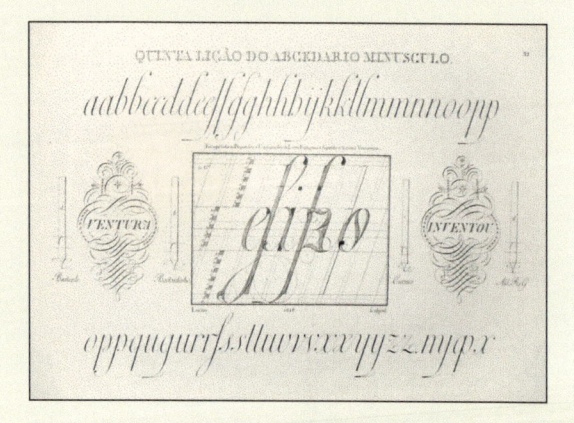

Proportions & Combinations of the Portuguese Script, according to Ventura's System

Ventura invented, Lucius engraved & Dino digitized the Portuguese Script from 1820 to 2007

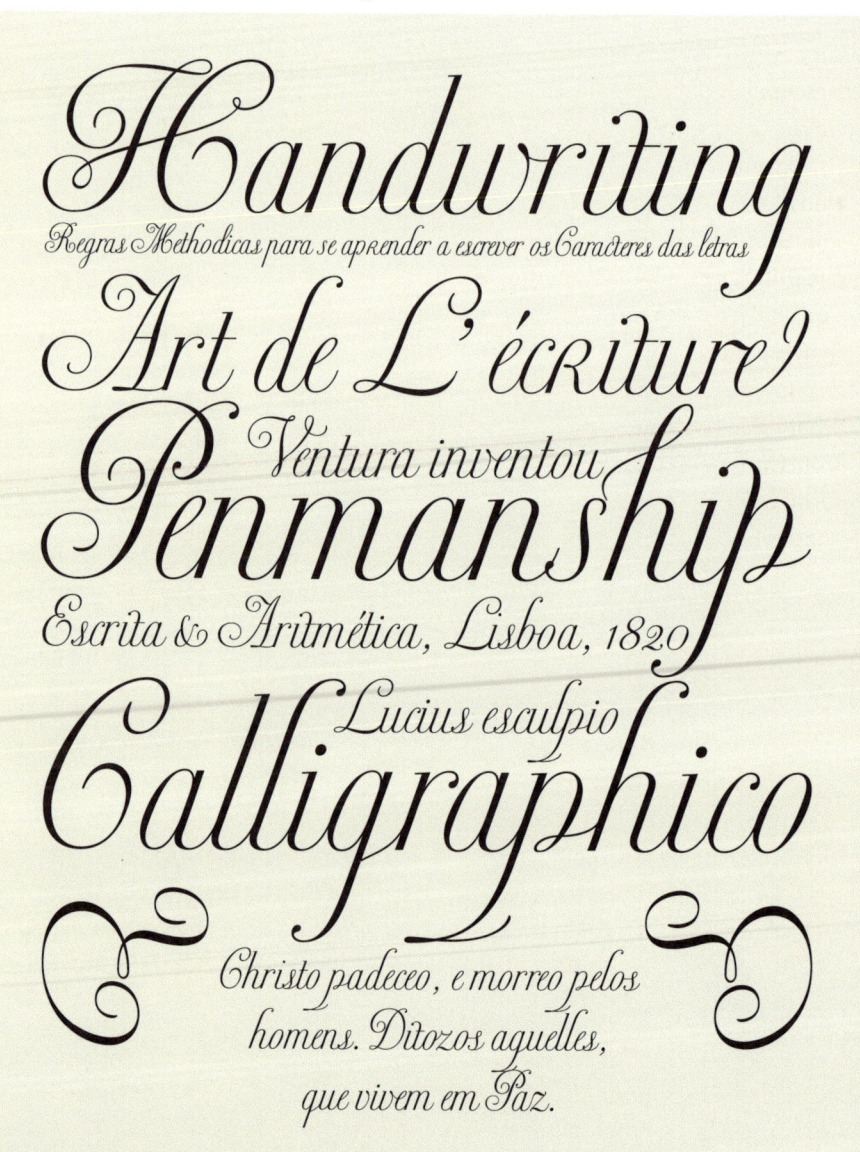

Ventura

Ventura is dos Santos' fine formal script, based on the early nineteenth century work of Portuguese calligrapher Joaquim José Ventura da Silva. The typeface comes as an OpenType font loaded with gorgeous extras, such as elegant alternates and an impressive collection of ligatures. Read more about Ventura's history on the opposite page.

Handwriting

Regras Methodicas para se aprender a escrever os Caracteres das letras

Art de L'écriture

Ventura inventou

Penmanship

Escrita & Aritmética, Lisboa, 1820

Lucius esculpio

Calligraphico

Christo padeceo, e morreo pelos homens. Ditozos aquelles, que vivem em Paz.

> *"History is one of the most relevant aspects of type design... but I also believe that we should take a step forward by connecting it to the present and the future through technology"* ESTA PRO

Ventura is one of your latest fonts, a "roundhand" script typeface based on an alphabet by a calligrapher named Joaquim José Ventura da Silva. Could you tell us more about the original and its designer?

Ventura da Silva was a Portuguese calligrapher and teacher from the nineteenth century, who in 1820 published an excellent book titled *Regras methodicas para se aprender a escrever os caracteres das letras Ingleza, Portugueza, Aldina, Romana, Gotica-Italica e Gotica-Germanica* (in English: *Methodical rules for learning to write letters in the English, Portuguese, Aldine, Roman, Italian Gothic and German Gothic styles*). It was the second edition of an 1803 book that was mainly about English script lettering. Ventura's work was influenced by English calligraphers like Charles Snell and George Shelley. At the time the British influence in Portugal was truly profound. The British army had defended Portugal from the Napoleonic invasions, and the gratitude for that support was visible in every aspect of daily life. Calligraphy was no exception.

However, in 1820 Ventura published this new version, which included samples of what he called the Portuguese Script. The Ventura font is a revival of those samples from the nineteen century, staying as close as possible to the original. The OpenType format allowed me to put in a single typeface several variations of the character shapes he designed, along with plenty of ligatures.

What do you think is the most important thing your students learn from you?

I usually say to my students that they need to enjoy what they do, that design is not just a profession but a daily attitude. In my classes everything can and should be questioned, even the teacher himself, but in an honest and thoughtful kind of way. For me, teaching is not just about passing my knowledge to the students, but providing the tools that help them build their own thoughts about design, type design and, above all, about the world they live in.

PREVIOUSLY PUBLISHED

Love of the Zoo
MODERNITY
Sacred Splendor
HOT PRESS
Modest allowance

Andrade Pro

▲ Dos Santos described Andrade as "my tribute to Portuguese typography and to the work of Manoel de Andrade de Figueiredo in particular." Andrade de Figueiredo was a typographer and calligrapher who was active in the early decades of the eighteenth century; his 1722 manual is one of forgotten treasures of Portuguese typography. It contains several early specimens of letterforms which we would now label as "transitional" (the style halfway between "baroque" and "classicist") which in Portuguese is called "leitura." Andrade is a convincing reinterpretation with large set of ligatures, swashes, beginning and ending alternates.

Christian Schwartz

AMPLITUDE ULTRA

FARNHAM DISPLAY REGULAR ITALIC SWASH

Although still in his early thirties, Christian Schwartz is among the most prolific and influential type designers in the USA, having published fonts with about half a dozen foundries. He has also created successful corporate type systems, such as the superfamily made for the German railways, for which he and Erik Spiekermann received the Federal German Design Prize in 2007. Just before we interviewed him, he had received news of yet another important award… *October 2007*

FARNHAM TEXT REGULAR

Christian Schwartz by Christine Tran

Christian, you've just received the Prix Charles Peignot of the worldwide typographers' association, ATypI. Congratulations! What did you think when they gave you the news?

I was out getting a cup of coffee when [then ATypI president] Jean-François Porchez called to deliver the news. He left a very funny, very cryptic message on my voicemail, instructing me to call back "immédiatement". Since he had never called me before, wouldn't say what he was calling about in his message, and it had been four or five years since the last Prix, I had some suspicion that this was what he wanted to talk to me about, but it was still a shock when he actually said that I was going to receive the prize. Although I have some really great collaborators, they're all far away, so I spend almost all of my time working in my little office at home, by myself, which makes my job seem very anonymous. It's a real honor to be recognized by my colleagues.

Apart from these special occasions, what is it that gives you most satisfaction in your work?
I have a lot of interest in following the news – local, national, international, all of it – and by extension I love reading newspapers and magazines. Books, too, but my first love is newspapers. Being able to contribute to the experience of reading publications is what I enjoy most about my work as a type designer.

It seems your relationship with typography began at a very early age – at three or four years old. How did that happen?
My father is an animator. He works with computers now, but when I was really young he still did everything by hand, including setting type with dry-transfer lettering for the occasional map or title. When he was done with these sheets, he would let me have the leftovers, for labeling my drawings.

You were fourteen when your first typeface, Flywheel, was published at a professional foundry. Was that a major event in your young life? Were you surprised?
I was very surprised. I felt a bit like I was getting away with something – I was accepted by the first foundry I submitted anything to! The difficult thing was following it up. Real curves turned out not to be as easy to draw as rounded rectangles.

How did you learn how to draw type?
The most important thing I did to help my development as a type designer was probably to look at a whole lot of existing typefaces, to analyze what really made them work (or not) – everything from Franklin Gothic to ITC Charter. Tobias Frere-Jones encouraged me to do this when I was an intern at Font Bureau during the summer of 1996, working under his direction. He taught me the essentials of drawing type – the rest has just been practice. David Berlow taught me about spacing during that summer.

Nuclear test
What's that rumble?
Lizard
IT'S GRAY, NOT GREEN

Farnham (Font Bureau, 2004)
▲ Johann Fleischman was a virtuoso German punchcutter who worked for the Enschedé foundry in eighteenth century Holland. Like his contemporaries Baskerville and Fournier, Fleischman took advantage of better tools and harder steel to achieve a remarkable crispness and "sparkle" on the page. His typefaces were largely forgotten as tastes changed, but the interest in Fleischman's work was renewed in the 1990s as several digital revivals were made. With Farnham, Christian Schwartz did not opt for a pure and faithful revival, but used the source material as a starting point for a very contemporary text face. Leaving out features he found distracting or exaggerated, he achieved a beautifully usable text font full of character.

FARNHAM DISPLAY REGULAR ITALIC SWASH

▶ Christian's custom type system for the Deutsche Bahn (German Railways) designed with Erik Spiekermann.

Silvero
FLAME & FORTUNE
Let's drive my sportscar to the hills
DERBY
a fine young man

Los Feliz (Emigre, 2002)

▲ Los Feliz is a district in Los Angeles that is full of amazing homemade signs. One such sign, for a company called Los Feliz Auto Parts & Service, was photographed by Schwartz's friend Matt Tragesser. Tragesser thought the hand-painted letters would make a good typeface, and sent the pictures to Christian. "I [had] spent 10 years trying to learn the 'right' way to draw type," wrote Schwartz. "When Matt showed me the Los Feliz sign, I realized it was an excellent time to take everything I've learned and turn it inside out to ask myself: 'If I didn't know what I was doing, what would I do?,' and to forgo tradition in favor of expressiveness." Tragesser's research to locate the sign painter resulted in a dead end, but months after Emigre released Los Feliz, Los Angeles magazine found him – a local craftsman named Cosmo Avila.

At what point in life did you decide to concentrate on type design?
I have tried to move away from type design a couple of times, but I keep getting pulled back in. When I graduated from Carnegie Mellon, I had every intention of using my graphic design degree for doing actual graphic design, but instead I ended up as an in-house type designer at MetaDesign in Berlin (starting an ongoing working relationship with Erik Spiekermann), then spending about two years working at Font Bureau before I moved to New York with dreams of becoming a magazine art director. It took me about 3 weeks of freelancing at Roger Black's studio to realize that I just wasn't cut out for magazine design. Roger had apparently anticipated this but had patiently waited while I figured it out for myself. He immediately had a lot of lettering and type design projects for me, and I haven't looked back since.

You've become Erik Spiekermann's right hand for most of his type design projects, and the two of you have created some impressive work together. Who does what?
When Erik and I work together, I take his big-picture ideas and translate them into typefaces. We also discuss details the whole way through – does the 'i' need a serif? Is the 'M' too wide? He's fond of saying that I always do what he asks, and then I do what I think is right. I've learned a lot from him about how to figure out what kind of family a corporate client needs. I also learned a bit about how to speak their language. It's nearly impossible to use aesthetics to sell a new typeface to people who are not very savvy about type. It's far more digestible when it's wrapped in a compelling story, and Erik is an excellent storyteller.

You've also continued to work for Roger Black, whose main speciality it is to do high-end magazine redesigns. What's your working relationship like?
Roger is much less interested in the micro level than Erik is. What I really enjoy about working with Roger is that he often describes what he wants in non-typographic terms. When we were working on the first round of sketches for the *Houston Chronicle*, he didn't say, "there's too much bracketing on the serifs." Instead, he told me, "You need to do something about those ridiculous bellbottoms!"

You belong to the first generation of designers to whom personal computers have always been around. Do you still think it is important to be able to draw by hand – or to know how the old technologies worked?
I did some letterpress work in college, and did a bit of old-fashioned paste-up work, with a waxer, blue pencil, and a light table at my job in high school, so I have some vague familiarity with the old technologies. I don't really think it's necessary to do beautiful drawings by hand to be a good type designer. I think my own sketches are

"In many ways the type business is a fashion business – some typefaces won't be used forever. That can be very freeing."

AMPLITUDE ULTRA

incredibly ugly, but they help me to quickly develop ideas, which is the important thing. The only potential issue I see with working 100% on the computer is that even the earliest proofs are seductively clean and crisp, so you have to be very careful to keep your critical eye sharp and not decide prematurely that the work is finished.

You've designed an incredible array of typefaces in an amazing range of styles, many of which are historically inspired. Is there a historical period of style that you prefer?
I'm not necessarily focused on one particular period. I think I'm more of an omnivore: I like to skip around and see what I can learn from various ways of making type – Granjon's italics are absolutely incredible, beautiful, and inspiring, but I don't think I could say I like them more than nineteenth century British Egyptians, or mid twentieth century Swiss sans serifs.

When you do a revival or reinterpretation – how much of your own heart and soul can you put into a typeface?
If expressing my innermost heart and soul through my work was my number one priority, I would probably go back to painting, or become a writer. The way I see it, my job is to make tools for other people, not to indulge myself through drawing wacky letters. I'm not saying that personal expression is a bad starting point for a typeface, just that it's not a way I feel comfortable working. I don't think I have interesting enough ideas for "blue sky" projects. I have to have a problem to solve, even for non-commissioned work. Amplitude attempts to adapt the engineering needed to make tiny type readable into a stylistic trait. Farnham updates Johann Fleischman's fantastic transitional faces to fit contemporary magazines.

How do you manage to come up with innovative ideas for each project? Could you mention any designers and books that have inspired you through the years?
It depends on the project, really. I often have a very pragmatic problem to solve, which makes it pretty easy to know where to begin. For example, Houston came from a specific project brief from Roger Black – how to interpret the model of Monotype's Italian Old Style for use as a news text face, specifically at 9pt on the *Houston Chronicle*'s presses.

I used to always carry a sketchbook, which I would gradually fill up with sketches of letters that I liked, but I've been doing that less and less these days. I've realized that I'm more interested in working initially from ideas and problems than from the formal side of things, unless I'm doing a historical revival.

My secret to coming up with good ideas is that I work with amazing collaborators.

THE PRINCESS AWAITS
Walking
in bed, above the town
RAW ONIONS!?
He eats too much candy, dear.

Fritz (Font Bureau, 1997)
▲ Fritz is based on various pieces of handlettering done in the early twentieth century by Oswald Cooper, a commercial artist and type designer best known for the popular display face Cooper Black. With Fritz, Christian Schwartz tried to "get into Oz Cooper's head," using the ideas underlying the lettering to draw a soft and flexible font for text and display. Being pretty self-critical, Schwartz later noted: "In retrospect, I wish I made the italic more cursive and didn't follow the rules of the text weights so closely when drawing the Robusto." As it is, Fritz works beautifully regardless; and its idiosyncrasies give it a lot of pizazz.

Sometimes these collaborators are type designers, like Paul Barnes, Kris Sowersby and Tal Leming. Sometimes these are clients: David Curcurito at *Esquire*; Mark Porter at *The Guardian*; Roger Black, on a number of projects. Erik Spiekermann manages to be both a co-designer and a client all at once. I have a much easier time designing a typeface once I can imagine how it will exist on the page. Paul Barnes and I spent several fruitless weeks coming up with sketches for *The Guardian* until we stopped thinking so hard about how we wanted it to look, and started to focus on what it needed to do – Mark Porter's assertion that the pages would be "modern and austere" got us out of focusing on endless variations of serif shapes and ball terminals, and gave us something to work towards.

When I was first getting serious about type design, many years ago, I was lucky enough to have the opportunity to work as an intern with Tobias Frere-Jones, who was still at Font Bureau at that point. He instilled a love for type history and an appreciation for type specimen books. However, while I love type history, I try to keep an eye on what's going on right now, not just in graphic design but also in fashion, music, television – serious culture and pop culture, all at once – so I buy more magazines than I care to admit. In many ways the type business is a fashion business – some typefaces are intrinsically attached to the time and place in which they were created, and so they won't be used forever. That can be very freeing.

What is it that makes a young type designer tick?
I have a really great little stovetop espresso maker. That is more or less what keeps me going.

"Drawing type is a real craft. I've learned it by doing it and by getting a lot of really terrible work out of my system early. Self-editing is the hardest thing to learn."

AMPLITUDE ULTRA

Amplitude (Font Bureau, 2002)

▶▶ Amplitude is an unusual sans-serif that makes for very different effects in text and display sizes. Schwartz took a functional device – the ink trap – and made it into an aesthetic feature. There's a precedent: Matthew Carter's Bell Centennial, probably the best known typeface with exaggerated inktraps. Originally designed for telephone directories, it was made to be used at very small sizes on absorbent paper. Deep inktraps were carved out to prevent ink from closing up sharp corners. As a student, Schwartz liked making "improper" use of Bell Centennial as a display face because its inktraps just looked cool. A few years later he made Amplitude do the same. When used in text sizes, it looks breezy and bright; used large, its deep cuts make for a striking image.

◂◂ Amplitude is used widely in editorial design to create a broad spectrum of styles; here *Wallpaper** and *Globe* magazines provide contrasting examples

Miracle worker
ABLE TO KEEP TRACK OF OVER 26,375 SIMULTANEOUS EXPERIMENTS

Toiling in the lab night and day
Never has time for lunch break
FINALLY ARRIVES AT AN AMAZING BREAKTHROUGH
Insurance claims down 62%

AMAZING

Doctor, it hurts when I move my leg like this
THEN DON'T MOVE YOUR LEG

Healers
VACANT EMERGENCY ROOMS

František Štorm

SERAPION II

FARAO BLACK

All type designers are individualists, but František Štorm from Prague is a special case. His historically inspired fonts are virtually unparalleled. He has arguably made the most interesting revivals of classic text faces by Jannon, Baskerville and Walbaum. But he also designed a large number of fonts that are less straightforward and pretty hard to pigeonhole: very personal and rather eccentric interpretations of classic and modernist traits and mannerisms. Fonts that serious typographers might think too fancy… if they weren't so well made and legible. *August 2007*

JANNON T MODERNE

Your biography states that you graduated from the Academy of Applied Arts in Prague, at the School of Book and Type Design under Professor Jan Solpera. What were the most important things you learned from Jan Solpera?
He was a guru to my generation of typographers. He taught us to be personal rather than useful, with an emphasis on an original, unmistakable attitude. When assigning semestral tasks, he always followed the individual nature of each student. That's very similar to what I'm doing with my students now.

Jan lives seven kilometers from my house in South Bohemia and we work together on his projects. He also helps out sometimes with consultations about my students, and comes to our parties, of course. When it's cold and rainy – we call it "typographic weather" – he comes to visit me and we drink tea, sitting at the computer screen and doing some Béziers.

▶ František Štorm is not only a prolific designer of digital type, but often turns his hand to music and is an accomplished graphic artist, as shown by these woodcuts.

When I first saw your early typefaces about ten years ago in a brochure on Czech design, I was amazed by their originality and unusual shapes. Did you actually set out to design type that was "different," or were these just forms that came naturally to you?
Both. Because being different is actually my nature. I have no clients at all, no boss, nobody tells me what to do. This can be very difficult at times, though. When I try to think of what to do and no idea comes, I know I'd better go chop some wood or cut grass to clean my mind. Then if still nothing comes, I go to a local pub to drink a few beers and consult the farmers. When I once tried to explain to them what typography is, they laughed: "are you stupid?"… "I am," I answered.

I suppose originality comes with freedom.

Besides digital type design and graphic design, you are proficient in woodcut, etching and photography. To what extent do these activities influence your typographic work?
Well, I have many more different activities. For instance, I do some music as well. It changes from time to time. I quit etchings, for example. For the moment, I also quit type design because everyone asks me about type design.

What is it that you like most about designing type?
I love all aspects, including research, exhausting computer work, printout samples, first public appearance, and… the money, because business is part and parcel of our occupation. I like to contemplate my sketches, compare them to existing typefaces, and select one of several possible forms. When I release a typeface, it's like a child being born, with lots of potential for growth. I love the silence in my studio, my tea on my desk, my music during endless hours of work at night.

A SPECIMEN
Perfectionist
1760 Birmingham
HANDY
Quick & Brown

John Baskerville

▲ Dissatisfied with existing Baskervilles, Štorm went back to the original source. In 1999 he studied rare volumes from Baskerville's printing office, produced c.1760, at Nové Hrady Castle in the Czech National Museum Library. Having selected the typeface that Baskerville used, among other things, for his 1763 folio Bible, Štorm designed what he calls a *transcription*: "The aim was not so much to be reverently faithful to the original, as to preserve the spirit of the typeface and to breathe new life into it." The result is one of the most readable Baskerville revivals ever made; a workhorse in the service of literature. Štorm's John Sans makes for an interesting sans-serif companion.

570 channels
cathode ray
WATCH
SQUARE PEGS

Etelka

▲ In today's digital office environment, products such as software no longer come with printed manuals. Installation CDs carry huge documentation, mostly in PDF format. To read these comfortably on the screen, we need extremely legible screen typefaces which are readable even in long lines. Etelka is for on-screen reading as well as print. Its design idea is a wide, open rounded square – like the shape of an old CRT monitor. It is suitable for all kinds of visual communication, especially corporate identity and orientation systems in architecture. The Pro version comes with useful ideograms and signs.

Many of your fonts are inspired by history. Some are serious and very thorough revivals, such as your excellent trio of Jannon, Baskerville, and Walbaum. Others seem more like playful or exaggerated variations of type from past centuries – I'm thinking of Serapion, Biblon, Farao and others. Is there an aspect of fun or irony to these designs? Do you think of them as parodies or pastiches?
That's right, I do. My life is full of grotesque experiences. You forgot Cobra, it's a pure joke.

For your catalogs and website, you have written numerous texts in which you re-write the history of type design in a way that is irreverent, witty and philosophical at the same time. Are you very critical of the "traditional" way in which the history and techniques of type are usually described?
I don't try to re-write anything, I want to explain a different point of view (mine) on historical material. I hope nobody regards me as a historian, and people reading my explanations should know the historical facts first. But there have been some stupid distortions, whose authors were led by the modern era's sickly penchant for simplification. For example, I hate the term "transitional" type, because it was invented in the past century, not in the age of Caslon and Baskerville. Also, some fonts which are named "Garamond" have nothing to do with Garamond, it is rubbish. I like to call things by their proper names.

Talking of Baskerville, what were your motives behind the revival you designed?
In the case of Baskerville, I wasn't satisfied with the existing digital versions. I never knew what to answer when colleagues asked me what version they should use for computer typesetting. I realized that many of the other renderings were poor – some

"When I release a typeface, it's like a child being born."

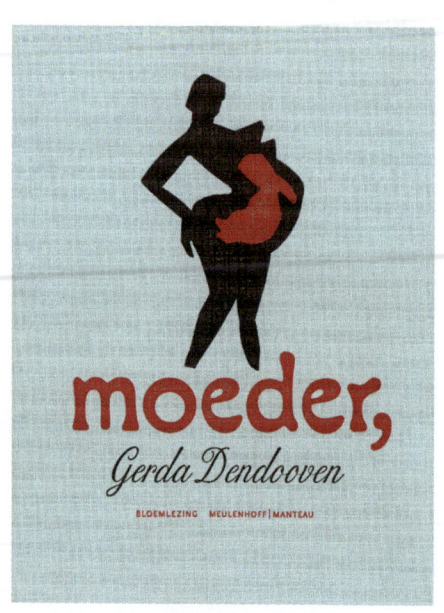

FARAO BLACK

◀ Book covers by designer Gert Dooreman with illustrations by Gerda Dendooven. *De lange weg naar huis*, a children's book based on the Odyssey, was designed with Štorm's Biblon and Teuton typefaces. Davidsfonds, 2008. *Moeder* was designed using Cobra and Excelsoir Script. Meulenhoff|Manteau, 2007.

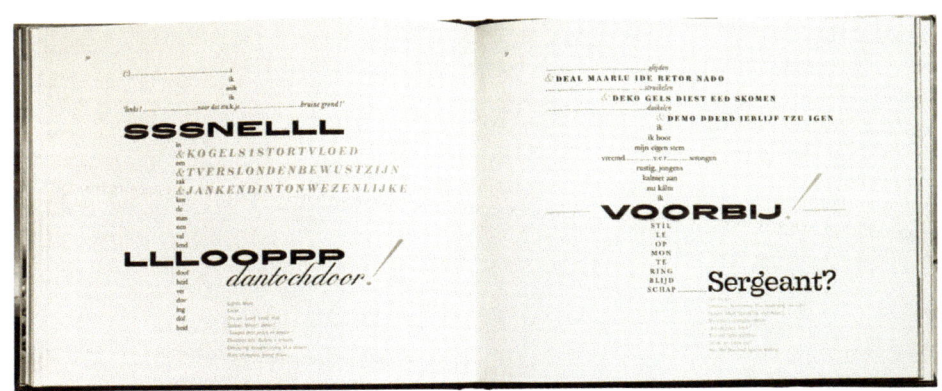

▸▴ Based in Gent, Belgium, typographic designer Gert Dooreman uses Štorm's typefaces frequently and brilliantly. *Niemand Land*, a war poem by Tom Lanoye, was set in expressionist style using many fonts from the Stormtype foundry (plus Rhode and Barcode from Font Bureau). "Every kind of expression I wanted to achieve was represented by those of typefaces," Dooreman commented. Prometheus publishers, 2002.

Splendid Quartett
▾ Štorm: "The division of a typeface family into four designs is common in most text faces. However, display typography calls for a richer tonal scale. Its purpose is to decorate, to represent and to please."

downright awful! So I took several original books printed by John Baskerville as a direct inspiration and ignored all later re-cuts, so that nothing stood between John and me. From that moment (with kind help of Otakar Karlas) my re-designing work ran very quickly. Now many books are printed with my Baskerville Ten Pro (including Cyrillics), which makes me very happy.

When you were in Romania to give workshops, you photographed stenciled street lettering and then gave these letterforms back to your hosts in the form of a free font. Are you always looking for possible sources of inspiration, everywhere?
Sure. Patzcuaro comes from Mexico, Teuton from the Sudetenland. I need local diversity, with specific design attributes. These should be preserved and developed in an original way, not mixed with incompatible folkloristic elements from other cultures. That's what today's world music does – but who needs Bavarian G'stanzl yodelling in Tamil-Nadu?

Romania is a wonderful country, and Manele music rules! Especially Nicolae Guta and Adrian Minune (search Manele on YouTube…)! And stencils too, each piece has its own story, often very personal and serious.

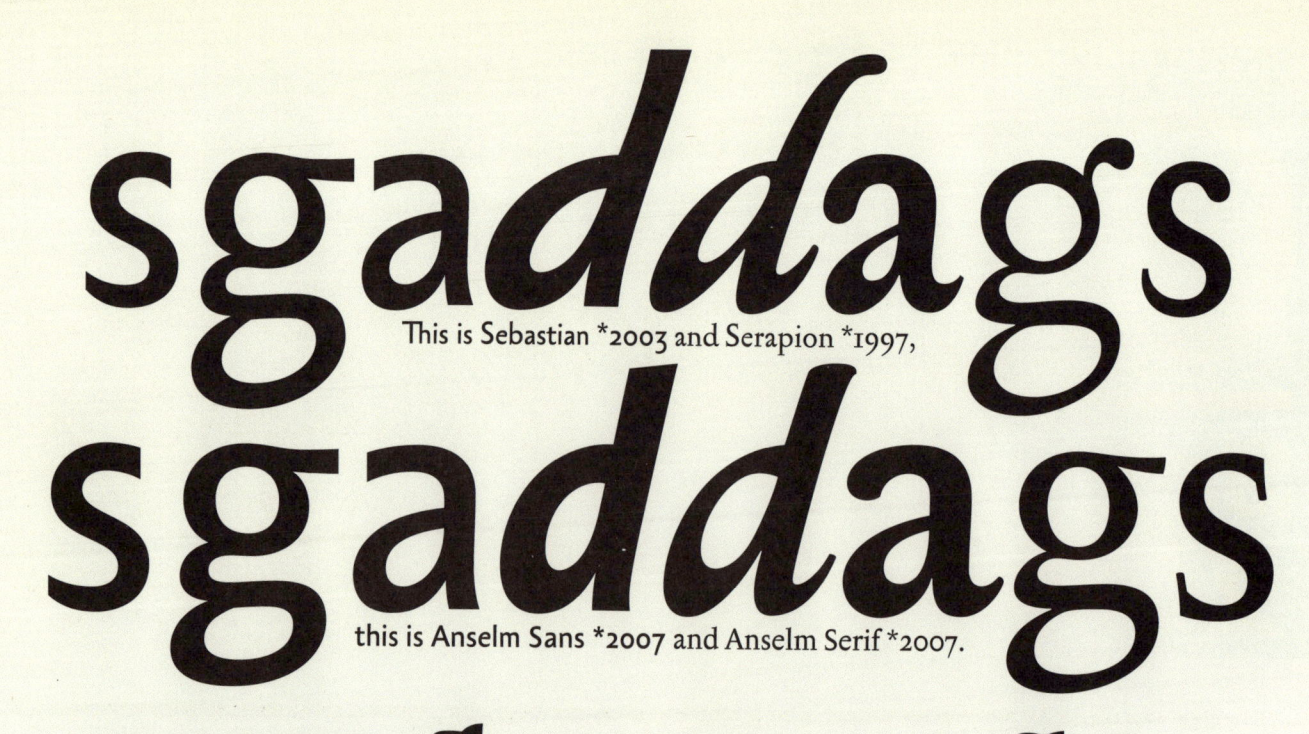

sgaddags
This is Sebastian *2003 and Serapion *1997,

sgaddags
this is Anselm Sans *2007 and Anselm Serif *2007.

monster monster
находится находится
γνωρίζουμε γνωρίζουμε
rohlenstayn rohlenstayn
Aucthors Aucthors
управляющим управляющим
μεταγλωτίσει μεταγλωτίσει
dobrodružný dobrodružný

&&&Ɛɛɛ@@@ ɞɞɞɛɛ@@@ &&&Ɛɛɛ@@@ ɞɞɞɛɛ@@@
&&&Ɛɛɛ@@@ ɞɞɞɛɛ@@@ &&&Ɛɛɛ@@@ ɞɞɞɛɛ@@@

Serif & *Regular* Serif & **Medium** Serif & **Bold** Ten & Regular Ten & **Bold**
Sans & Light Sans & *Italic* Sans & **Medium** Sans & **Bold** Sans & **Black**

◀ Farao and Serapion on *Cultuur in Gent* brochure by Dorp & Dal

Nine tana leaves
Egypt
Foot-drag
EGYPTIENNE LOVER
Boggy slumber

Farao

▲ Egyptiennes are cheerful typefaces. In the early nineteenth century, when they were first developed, a lot of experimenting with new letterforms was going on. Therefore, many Egyptiennes (also known as slab-serifs) had design flaws – uneven spacing, letters falling backwards and bizarre details – for which they were avoided by "serious" typographers. In the course of time, however, it was realized that such oddities could be quite pleasant and inspiring. Based on nineteenth century sources, Štorm's Farao is soundly imperfect, which makes it stand out from other, colder slab-serifs.

They also took us to visit the Academy in Bucharest – which was kind of shocking. The students are regarded as complete idiots by their aging professors, just like in Prague some 50 years ago. But we also met open-minded young people, who resist all that bs, doing great graphic design and making public lettering with stencils, in defiance of the school.

Many type designers will say that making type is like providing practical solutions: making little machines for reading. But what about fantasy? Decoration? Seduction? Whatever it is, it must be legible. There is no type without the reader, no font without customers. That's what I keep saying to my students. Then comes art, but it always comes second.

In the past ten years, your type library has been growing at amazing speed. You've also managed to improve and extend existing families. Among your own typefaces, which are your favorites at the moment?
Always the one I'm working on, my last type system (Sans&Serif). It shall be out very soon. It will have Latin, Slavic, Cyrillic and Greek; something huge and ambitious. Of course, I'm not sure yet whether the result will match my expectations…

RIGID DIRIGIBLE
Afloat
Lighter than air
Luftschifffahrtsgesellschaft
AIRSHIP

Zeppelin

▲ Originally designed in 1998 as an all-caps font, Zeppelin was inspired by the shapes of the famous airships of that name. More recently a lower case was added, as well as a narrower version. Zeppelin's design is simple and consciously impersonal; as the designer notes: "…its consistent monolinear drawing is nearly naive, with no trace of expression." Zeppelin is ideal for a wide range of contemporary applications: from magazines and advertising to information and signage systems.

What other plans do you have for the next few years – professionally speaking?
First, I'll quit teaching at the Academy of Art Architecture and Design in Prague. The state scholar system only parasitizes on my enthusiasm, giving me no reason to stay. After that – I don't make fixed plans, because they could go wrong.

◀ Some historical models are repeatedly revisited throughout Štorm's body of work, receiving sterner or more frivolous treatments according to the designer's mood. Anselm goes back to Štorm's Jannon, a reinterpretation of the typefaces by the French punchcutter of that name, as well as the 1997 Serapion, a capricious typeface derived from Jannon's work. Anselm succeeds it after ten years of evolution – a more sober, reliable workhorse typeface. Its sans-serif companion was developed from the earlier Sebastian. The most significant difference between Sebastian/Serapion and Anselm is the large x-height of the latter's lowercase, which makes it very suitable for application in extensive texts.

Tomáš Brousil

ATRAMENT

BISTRO SCRIPT

Based in Prague, Tomáš Brousil's Suitcase Type Foundry is one of those one-person font foundries that have been instrumental in raising the bar for emerging type designers. Brousil's fonts are intelligent and original, well-made and useful. He also masters an amazing range of styles. Meet Tomáš Brousil, a man of many faces. *August 2008*

DEDERON SERIF MEDIUM

Tomáš, were you always interested in type and lettering? Or did you have in mind a completely different kind of career when you began your design education?
After graduating from what we call "middle school" I started my career as a graphic designer in a small agency. My plan was to learn about the technical details of print production and pre-press technologies first, and then after one or two years enroll into Jan Solpera's typographic studio at the Prague Academy of Fine Arts, which holds admission exams every year in January. Of about 30 people that usually sign up, only one to three people get through. I was not accepted until five years later. Each year I learned more about type design and consequently I became totally addicted to type. When I finally began my studies at the academy, I had a clear idea of what I wanted to do – start up my own type foundry.

Photo by Radeq Brousil

mail@receiver

You were a student of František Štorm. What are the main things you learned from him?
František began teaching at the Academy in the same year when I began studying there. He took over the typographic studio from Solpera one year later. I owe the majority of my design skills to him; he also taught me the technical ins and outs of glyph construction and the necessary production know-how.

Štorm has developed a very personal, idiosyncratic style of type design. Your typefaces seem to be less emphatically expressive, more neutral. Is this simply a question of personality, or did you consciously move away from your master?
It is probably a combination of several elements. One of my concerns when I started my foundry six years ago was that my catalog should somehow be complementary to Štorm's. He mainly produced fonts for book-setting at the time and I missed quality fonts for designing posters, corporate styles or logotypes – simply contemporary typefaces. I don't have the same special interest in baroque or renaissance styles as he does. I am more fascinated by the innovative typography of the 1950s and '60s and its simplicity and coldness.

As a former student of František, I feel I am under constant scrutiny from other designers. As soon as I do something that remotely resembles his work, I am told it is "too Štorm". It is frustrating sometimes, because my approach to type design is completely different.

Would you say that there are aspects of your work that are typically Czech or Central European? Has the massive amount of diacritic signs in Czech or Slovak influenced the structure or proportions of your letters?
I don't think that today our typefaces are specifically Czech. One could think of typefaces that refer to our classic twentieth century designers like Preissig or Menhart, but this has already been done and it could become a bit boring. In fact, there have been more interesting type designers in the past, even though their designs were not as expressive.

The frequent usage of diacritics in Czech accounts for longer ascenders and lower capitals in many of our alphabets. But what is important to me here is a high sensitivity to the placing of diacritic marks – not just for Czech but for all languages. Too often, graphic designers who want to use fonts from foreign foundries for Czech or similar languages need to have them furnished with new quality diacritic marks.

Cleen-O-Matic Scrubbed Bagging clothes

BistroScript
▲ BistroScript was selected by designer Nick Sherman as one of Typographica's Typefaces of 2007. He wrote: "There is no doubt that this face got its inspiration from mid century 'retro' handlettering, but BistroScript moves beyond what John Downer would call a revival, instead holding its own as a contemporary tribute to the script styles of yore. Like Underware's Bello, BistroScript is one of few typefaces born from classic cursive brush scripts which can hold its ground in contemporary contexts without seeming gaudy or revivalist."

▲ The very rare Suitcase t-shirts with Metalista and Bistro Script

Inflatable Raft Handle Hook/Line/Sinker COLD ONES

Fishmonger
▲ Fishmonger originated as a custom-made font for a seafood shop. As soon as Brousil had sketched its basic principles, the idea arose to expand it into an extensive series with a large number of styles. The result is a family of five widths in five weights, each with its respective italics: 50 fonts in all. With its unmistakable silhouette, Fishmonger is a functional, clean design that is ideal for lending a unique identity to an arts event or a trendy product.

What is it you like most about designing type?
I really love the early stages of a typeface: sketching, looking for shapes, and arranging the basic characters. To me, those are the best moments of designing type. The rest is more or less routine, and not much fun. And what is really hard for me is to come up with a name for each new typeface.

You belong to a generation that has more or less grown up with computers. How about manual work: techniques like drawing, calligraphy, and woodcut… Is it still important?
I begin most typefaces by sketching and hand-drawing. It's not necessary for all typefaces, but it usually helps to establish the basic ideas. All the other steps are simpler when done by computer; the mouse and the keyboard are natural tools for me to work with. But I certainly think drawing is important. I have hundreds of sheets filled with character studies. I am convinced that this helps to grasp the construction of an alphabet and the relationships within the font.

"It is not so simple to choose favorites because every typeface has its own interesting story"

DEDERON SANS MEDIUM ITALIC

Considering that your Suitcase Type Foundry was founded a mere five years ago, your output has been quite impressive. Do you use special methods or techniques to keep up a high production?
It is really quite simple. Most of my fonts were originally developed during my studies at the Academy. My production was imposed by the rhythm of the school: twice a year we had to show a minimum of one or two typefaces, or rather type families. This compelled me to make optimum use of my time, simplify the process of creation, think forward and work on more than one font at a time.

Of your own typefaces, which are you favorites, and why?
It could be RePublic, a typeface originally named Public and designed by Stanislav Maršo in 1956, which I redesigned in 2004. Public was closely linked to an era of standardization in our society; one of its main uses was for the communist party newspaper *Rude Pravo*. So for an older generation of designers the typeface had negative connotations and they advised against reviving it. I did it anyway, and today RePublic is widespread and quite popular. I think I managed to rehabilitate an interesting typeface.

◀ Brousil's noteblock with sketches that would lead to the design of Dederon Serif.

▶ Pages from the *Comenia* type specimen, designed by Tomáš Brousil. The family was specially developed for use at schools and universities by three Czech designers: Brousil (Sans), František Štorm (Serif) and Radana Lencová (Script).

Comenia
School Typeface System

BROUSIL / LENCOVÁ / ŠTORM

So, why do we object against the most common fonts, that is, Times New Roman and Arial supplied with every operating system? In the first place, they are not well designed and they do not fulfill the requirements for faces used in schools, because they were made with a different purpose in mind.

Times New Roman was designed by Stanley Morison in 1931 for the British newspaper The Times. It fulfills all the requirements for a good quality newspaper type – narrow letters, tall x-height and strong contrast; these characteristics, however, make it unsuitable for teaching purposes. Besides, the digital versions used today feature wrongly made diacritics. The Arial typeface (originally called Sonoran Sans Serif) was designed in 1982 by Robin Nicholas and Patricia Saunders for the Monotype Imaging company. It is essentially a system font, originally designated for use in laser printers with low resolution printing.

Hustá síťovina
TIMES NEW ROMAN

Šíleně alergicky
ARIAL ITALIC

These are typical random examples of the faults seen in system fonts. Poor quality Czech accents: apostrophe used in place of a caron with the letters t and d in Times, or wrong position and shape of accents in Arial. Besides, the italics in Arial is only a strongly slanted regular cut without the necessary differences in the shape of letters.

Hustá síťovina
COMENIA SERIF REGULAR

Šíleně alergicky
COMENIA SERIF ITALIC

S

Serif

Comenia Serif Regular, *Italic*, **Bold**, ***Bold Italic***

Comenia Serif is a modern Roman type with large, open counters, best suited for long texts in textbooks, theses and academic prints, but also for primers. The construction of letters abides to this principle. Short, distinct serifs clearly connect to the letter stems, it has well-balanced round strokes and good relation between the letter stems and the other strokes; all these ingredients make for a harmonious typeface. Accents fit with the lower and upper case while fully respecting the characteristics of Czech, Slovak, Polish, and other Central European languages where accents are used aplenty.

VYJMENOVANÁ SLOVA PO „L"

mapa
Zameškané hodiny
okraje
Matematika
Zakládání betonových staveb
ZVONĚNÍ
František během vyučování neustále vyluzuje bručivé zvuky.

Sans

Comenia Sans Regular, *Italic*, Medium, *Medium Italic*, **Bold**, ***Bold Italic***, Condensed Regular, *Condensed Italic*, Condensed Medium, *Condensed Medium Italic*, **Condensed Bold**, ***Condensed Bold Italic***

Comenia Sans has the same upper and lower case height as Comenia Serif. They are alike in the length of ascenders and descenders and in the colour of each weight cut. This is why they may be used together on a single line of text without disturbing each other. Comenia Sans, however, has been stripped of all decorations and variations in stroke weight, which are pleasant and lively in long text blocks but unnecessary in short pieces of text. Still, Comenia Sans retains a soft, pleasant feel and also a few little details which lend it distinct character without compromising its legibility and overall utility.

Biochemie
Dne 1. 9. byla Tomášovi udělena ředitelská důtka.
pastelky
DĚJINY LOUTKOVÉHO DIVADLA
Index
Pythagorova věta
SBOROVNA
Technologie oprav letadel

The character set contains some letters with **multiple variants**. Usually, we prefer certain shapes of letters ever since we remember – maybe our parents or grandparents wrote that way, too, and we came to like it, or we choose them simply as an expression of our freedom. Four letters and two figures have two shape options. Children may try both, choosing the one which suits them best; or they may use both as they like.

RR aa ff kk
33 44 yy

Serifs are important for good legibility and they help in the writing process, too. This was true in the Carolingian minuscule script and it remained true even later, in Venetian italic scripts. The serifs don't need to be too large, what matters is the acknowledgment of the beginning of the letter stroke.

imh

Libraries gave us power
WORK
Helden der arbeit
Wealth, the great comforter
Around 360 BC
Centralised
He tends not to ruffle feathers

RePublic

▲ Based on Stanislav Maršo's Public, originally designed in 1956 for the Czech communist newspaper *Rude Pravo*, RePublic is as good an example as any of how typography, even when born of bureaucracy and standardization, can be a highly emotive subject. Revivals and rediscoveries need not be limited to romantic scripts or heroic uncoverings of lost masterpieces.

Or it could be Sandwich, the first font with automatic vertical aligning of glyphs. Or maybe my first typeface Katarine, which is named after my fiancée and which I re-designed last year, when my daughter was born. It's not so simple to choose because every typeface has its own interesting little story.

Could you mention some typefaces that you wish you had made?
This really is the hardest question of all. For a recent discussion, I wrote down a list of typefaces that I'm kind of envious of. There was Bryant by Eric Olson, Enigma by Jeremy Tankard, Lapture by Tim Ahrens, Merlo by Mario Feliciano, Moderno from Font Bureau, Omnes by Joshua Darden, Plumero Script by Diego Giaccone. I later thought of two more typefaces, Olga by Christina Bee and Tisa by Mitja Miklavčič.

You have designed a display font called Metalista, which you have made available for free and which you describe as "an expression of undying admiration for the persistence of the metal culture." Are you a metalhead? Apart from Metalista, has music influenced your type designs?
Oh no, I am not a metalhead. I just admire people who manage to conform their own lifestyle to some style of music. Heavy metal has a long history and a strong position in my country and the fans look the same today as when I was a child. I find that incredible. Otherwise I play music non-stop while working, but I don't think it has some special impact on my typefaces.

"Each year I learned more about type design and consequently I became totally addicted to type."

DEDERON SANS MEDIUM ITALIC

MIDNIGHT
BEWARE THE BEAST
CHOMP

Sandwich

▲ Sandwich is another clever toolkit for building visual identities. This all-caps display face comes with a series of alternate, rounded characters for letters like 'A', 'E', 'M', 'N' and 'Y'. Its most unusual feature is a series of about forty "ligatures" or vertical catchwords — articles and prepositions in several languages, as well as the possibility to compose your own vertical two- or three-letter words.

What is your biggest ambition for the foreseeable future?
My next project is a typeface that can change style within the framework of the family. It could be a great typeface for setting magazines or newspapers. Other than that, I don't have any special long-term ambitions. What I do plan is to produce printed catalogs to support the foundry. I have a type specimen in its final stage in my computer, and I am looking forward to printing it. ❧

Dederon Sans & Serif

▶ Dederon Serif is a beautifully drawn typeface for book typesetting. Some of its characteristics can be traced back to the Liberta typeface published by TypoArt in former Eastern Germany, but its details are wholly original and contemporary. There is no better companion to Dederon than Dederon Sans — a matching sans-serif based on the same principles but sufficiently different to stand out, creating the perfect dynamics between the various sections or levels of a design.

Swasemis
EXPECTA D. LADED
Aque pardalque
Kaming
«La pard dontre juse»
(1970 Corman)

ADVAGIATON. 681
Dørned Kjældemmed
24 cona
[Ah! - Maistaie.]
STRAGGIONO

Ronna Penner

AMELIE REGULAR

POINTED BRUSH

The growing interest in script and handwriting fonts has resulted in some remarkable success stories. Canadian lettering artist Ronna Penner submitted her first fonts to MyFonts years ago. Sales remained slow for a while and she concentrated on other activities. Then in 2007–2008, when the script craze hit, her foundry Typadelic made a convincing comeback, hitting the top of the bestseller lists with Sweetheart Script and Cookie Nookie. And there's more where that came from. March 2008

MOONBEAM REGULAR

How did you become interested in lettering and fonts?
I've been making them all my life, really. When I was a kid I would scrawl alphabets on every scrap piece of paper I could find. I used to experiment with different type styles, from chunky lettering to pretty script faces. I'd fill page after page with alphabet scrawl until the white of the paper was obliterated.

When I was a kid in school we had penmanship classes and I took great pride in my handwriting, occasionally winning penmanship contests. Not hard to do when everyone else was outside climbing trees… I just wanted to draw letters! I still have books filled with my handwriting samples and actually used one of my early samples to create Velvet Script. In that font you can see influences of The Palmer Method as it was taught in schools in the 1960s.

I think it's a shame that penmanship is no longer taught in schools today. Good handwriting is an art and is beautiful to look at. Compare the penmanship of days gone by with what passes for handwriting today!

When I decided to go to college for graphic design in the early '90s, my interest in lettering and (especially) fonts came to the fore. Computers were not tools we had access to at that time so we made do with Letraset or we designed our own lettering for titles or logos. This was right up my alley and I really enjoyed it.

Once I graduated I bought my first Mac and shortly after that the internet found its way into my life. It didn't take long for me to become a font junkie.

Which type designers inspire you?
About 10 minutes after I connected to the internet for the first time, I found Font Diner and fell in love with those fonts and with the site itself. What could be cooler than a font vending machine?

Chank Diesel's site was another one I visited often, and if I remember correctly, I learned how to make fonts using a tutorial that is still found on his site. Thanks Chank! From afar I thought he was a pretty cool guy and one very prolific font designer.

You were a "concept designer" in the greeting card industry. What does a concept designer do? Is lettering or type design part of the job?
My job as a concept designer was simply to develop concepts for low cost greeting cards. Interesting lettering is definitely a part of greeting card design. It has to evoke some kind of emotion on the part of the buyer: happiness, a sense of playfulness, etc, and to ultimately communicate what the buyer wants to express. That seems like a rather big job for a typeface to accomplish, and that is where my desire to develop typefaces was born. I spent many hours searching for just the right font for the job, and – not always finding it – decided to develop my own to express exactly what I needed.

You've developed an impressive ability at designing script fonts. Who taught you?
I'm totally self-taught. Dogged determination, an obsessive-compulsive tendency as well as neurotic perfectionism are my secrets to building script fonts.

For me, scripts are probably the most difficult type of lettering to develop. It's also extremely difficult to achieve the free-flowing, spontaneous nature of handwriting, and to get the letters to join properly as you type on your keyboard. I developed a technique I'm comfortable with, which works for most of my script fonts, so I stick with it.

2 Breaks Jumping Rope Recession

Inkster
▲ Inkster breaks all the rules – it is capricious and unpredictable. Some letters have serifs, some don't. Some are condensed, some are impossibly wide. Some lowercase letters have uppercase shapes. The contrasting characters bounce all over the baseline. It isn't hard to imagine a book cover design using this font in slightly varying sizes to add to the fun. A powerful calligraphic roman, Inkster is your shortest route to a distinctive lettering style. It's part of Typadelic's Most Popular Collection.

Sweetheart Script
▼ Sweetheart Script, Typadelic's most popular typeface, is a charming upright script drawn with great care and sensitivity. Its lowercase letters connect impeccably, giving the typeface the gentle flow of a classic piece of hand-lettering. Romantic without being cheesy, cheerful yet restrained, Sweetheart Script is one of the most balanced connected script fonts recently published. The caps are meant as initials with the lowercase – so don't use in all-caps!

You're a Sweetheart!

Conversation
The One I Love

Pear stack 69¢/lb Greengrocer's Fresh!

Pointed Brush
▲ Pointed Brush evokes the elegant look of hand-painted calligraphy using a pointed brush. It gives your headlines the confident dash of expert lettering, alternating connected and disconnected characters with a great sense of freedom. It works admirably in longer texts as well.

I love seeing a script font come to life! Really, the hard work for me is building the font in FontLab, then outputting it and testing it to see what's working and what needs tweaking. I tweak to the point of distraction. I often wonder why I make script fonts because they have a tendency to frustrate me, but I get a lot of satisfaction in seeing the final product.

Your Sketchley font family won an award in the 2001 worldwide type design competition Bukva:Raz!. Did that influence you to specialize in type design?
Winning the Bukva:Raz! award was in my early days of typeface design and it absolutely influenced my decision. Sketchley was an experiment to see if my designs had a viable audience. To get some recognition early in my type designing career confirmed that there might possibly be a market for my fonts out there.

So I began working on a few typefaces and developed Typadelic as a showcase for my designs. I haven't looked back.

Your other website is Scrapadelic, devoted to the art of scrapbooking. Could you tell us a little more about scrapbooking – and about the link with your fonts?
I've always been a scrapbooker, even before I knew there was a name for it. I've always kept my family's pictures in albums and, later on, added titles and dates and a few tacky floral stickers here and there to make the pages look interesting.

At one point MyFonts asked me to develop an advertisement using my own fonts for a scrapbooking magazine. I didn't know such magazines existed. After doing some research and creating my ad I soon realized how well my fonts suited digital scrapbooking.

> *"Dogged determination, an obsessive-compulsive tendency as well as neurotic perfectionism are my secrets to building script fonts."*
>
> AMERICAN WRITER

Cookie Nookie

Digital scrapbooking really appealed to the graphic designer in me. Developing fonts can be a colorless and sometimes mundane job but scrapbook design is full of glorious color, a definite change of pace from font making. I started designing scrapbooking kits and selling them online. While I experienced some measure of success and still love the scrapbooking industry, my heart is in fonts and always has been.

Two of your fonts, Sweetheart Script and Cookie Nookie, have been extremely successful lately. Were you surprised – and has it in any way changed your plans for the immediate future?
Sweetheart Script was first released in the digital scrapbooking market as an experiment to see how well it would sell. It had a very limited character set and a low price. I was surprised to find that sales were lower than expected even given its low price, and it was one of the reasons why I decided to pull it from the market. The finished font sat on my computer for two years while I developed my scrapbooking business.

I released Sweetheart Script at MyFonts in December 2007 – and it got a much better reception! That font is my personal favorite and I am pleasantly surprised to see it do so well. It hasn't changed my plans for the future other than to develop more script fonts. I have to chuckle when I see the name Cookie Nookie. Can you tell I didn't know what to name it? To me, naming fonts is like naming race horses. The names don't always make sense.

Your fonts are usually priced at just under 20 dollars, which is very reasonable. Cookie Nookie costs much less. Why did you make it so cheap?
Another experiment. I've spent a few years in the digital scrapbooking industry where products are very under-priced. I personally don't know many scrapbookers who are willing to pay full price for a font they may use once or twice, so my strategy was to make a really usable, reasonably priced font (read: cheap!) for both the graphic design industry and the scrapbooking industry.

Could you mention two or three typefaces you wish you had designed? What kind of font would you most like to design if you had unlimited time?
I wish I had designed any one of Rob Leuschke's stunning fonts. His Inspiration is a wonderful, playful, flowing typeface that I use on many of my scrapbooking layouts. Sloop Script from the Font Bureau is a gorgeous typeface and I wish I had the discipline to design something like that. I've just discovered Canada Type who also have some beautiful typefaces. If I had more time I'd like to work on vintage handwriting fonts like some I see from P22, or The Type Quarry.

Until the foundry Cheap Pro Fonts issued a "Pro" version of your Black Jack, you used to give it away for free – why ?
The truth of it is, I didn't much like that font and couldn't see charging for it. I have to really like my fonts to release them for sale. However, I thought it would make a really awesome free font! I see Black Jack used everywhere and still can't say it's my favorite. The funny thing is, I do feel some pride when I see that someone liked the font well enough to use it on their signage, or packaging. I always say to myself, "I designed that!"

7th Circle
AUREI, PLEASE
HADES
Stygian Ferryman

Garden Party
▲ Garden Party belongs to the same category of calligraphic romans as Inkster, but it's a more regular and therefore perhaps easier to use. It will work wonders on an illustrated book or brochure cover, standing out more than your regular brush script font.

Cattapilla
The cattapilla does all the work but the butterfly gets all the publicity.

Cyrus Highsmith

ANTENNA THIN

DISPATCH BLACK

Cyrus Highsmith is a senior designer at Boston's Font Bureau. With his contemporary body of work, he has established himself as one of the truly original new voices in American type design. He's somewhat of a *designers' designer* – many of his peers hold him in awe for the sheer audacity of his letterforms. Jean-François Porchez, himself one of the most respected type designers in France, called him "the W.A. Dwiggins of today." Meet Cyrus Highsmith, a natural draftsman. *February 2009*

ZOCALO TEXT REGULAR

Cyrus Highsmith by Mitch Wiess

Contrary to many other type designers, you never had a previous life as a graphic designer, lettering artist or illustrator. So you must have realized at a pretty early stage: "I am going to be a type designer!" When did that happen?
Actually, I did not realize I wanted to be a type designer until fairly late. I studied painting and fine art for a while and eventually landed at RISD to study graphic design. While there I got more and more interested in typography. It seemed to me that to be a good graphic designer, you had know about type. So I wanted to learn about that. To create the typography I wanted, I started to draw my own letters. Drawing letters quickly became the most interesting part of the project for me. Making type was more fun than just using it. But more than that, drawing type felt to me like a very pure form of drawing. It was distilled down into just black and white, form and counter-form, contour and shape. I felt like I really found something I could do.

Like many designers in my generation, the first type designer I had ever heard of was Zuzana Licko of Emigre. In fact, I wasn't really aware you could be a type designer until I became of aware of her work, which was new and exciting, and it was changing the way things looked. It made a big impact on me.

At RISD, there were no classes in type design. It is too specialized and until recently, it wasn't really technically feasible for an individual to make a typeface like it is now. In addition, at that time, I think the department was skeptical of the idea of making new typefaces. The classic ones they were accustomed to using seemed to be working just fine. But despite any modernist misgivings, the faculty at RISD was very supportive in the sense that they connected me with Font Bureau in nearby Boston, got out of the way, and mostly left me alone. It was exactly what I needed. I thrive when I can work independently in a more unstructured environment.

As a student, I would visit Font Bureau every few months to show them my work, ask questions, and get feedback. After I graduated I went up for another visit and eleven years later I still haven't left.

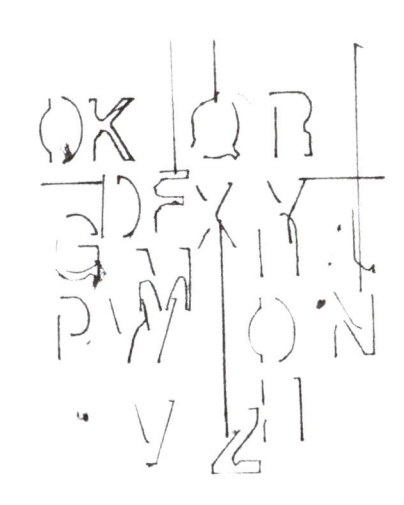

▲▼ Pages from Cyrus' sketchbooks

"The best advice I ever got as a student was 'Quit school!'... If you are not into school, don't waste your time and money." ZOCALO DISPLAY REGULAR ITALIC

Daley's Gothic

▲ Highsmith's first typeface published at Font Bureau, Daley's Gothic (1998), was the outcome of a series of experiments with a steel brush and ink on paper. Dark in color and consisting of straight lines only, the typeface is not a model of legibility, but it doesn't have to be. As an expressive headline face, Daley's Gothic is outstanding. Cyrus named the family after his mother, who taught him how to draw in the first place.

Antenna

▲ Antenna presents a fresh look at the sans-serif genre. It is calm and regular, but never bland; it is clean and businesslike, but has an attractive rhythm and a certain loungey coolness about it. Through seven weights in four widths, with matching italics, Antenna's subtleties show a remarkable sense of proportion. Its many styles make Antenna a versatile typeface for newspapers, magazines, and book cover design.

Who taught you how to draw type?
I was mostly self-taught until I got to Font Bureau. My apprenticeship there lasted three or four years. I was very lucky to have been able to work as an assistant for some of the best – Tobias Frere-Jones, David Berlow, and Matthew Carter – which was pretty amazing. Looking back, each one's lessons ended up being distilled into different aspects of type design. From Tobias I learned a lot of the production tricks and methods that go into making fonts. But the main thing I learned from him was how to see type and how to explain this to other people. From David I learned about spacing and approaching type design using systematic thinking. And from Matthew I learned about craftsmanship and drawing. I still work closely with David and Matthew, although our relationships have evolved.

My biggest influence on the way I draw was my mother, who is an artist. She taught me to look at negative space. The lesson came one day when I was frustrated that my drawings of trees never really looked like trees. They just looked like a bunch of lines. I could not get a feel of the shape or structure of a tree. She taught me to draw the shapes between the branches instead of the branches themselves. When you do that, you quickly come a lot closer to actually drawing something that resembles a tree. When I am drawing letters I use the same approach. I am drawing the white shapes, not the black strokes. So the relationship between the white shapes on the inside of the character and the outside of the character is something I am very interested in.

If you had not discovered type design, or it hadn't discovered you, what do you think you might have become?
Who knows? I cannot remember a time when I didn't want to be some kind of graphic artist. Actually, that's not true. When I was five or six I really wanted to be a garbage man. Specifically, I wanted to be the guy who got to hold on and ride on the back of the truck.

Many type designers today look at historical models for inspiration, but you don't seem to do so as much. Apart from a few exceptions, such as Relay, your typefaces seem to have no stylistic precedent. Each one tackles the age-old problems of readability and personality in a very personal and innovative way. How do you do it? How do you generate ideas for new typefaces?
My philosophy is that when an artist really pays attention to the needs of the audience, and is serious about craftsmanship, the result will be work that is imaginative and inventive. Original work, in other words. This doesn't mean it comes from nowhere, or is a complete break from what has preceded it. It means that the work adds something new to the world. The effect of a new addition can be subtle, or it can rattle the whole ecosystem.

Today, there are more typefaces available than ever before. So do we still need new ones? Maybe. Maybe not. But it's what happens when it's done right. Of course, no one can do it right every time. When you create for a living, sometimes your efforts can fall short for a whole variety of reasons. But you try. I think these things are true for any creative pursuit.

But to be honest, at the same time I don't really know where my ideas come from. It is terrifying in this sense. I am a pretty disciplined person but there is a part of my creative process that is out of my control and I just have to be grateful for it when it works.

◀ Danilo Black used Amira in their 2004 redesign of *Natural Health* magazine.

As you just pointed out, you've spent your entire career so far as a type designer at Font Bureau. Did you ever consider going anywhere else, or becoming independent?
I have been there so long because it is a symbiotic relationship. Both Font Bureau and I are happy when I can focus on drawing. I have the kind of space and amount of independence I need within the organization to do that. It is very unstructured. This can drive some people crazy but for me it is great. Plus I like the people I work with. It is a small group but we all respect and support each other.

Do you get to decide for yourself what projects you take on, and which typeface you're going to work on next?
Yes, mostly. In the past, I worked a lot on commission, responding to requests from publication designers. Lately, I work mostly on self-initiated projects which they publish and promote. There are a couple of publication designers whom I continue to work with, and sometimes Font Bureau throws something on my desk that needs to get drawn and I am happy to do it. The most consistent kind of thing on my desk is making new additions to my older work. It seems like there is always something that needs italics or small caps or another weight or something to keep me busy when I'm between new projects.

Amira

▲ In spite of his reservations about calligraphy, Highsmith became interested in the possibilities and conventions of writing, especially the diagonal stress between thick and thin strokes that lends coherence to words and lines. Out of these explorations came Amira, one of the first "calligraphic sans-serifs" of the decade. Highsmith: "I was curious to see how other type designers approached this theme but I didn't find many examples – it was relatively uncharted territory. That was part of the attraction of this project for me. I didn't do any actual writing with broad-nibbed pen but I have enough experience with the principles that I can visualize the effects when I am sketching with a pencil. Again, my approach to drawing was very much focused on the negative shapes rather than the black lines." (Highsmith in an interview in Eye 59, 2006)

"Drawing type felt to me like a very pure form of drawing. It was distilled down into just black and white, form and counter-form." ZOCALO DISPLAY REGULAR ITALIC

177

FAST TURNING EVENT
Square peg
Your pen might be magical
Quickly
A sharp perspective
CONTRA

Prensa

▲ Prensa (that's Spanish for printing press) is possibly Highsmith's most successful text typeface to date. The family explores the possibilities of a creating a contradiction between the outside and the inside curves of the characters. Highsmith consciously borrowed this device from the great W.A. Dwiggins, who first used it in his book face Electra. "I liked Dwiggins' modular approach to letter drawing," he says. "It confirmed my ideas that there are different ways to approach type design than from a calligraphic point of view."

▼ Prensa as used in *Inc.*, a New York City-based magazine for people who run growing companies.

Your other job is as an instructor of typography, if that's the right title, at Rhode Island School of Design. In what ways does teaching influence your work as a designer?

I think my official title at the moment is "critic", which I have mixed feelings about. But it doesn't matter much what they call me. I am a designer and an artist, and I work with the students as a designer and an artist. My role is to show them what I know how to do, and get out of their way. Students are already connoisseurs and critics by virtue of being engaged enough with their medium to decide they want to pursue it as a profession. Their education hopefully can broaden their horizons. Art history is important. However, skill needs to be the primary focus of an artist or designer's training.

I teach two classes. "Typography 1" is the first of three required classes in typography all the graphic design majors take. It is often the first typography course the students have ever taken so it is basic but we get really deep. It is a foundation that prepares the students for the next classes in the series where they learn about setting type in different kinds of documents.

The other class I teach is a type design elective for the advanced students – a crash course in letter drawing. Its goal is not to educate type designers: I want the students to become more sophisticated users of type. Drawing your own typeface is a way to sharpen your eyes so you can make smarter decisions when it comes to choosing a typeface and setting type. The goal, in other words, is to make them into better typographers. And if they decide to go further with type design, they'll be off to a good start.

So I see the students at the very beginning of their design education and some of them again at the end. I don't know much about what happens in between, and I kind of like that.

The reason I teach is that it offers me another point of view from which I can approach the subject of typography. I enjoy figuring out the structure of the class and figuring out ways to explain things for a lecture. But the more time I spend in an academic environment, the more I want to get back to my studio so I can draw and work on my own stuff. It reminds me how important actually making things is for me. The students are at the exciting stage where they are manic to learn as much as they can, as fast as they can, about everything they can. I am more focused on the slow and often tedious process of getting through a project, trying to get it right while making mistakes and getting lost along the way.

Which are the most important things you're trying to impart to your students?

I try to impart all sorts of things but I never know what sinks in. The best advice I ever got as a student was "Quit school!". I had already dropped out by the time I got it but it was nice confirmation. If you are not into school, don't waste your time and money. My best students are often the ones who have taken time off previously or went to the wrong school first. When they get to my class, they are focused and ready to learn.

Stainless/Dispatch

Dispatch is a slab serif typeface that is radically different from the geometric slab serifs of the early twentieth century (such as Stymie or Rockwell). It has a nuts-and-bolts quality, without being purely mechanical. Its originality and brashness have made it a popular face for magazines and advertising. After Dispatch came Stainless. Highsmith: "I started cutting off the serifs from Dispatch one day just as an experiment. I liked the results so I kept going. The important thing was that the sans-serif design should not appear to be Dispatch with something missing." Stainless has lower contrast, and reworked shapes to compensate for the missing serifs; yet the two families are highly compatible and can successfully be combined in the same project.

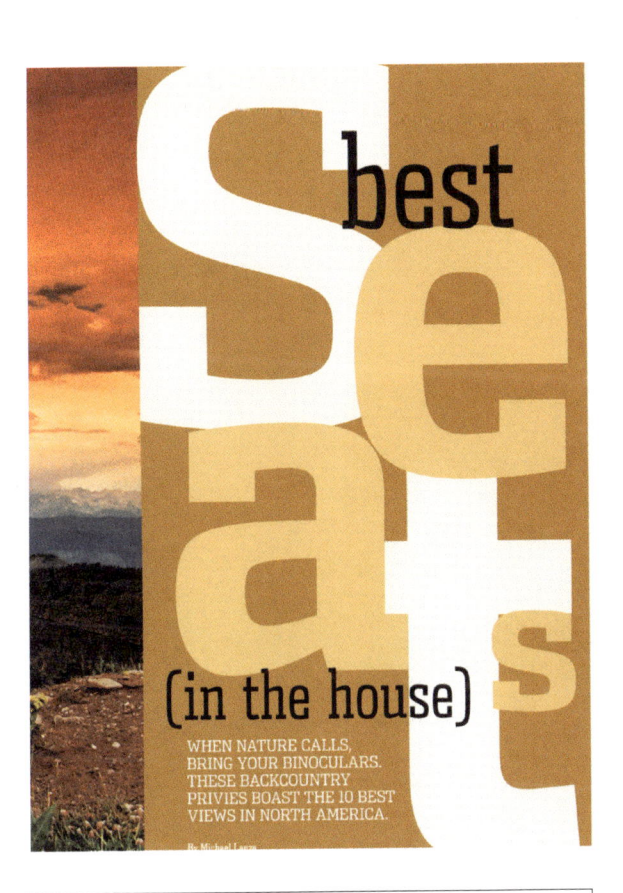

▲▲ Stainless in use in *Backpacker* magazine.
▲ Dispatch and Stainless combined in one project: *Type at Work*, written and designed by Andreu Balius, BIS Publishers.
▶ Dispatch used in combination with Font Bureau's version of Nobel for the 2004 design of *Morf*, a Dutch magazine for design students. Published by the Premsela foundation, design by Office of CC (Chris Vermaas).

The Hollywood Reporter

ANTENNA NARROW

For their dramatic redesign of *The Hollywood Reporter*, a daily paper which reports on the business of Hollywood, New York's Reyman Studio used a variety of Cyrus Highsmith typefaces. "All of them worked very well together," says designer James Reyman. "Quiosco was the text face with a custom small caps version Cyrus drew for me. The Prensa family was used for the headlines; a versatile and fantastic display face with just enough personality for the project. Antenna was the sans serif family and it, also, is a magnificent, versatile face with personality and variety. Together they all made for a handsome and accessible read for *The Hollywood Reporter*." The new look began with a new logo, based on Antenna's Compressed version – authoritative, accessible and immediate. To orchestrate the pacing of the magazine, Reyman introduced new visual navigation aids to help the reader find that information quickly. Reyman's redesign convincingly met the brief – which the studio summarized as "essentially, to bring the publication into the 21st century." Reyman was awarded a gold medal in the 2008 *Folio;Ozzie* award competition (Best redesign in the B-to-B magazine category).

QUIOSCO ONE

▶ A page from Highsmith's sketchbooks

I've heard you're writing a textbook about type.
Yes, I am working on a book. It grew out of the lecture series I developed for the basic level typography course I teach at RISD. It is about what goes on inside a paragraph of text, written from my point of view as a type designer. It gets into typography on a molecular level. But the idea is not to go crazy explaining everything in a super technical way. The goal is to help the student form a foundation for all the typographic knowledge they will get from other books, teachers, and experience. There are a lot of good books on typography but most of them are written more like manuals, with lots of details or bits and pieces. Hopefully the book I am working on will help the student put all those details into context and see the relationships between the bits and pieces.

With the advent of OpenType programming and multi-language character sets, type design and production has gone through some big changes recently. Have things changed for you?
Yes and no. In terms of text faces, we have been producing typefaces for a long time with large character sets, different sets of figures, ligatures, and a lot of the sorts of features you find in what some foundries call "pro" OpenType fonts. However, these typefaces had to be split up into different fonts and the additional features were hard to get to and really only available to the users who specifically asked for them. OpenType has sort of simplified this. There are still a lot of headaches for users when it comes to accessing the features and special characters that are the result of design flaws in typesetting software and in the font specification itself. OpenType is a step forward though and there are more improvements on the horizon.

With all this in mind, Font Bureau has recently written a new specification for text faces that all of our new text and text/display series will follow. The new specification is not format specific but from it we can extract OpenType fonts that will have some nice typographic features. We published this specification and a new series I developed to prototype it called Ibis.

In more experimental terms, I have been working on a set of borders and ornaments that magically assemble themselves using OpenType programming that I am pretty excited about. I don't write much code but every once in a while an idea for something will come to me more or less in a dream and I try to make something with it.

Finally, a more private question: You became a father recently... what effect did that have on your professional life?
It has been very liberating. It is easy to get too wrapped up in your work and inflate its importance. Every day my daughter reminds me of what the important things really are. I still have as much interest in my work as ever but I feel more relaxed about it and willing to take more creative risks. ❧

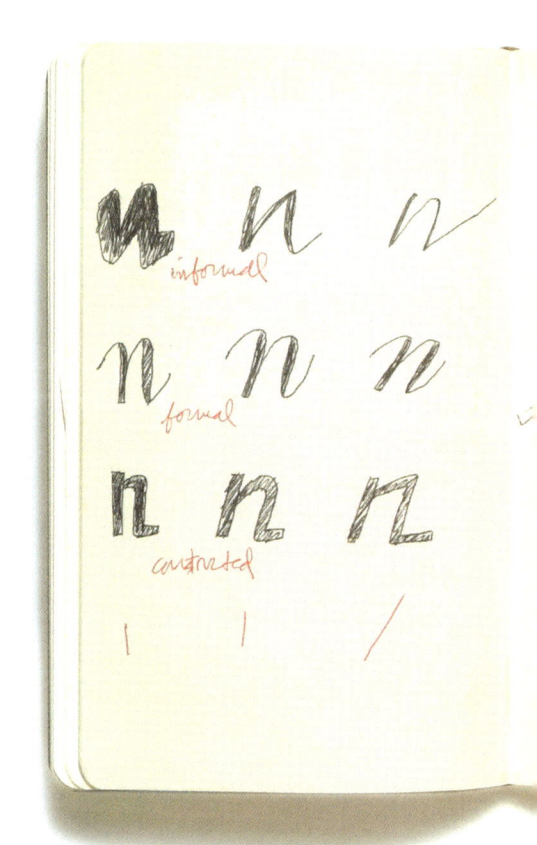

Calaveras de azúcar
¿Qué pasa?
In the desert by 3 o'clock
Mescalito
Doffing Baja jackets
FRUTAS
El Distrito Federal

Zócalo Series
▲ The Zócalo Series was commissioned by Eduardo Danilo for his dramatic redesign of *El Universal*, a leading daily in Mexico City. Zócalo is among the most innovative newspaper typefaces published in recent years. Inspired by sources as diverse as the romans by 17th century Transylvanian émigré Nicholas Kis, and Chauncey Griffith's classic news face Ionic, the lively text face is both strikingly original and pleasant to read. The raw energy of Mexico City pulsates in the more contrasted Zócalo Display. Zócalo Banner was designed for intermediate sizes: it is more subtle than Zócalo Text but has less delicate hairlines than the Display.

3 Underware

They began working together more than ten years ago when studying type design and typography in The Hague, the Netherlands. They gradually became the type world's best loved design collective. They are Underware: **Akiem Helmling** (German, living in The Hague), **Sami Kortemäki** (Finnish, Helsinki) and **Bas Jacobs** (Dutch, Amsterdam). Besides making strikingly original typefaces, Underware publish books and magazines, give hilarious lectures and inspiring workshops, perform in art galleries, and are co-founders of Typeradio, the world's only traveling radio station dedicated to typography. Meet Underware, three guys who know how to have fun with type. *January 2008*

Underware is a studio whose members live and work in three cities in two different countries. How did you get together?
After combining forces on various projects while at the Royal Academy of Arts in Den Haag, it was a natural step to continue our cooperation after graduation. Some call us "a virtual studio" but that is not correct. We have one shared bank account and discuss all projects together. If the three of us worked at the same location it wouldn't change a lot. But as we all prefer to live in the city which we inhabit, it just turned out be Amsterdam, Den Haag and Helsinki. Let's say Underware is a multi-locale-studio.

Your typefaces claim to be "collective" designs instead of being credited to one individual designer. How does this work in practice? Do you really design type together?
For typefaces it's not so common to have several people credited as designers. But our activities overlap so much that they are impossible to separate.

Contents

Stick out your thumb & HITCH HIKE!

« COMMERCIAL PREFACE X 3 PAGE 3 »

KATHERINE GILLIESON *Vignettes of* **a hitch-hiking trip** PAGE 6

Back some 30 years ago we had a dream… by Teija Niemi, page 8

Wrong way isn't always wrong

In practice, of course, a new typeface usually starts with one person. Others might take over after a while, might just criticize it, might bring up new ideas, might start making another weight or an italic, etc. The most important thing, however, is to define a typographic palette – define what a typeface should be able to do and what not. This is always discussed and specified together, and is way more important than "who is the one actually making it."

How have you managed to stay together over the years?
That is an interesting question, because that is much harder and it takes more alertness than starting up a cooperation. While studying we didn't only spend lots of time together on projects, but also in the pub and on the beach. Now, with our multiple locations, it can easily happen that we only discuss work and drift apart on a personal level. That's why we get together a few weekends a year, where we do nothing but have a sauna.

The main thing is trust. If one of us does something stupid, we don't lose faith. Next time it will be the other guys' turn to make a foolish mistake. What keeps us working together is that we keep appreciating the differences. We still get surprised by the stuff on the other side of the wire, and we're aware that none of us would be able to achieve on his own what we can do together.

Auto

▲ With Auto, it's the italics that make the difference. Auto (the roman) is a friendly, open sans serif typeface with a humanist touch, not unlike Fedra Sans or Relato Sans. What makes Underware's Auto unique is its range of three markedly different italics, each with its own typographic flavor.
The italic for Auto 1 (used for text throughout this book) is straightforward and restrained. Auto 2 Italic has a more personal touch, a friendly flow. Also, it contrasts more strongly with the roman, and therefore is great for emphasis in dictionaries or listings. The italic for Auto 3 is the most provocative of the lot, almost upright, with open counters and strategically placed serifs, loops and swashes.
The user can choose an Auto for a specific occasion. Use three Autos within one corporate identity, so that different kinds of publications can be given their own flavor. Use the three Italics for multi-lingual texts or to differentiate between speakers in a play… the possibilities are endless.

> "The only way to test drive a font is by installing it and using it. Would you ever buy a new car straight from a catalog or a car simulator?"
>
> <small>AUTO 3 BOLD ITALICS</small>

Bello

▶ The members of Underware are experienced lettering artists; the paint brush is one of their favorite tools. Bello convincingly mimics the work of the sign writer. It adds character to menus, magazines and logos – and it would provide perfect signage in a beach bar. Bello is big, beautiful and well-equipped. Its glamorous ligatures and swashes allow the user to give each word its individual layout. Besides the appealing flow of the Bello Script face, there's the upright and sturdy Bello Small Caps. In Bello Pro, the OpenType version, the Small Caps are integrated, together with a set of striking word logotypes. When you opt for the separate logotype font, Bello Words, there's a companion font of drop shadows to play around with in different colors. Bello is the ultimate brush font toykit.

▼ Bello t-shirt by Nick Sherman for Oath Threadline, photography by Gennessy Martinez

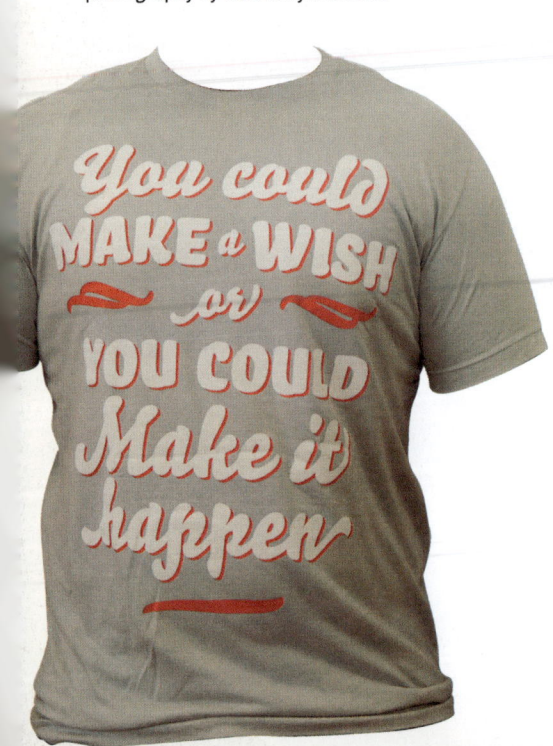

Also, we give each other lots of freedom. If the weather's good, Akiem goes riding the waves with his surf board, Sami goes training his six-pack with eighteenth century cannon balls and Bas bikes around Amsterdam in search of a 5-kilo jar of Nutella. If it's raining, we work out our brains. If one wants to sketch ideas for an all new typeface, he can do so, even when there's other stuff on the desk. Instead of killing each other's budding ideas, we let them grow freely. After some time we get together to decide which ideas are worth continuing.

What would you say are the best and the most difficult aspects of publishing your own typefaces?

Best aspect? Defining our own challenges. Which, in fact, is also the most difficult aspect. Other challenges: to get your typeface known, and to set yourself a deadline. It is not easy to make your typeface stand out among those other 60,000 fonts. As for deadlines: we are very good at endlessly developing and improving our fonts, never considering them good enough, and before you know it, another year has gone by! As you see, we don't have a fool-proof production line for our retail fonts. We also don't have a master plan about what our font library should look like in ten years. We follow our intuition and current motivation, and we cherish that freedom.

Example: for the typeface Auto we first made one italic style. But we felt that something was missing - that in fact it would be groovy to have a palette of three different italic styles to pair with a single roman. Then we saw that in practice the choice of italic also miraculously changes the feel of the roman! We would not be aware of these things if we didn't take so much time developing the fonts.

For the first two Underware type families, Dolly and Sauna, you developed a unique and courageous sales system based on trust. A CD with the complete family was included with the specimen booklets, leaving it to the users to buy a license when they find themselves using the typeface. Did that work for you? Would it still work today?

The idea is to (try to) understand the position and the needs of the end users. If you want them to use your fonts, you must listen to their needs. Graphic designers often depend on their customer's decisions; they may need to test-run a font to see if it actually works for their specific situation. It's good if the type designer can give them the possibility to do just that. Therefore our publications come with the CD. The trust-each-other system is clearly described on the CD, and users seem to understand and appreciate this.

The current OpenType jungle actually shows that most people don't know exactly what they're buying. The only way to really test-drive a typeface is by installing it and using it. All other ways (like online test-drivers, etc) offer a preview, but will never be a satisfying substitute. Would you ever buy a new car straight from a catalog or a car simulator?

NOW SOME 2nd chapter ITALIANOS!

don't miss

That abbello had such

BELLO PRO WITH AUTOMATIC OPENTYPE LIGATURES & ENDING SWASHES

an odd character

Bello

▲▶ Cover and double-page spread from *Read Naked*, the Sauna specimen produced in collaboration with Dutch designer Piet Schreuders and a host of contributors.

Sauna

▲ Like the Finnish invention it was named after, Sauna has a warm and comfortable feeling. It is a type family that is hard to define. Its basic silhouette is rather square, but it is round and cozy in its details. It is an attractive headline face with an unmistakable character of its own, but it has been successfully used for long texts as well.

The Regular and Bold weights are far apart, so that they provide strong contrasts within a piece of text. The Black weight is extreme in every sense, and is only recommended for sizes ranging from large to huge. Each weight of Sauna comes with two italics: the regular italic is formal and dependable, the swash italic is frivolous and cheerful. To top it off, Sauna offers three sets of ligatures with swash italics for making really fancy headlines.

Did the system work for us? People do license our fonts – first they buy a book, then they come back to purchase a license. So there are still honest people around. But it's hard to measure how effective this system really is. And yes, we will do it again. Our next publication will also have a CD including the fonts for testing.

Those early specimens, designed by Dutch designers Wout de Vringer (Dolly) and Piet Schreuders (Sauna) were beautifully produced. The Sauna specimen especially was quite spectacular. Titled *Read Naked*, it was printed on heat- and moisture-resistant material, and some texts were printed with special ink that only became visible at sauna temperatures. Early presentations of Sauna verged on performance art, involving lots of hot water and steam. Did you do it just to have fun, or was there a conscious strategy behind it?

We can get very enthusiastic, sometimes overenthusiastic, and when this happens we tend to lose sight of the big picture. This prevents us from precisely planning what we are doing. We just jump into a project, and then see where the rocket ends up; like untrained astronauts pressing the "start" button. We like to think big, without knowing where that will take us.

At the moment we are working on a publication on "voluntary suffering." Not sure where this will take us, but the subject is engrossing. Then the rest of the process of making this book just has to grow naturally.

A conscious strategy behind our publications? Here's one of our goals: to give kudos to our mothers while they're still alive. At least, for that reason we invited them to be our three cover girls in the *Is Not take-away #1* publication.

186

◀ A leaflet designed with Fakir for the Amsterdam rock group organization GRAP by Underware's Type Radio partner, Donald Beekman.

Fakir

▲ Fakir is a contemporary take on the blackletter genre – a streetwise gothic, so to speak. It examines the edgy structure of the textura alphabet as it was written with broad-nibbed pens for centuries, but also looks at lettershapes used in graffiti pieces. For decades, blackletter was abandoned – it was almost a taboo, with its confusing connotations of fascism, heavy metal rock, and beer. But the genre has seen a remarkable revival, and it's cool again to use and wear it. Underware taps into that newly found popularity, hoping "to give our generation a blackletter from the here and now." Fakir is not a revival, but "an all-new 21st century blackletter uncorked in 2006, after 5 years of aging."

A question about type and technology. You are all very computer-savvy, you program websites and have designed fonts that play with the pixel grid. Yet you always emphasize the importance of sketching and drawing by hand. Would you say it's crucial to start each project by turning your back to the computer screen?
More important than which direction to look, or which tools to use, is the processor: our brain. Sitting at a computer screen is not always the most inspirational environment, most ideas are born somewhere else. But yes, you are right. We find sketching by hand very liberating. It can be very rough, in the train on an old newspaper, or more accurate behind your desk in a sketchbook.

Mostly we do not scan the hand sketches in order to digitize them 1:1. They're a tool that helps us define the basic form and concept much quicker than a computer. We sketch complete words, not just single letters – that makes it easier to see each letter in the right context. It immediately gives an idea of the spacing, rhythm and style. Relatively soon we start to enhance this sketch digitally. For a while the digital and analog sketches develop simultaneously. But then there is a period of around 2 years where a type family gets further designed and produced on the computer.

Child of the 1950s
STRIPES
Willow, Wisconsin, USA
GLANCE
pointed eyebrows
BANGS & TAIL

Dolly

▲ Dolly is a book typeface in the best Dutch tradition – made for optimum legibility, inconspicuous yet beautifully detailed, suited for conventional typography but also for elegant display work. The Roman is a low-contrast text face that works well in both small and display sizes. The Italic is slightly lighter in color and provides subtle emphasis. Dolly Bold is nice and dark, which works perfectly when extra attention is needed. Providing solutions to most problems encountered in book typography, the Dolly family is proof that small can be quite beautiful.

We find it easier to create a personal, evocative style when we sketch by hand. Probably not one of our typefaces is "neutral," all are expressive and peculiar. Our typefaces are meant for reading, but at the same time have an emotional or aesthetic added value. The last aspect is often over-exposed, while the first aspect, the user-friendliness, is much more important. Finding a balance between the two is an intriguing process.

You've worked out a rather unique system of typography workshops and a website to support it. Could you tell us more about the kind of workshops you offer? Does working with students influence your own design practice?
If there's a formula for our workshops, it would be something like: problem + group of people + type design knowledge + unconventional application = surprise = motivation = energy.

Most of our workshops take place in various academies, with a local organizer helping us to realize the event. The longest workshop so far ran for two weeks and the shortest for just a couple of hours, but 2–4 days is typical.

The end result can be anything. Although the 3D results are more immediately eye-catching than something very specifically 2D, the subject can be anything. We enjoy type, and if others enjoy type as well, we can have an entertaining and inspiring time together. It's amazing to experience that what we find fascinating is also interesting to others. We influence and get influenced, and sometimes participants from different workshops even start to discuss with each other.

There has always been something subversive about Underware – from your name and working structure to the individual typefaces. Lately, you've participated in the redesign of the Daimler identity, developing that luxury car company's new logo. Did that feel like some kind of contradiction? A triumph? Entering a different world? Or just another job?
The design approach is very much the same for every project. Doesn't matter if it's a local underground record label called Sic-Rec, or a multi-national company like Daimler. You always try to find the best typographic solution. Of course, seeing your logo applied worldwide can cause a sense of triumph, but you also get that when seeing somebody very proud and happy with the new logo for his record label (which is his life's passion). You can't compare the two. Probably the biggest triumph is to be asked (and appreciated) for your work by two very different parties.

Working on a custom type project is quite a different story from working on our own retail fonts. Corporate type should pay tribute to the client, not to us. It was very intriguing to see that such a high-class luxury brand could have potential to carry a "beyond style" logotype. Something very subversive could also have worked, and the brand would still be a luxury brand, because everybody already knows and values the brand.

"We're like untrained astronauts pressing the 'start' button. We like to think big, without knowing where that will take us."

AUTO 2 BOLD ITALICS

LIZA PRO LETTRES D'AMOUR

Outofink feature

Damn, I'm out of ink

✷ Liza Pro contains a feature which simulates real-life characteristics of sign painting. At a certain moment you're out of ink, and you have to dip the brush in the ink again. This causes an interruption of the continuous script lettering. The typeface Liza counts the amount of ink being used, and automatically interrupts the ongoing flow once you would be out of ink. OpenType technology takes care this all gets done automatically. You only have to type, while Liza takes care of your ink.

When you're not designing typefaces or logos, what other types of design work or art are you working on?
Unfortunately we are not biomedical scientists,† but we love playing the piano, running an art gallery, pimping up wooden boats, riding bikes, developing our masculinity with girya kettlebells, playing kamikaze chess, watching clouds, running our own radio station, making the ultimate espresso, publishing type specimen books, playing panna with kids, jumping into a hole in the ice, serving green tea, cooking, culture and any kind of sub-culture.

What new type projects do you have in store? Is it more difficult now than it was, say, five years ago to come up with original ideas?
We have around eight font families under construction at the moment, and some publications. It hasn't become more difficult to think of new ideas, it's just that finishing a project isn't our strongest point. We always try to be better than last time. And as long as there's no deadline, a typeface is never good enough but can always be improved. Some fonts have been in progress for as long as five years now. Last weekend we sat down together again, and defined which fonts to finish first. "The next font we release will be a fully loaded script typeface, based on the Typeradio logotype".✷
    Then we jumped back into the sauna.

typeradio.org

✷ Since this interview was conducted in 2008, the Typeradio logo has indeed become a fully fledged typeface, called Liza

† Unlike Font Garden's Ellinor Rapp, for example

Acknowledgements, etc.

This book is based on monthly e-mail newsletters that were (and still are) sent out to users of the font distribution platform MyFonts.com. The archive of these newsletters can be viewed online under www.myfonts.com/newsletters/cc/.
Many thanks to the MyFonts team for their ideas, support and proofreading: John Collins, Kevin Woodward, Chris Lewis, Laurence Penney, Adam Twardoch, Joshua Lurie-Terrell, Chris Dargue. Additional proofreading was done by Anthony Noel, who also did the book's layout. The original design concept of the newsletters was created by Nick Sherman, who also designed the bulk of the black and white type samples used both in the 2007–2009 *Creative Characters* newsletters and in this book. Thanks! We greatly appreciate the patience and cooperation of the interviewees, many of whom provided us with new visuals and type specimens. Many thanks to the individuals and organisations who made available imagery of typefaces in use, and whose names are acknowledged in the respective captions.

All the work shown is copyrighted, and cannot be reproduced without prior consent from the publisher and the designer(s) involved. All typefaces shown are the work of the designers mentioned and may be copyrighted in certain areas. Copying these typefaces is an infringement of intellectual property rights and of common decency. Anyone desiring to use the showings of typefaces as a starting point for a font is informed that this, too, may be an infringement of copyright. Aspiring type designers are encouraged at all times to conceive their own forms instead of imitating those created by others.

About the author: Jan Middendorp is an independent designer and writer living in Berlin, Germany. He is the author and co-author of several books on typography and graphic design, including "*Hey, there goes one of mine*" (2002), *Dutch Type* (2004), *Made with FontFont* (with Erik Spiekermann, 2006) and *Playful Type 2* (2010). He teaches in Antwerp and Berlin. He has been the editor of MyFonts' newsletters since 2007.

▶ Optical illusions can be fascinating within typography. This recent poster by Underware using Liza shows a word which can be read both as 'Yes' and/or as 'No'. The MyFonts logo with its 'hidden' hand, also designed by the Underware team, is another example of that same fascination.

Say No